WISDOM
FOR THE ROAD

WISDOM
FOR THE ROAD

*Daily Reflections
of Our Designer*

MITCH KRUSE

credo
house publishers

Published in the United States of America by Credo House Publishers,
a division of Credo Communications, LLC, Grand Rapids, Michigan
credohousepublishers.com

ISBN: 978-1-62586-182-5

Cover and interior design by Sharon VanLoozenoord
Editing by Pete Ford

Printed in Canada

First edition

INTRODUCTION

I STUMBLED up the back stairs of an office building to meet the wisest person I knew in an unfinished storage room lined with bookshelves encasing hundreds of theological, psychological, and legal works. He looked me in the eyes and asked if I would consider pursuing wisdom, rather than money, as the scorecard of my life. I remembered Solomon had asked for wisdom, but I didn't know what it was or how it applied to my marketplace endeavors.

I wrestled with this as I pondered how I had wandered from my faith after a decade of owning my auction business. Growing up going to church three times a week had not fully prepared me for my collector car auction life where conflict was everywhere. Buyers wanted to purchase at the lowest price possible, and sellers desired the most money attainable for their rolling sculptures. As the auctioneer, I facilitated their meeting in the middle.

If God cared about my marketplace world, I needed to keep Christ at the center instead of controlling my own life, merely placing my faith on a shelf as an insurance policy. Without Him as the focal point, I would avoid heart transformation.

That day in the storage room was the beginning of pursuing wisdom that combined God's heart with street smarts—a picture of the vertical intersecting with the horizontal, like the bookshelves that lined the room. I left that encounter with a copy of the Book of Proverbs, complete with fourteen studies and a concordance. Today, that tattered, worn, broken-cover book lies in my top right-hand desk drawer, serving as a reminder of how God transformed my heart, my company, my family, and my relationships.

When I bent the knees of my heart to God, just like I had bent the knees of my physical body to climb those stairs to the storage room, I took the first step to experiencing His wisdom. As I applied what I read each day in the Bible, I witnessed firsthand His restorative power, offering my life as a minister of restoration. Looking back, after the sale of my company to eBay, I see how God's vision was followed by His provision.

In my first book, *Restoration Road,* I shared how God desires to restore us to His original design. In *Street Smarts from Proverbs,* I illustrated the twelve purposes of Proverbs with practical tools to help readers navigate through conflict to community. Now in *Wisdom for the Road,* I want to help you invest a few minutes each day to recalibrate your heart with God's. In our world filled with uncertainty, disappointment, fear, and discouragement He offer purpose, hope, faith, and encouragement, which shape us to be more like Christ.

Maybe you're a business executive, church leader, entrepreneur, student, athlete, or the CEO of your household—you need to know God indeed cares deeply about every detail of your life. He has uniquely prepared the road ahead for your journey, and my hope is that the devotions in this book will help you encounter the wisdom only God and His Word can provide. Each day we will dive into the markers that define our faith to help you experience Christ's transformation of your heart and life. The first six months, we will focus on restoration. The second half of the year, we will delve further into wisdom, the means and the end of Christ making us new again.

My prayer is that you will engage with your Designer, learn from the Bible, and then surrender to the Holy Spirit who will connect God's wisdom with the hearts of those around you, as you begin to see every encounter as a divine appointment to guide others to restoration in Christ.

Lost Treasure

Revelation 21:5

IN the early 1930s, famed car designer Ettore Bugatti crafted the world's seven greatest classic cars, the Bugatti Royales. Each was a uniquely-designed work of art with a length exceeding twenty-one feet, about five feet longer than our vehicles today, and powered by a 300-horsepower straight-eight engine. The Bugattis were rolling sculptures. However, two had remained lost for decades.

The pursuit of these lost treasures prompted racer and car builder Briggs Cunningham to approach the wrought iron gate of Bugatti's estate, not long after the unconditional surrender of the Axis powers to end the Second World War. Once inside, he noticed a brick wall that appeared out of place. After one swing of his sledgehammer, he peered through a hole in the facade, finding the two lost Bugattis. I recall Briggs telling me he purchased both vehicles that day for $50,000 and two refrigerators, which were held at a premium in Europe after World War II. Today, both Royales are worth millions of dollars.

Inside each of us is a lost treasure, hidden behind a brick wall that has hardened in our hearts. We discover our original, authentic design when we surrender that wall to the Restorer. Jesus said: "I am making everything new" (Revelation 21:5). What brick wall do you need to surrender to Him today?

Authenticity Versus Pretense

Philippians 4:7

AUTHENTICITY is said to be the highest value in our post-modern culture because it aligns our lives from the inside out. Consequently, we deconstruct every person we encounter to discover whether he or she is truly authentic, the same down to the core of his or her being.

Pretense, the opposite of authenticity, misaligns our lives from the outside in. It focuses on the outside at the expense of the inside. In the collector car world, we call this a cosmetic restoration: A vehicle is spruced up on the outside just enough to fool others that it is restored. It is only a matter of time before the concealed truth about the vehicle's cancerous undercarriage is revealed, followed by another outside-in attempt at restoration. This process never satisfies.

Authentic restoration in our lives begins when we surrender our pretense to the Restorer, who aligns our lives from the inside out, giving us peace. Paul wrote: "And the peace of God, which transcends all understanding, will guard your hearts and your minds in Christ Jesus" (Philippians 4:7).

Are you pretending from the outside in? Surrender to the Restorer who will align your life with His from the inside out.

Basket Case

Matthew 11:28

IS there anything in your life that you would like to be made new? Like a classic car that needs restoration, each one of us must surrender our old basket case of a life to the Restorer, who disassembles and renovates the components of our lives, piece by piece, whether they are unrestored or self-restored. As the restoration process unfolds, we learn that we are designed to bring authentic restoration to others. We surrender the new for this purpose and continue to surrender any old parts that corrode again over time.

On our restoration journey, our resolve can fade, tear, wear, grow tired, and become rusty as we occasionally turn from God in an attempt to restore the individual pieces ourselves. Pride deceives us into either believing that our self-restoration attempts are working—or thinking that we cannot bring a particular piece to Him more than once. Consequently, pride leaves us questioning how we are supposed to surrender that piece of our lives.

Surrender says to the Restorer, "I can't. You can. I can't restore my life. You can." Jesus said: "Come to me, all you who are weary and burdened, and I will give you rest" (Matthew 11:28). Is it time for you to tell Him, "I can't. You can"?

Pride Is the Lock; Humility Is the Key

Matthew 16:19

PRIDE is the lock on the human heart. Humility is the key. Imagine the inner workings of a lock fashioned with two concentric cylinders that are held together by four spring-loaded pins. The inner cylinder represents our spiritual heart.

A key is the perfect combination for each respective lock. It pushes up the spring-loaded pins high enough so that the innermost cylinder can turn freely inside the outermost cylinder, unlocking the door. Partially surrendering the key into the lock will never open any door. Only fully surrendering the key will unlock it.

The same is true for our lives. God told the prophet Jeremiah that partial surrender is only pretense (Jeremiah 3:10). In order to be restored to authenticity, we must fully surrender our hearts to the Restorer who holds the Master Key, Jesus Christ. Jesus spoke of similar keys when he said to his disciple Peter: "I will give you the keys of the kingdom of heaven; whatever you bind on earth will be bound in heaven, and whatever you loose on earth will be loosed in heaven" (Matthew 16:19).

When we fully surrender the key of humility into the lock of our human heart, we open wide the gate to the kingdom of heaven in our lives. When we partially surrender the key of humility into our prideful heart, the gate to the kingdom of heaven remains locked—both in this life and the next.

Sand and Stone of Pride

Proverbs 27:3

PRIDE is a hard heart, one that makes itself higher than others. It comes in two forms: sand or stone. A sand heart focuses on people and tasks at the expense of God. It is loose and requires a storm to be shaped and restored. A stone heart pretends to focus on God at the expense of others. It is legalistic and requires tooling by a sharp instrument to be shaped and restored.

Ironically, both sand and stone are the same substance, just a different aggregate. In essence, sand is just tiny pieces of crumbled up stone. However, neither reflects the wisdom of our Designer and Restorer because proud sand and stone hearts are foolish. They break apart the vertical from the horizontal, creating four walls that form a prison. The result is the incarceration of pride.

Solomon observed: "Stone is heavy and sand a burden, but a fool's provocation is heavier than both" (Proverbs 27:3). Which substance represents the condition of your heart? Surrender it to the Restorer today.

Master Key of Full Surrender

Revelation 3:7

THE Master Key that fully surrenders our hearts to the Restorer is cross-shaped, the perfect combination of the vertical intersecting with the horizontal. The vertical axis is our relationship with God. The horizontal axis is our relationship with people. In order to fully surrender the Master Key into the lock of pride on the human heart, we must humble our heart vertically to God and horizontally to others.

The Bible tells us that Christ the Designer (Colossians 1:16) and Restorer (Colossians 1:19) holds the restoring key that unlocks the kingdom of heaven. What He opens, no one can shut; what He shuts, no one can open (Revelation 3:7). He has unlocked the door to abundant and eternal restoration to those who humble their hearts to Him. In order to discover who God created us to be, we must gather the courage to travel into the mystery God will reveal to us as He unlocks the condition of our hearts, our desires, and our three resources of life (which we will explore soon) for the advancement of His kingdom.

Are you overdue for an appointment with the Restorer to unlock the gate of your heart to Restoration Road?

A Clay Heart

Isaiah 64:8

A CLAY heart is a humble heart that lives in the sweet spot where our vertical relationship with God intersects with our horizontal relationship with others. In fact, the words *humility* and *humanity* come from the same Latin word, *humus*, which means, "from the ground."

Consequently, humility is bending the knees of our hearts, "to make ourselves lower than" God and others.

Whereas a sand heart is a picture of license, and a stone heart is a picture of legalism, a clay heart is a picture of love. It is a humble heart, malleable in the hands of the Restorer who breathes life into the substance that is void of meaning unless it is shaped and restored by the heart and hands of the Restorer. The prophet Isaiah proclaimed: "Yet you, LORD, are our Father. We are the clay, you are the potter; we are all the work of your hand" (Isaiah 64:8). Like when He breathed that first breath of life into the clay, God continues to breathe into, shape, and restore those whose hearts are fully surrendered to Him.

CLAY

Matthew 11:29

CLAY is an acronym that helps us remember how to live with a humble heart. First, we *confess* to God our proud sinful hearts of sand or stone. Second, we *learn* His design for our lives from the Bible. Third, we *apply* what we learn from the Scriptures to our daily tasks and relationships. Fourth, we *yield* the outcomes to God. We experience the design of the Designer when we confess, learn, apply, and yield.

Jesus, our Designer, proclaimed He was humble in heart (Matthew 11:29). He was the authentic picture of a clay heart surrendered in communion with the Father and community with others. All of Jesus's time, talent, and treasure were completely surrendered to the promptings of His heavenly Father. Jesus glorified the Father by coming to earth as a sacrifice for sin, and in return the Father restored Jesus to the glory of heaven (John 17:1–4).

Jesus invites each of us to be restored to authenticity, to the unique expression of the Designer in us. Are you prepared to confess, learn, apply, and yield to Him? When you become CLAY in His hands, you begin to walk Restoration Road, as He makes you new again.

Outside-In Versus Inside-Out Living

Matthew 23:26

CHRIST the Restorer came to earth to inaugurate the kingdom of heaven, the biggest restoration project in the universe. He came to restore the unique expression of the Designer in each one of us.

Unfortunately, we turn away from that design. Often times, we sign up for self-restoration, which takes place from the outside in. We think that if we go somewhere, we can do something, and then we will be somebody without first addressing our hearts or our desires. This is diametrically opposed to God's design. Referencing the Pharisees' futile outside-in restoration attempts, Jesus taught: "First clean the inside of the cup and dish, and then the outside also will be clean" (Matthew 23:26).

Living restored to authenticity occurs from the inside out. This is the be-do-go of full surrender. Who we are designed to be determines what we are designed to do, which determines where we are designed to go. Who has God designed you to be? What has He designed you to do? Where has He designed you to go?

The Day the Colors Came Alive

Ephesians 2:10

THE Artist imagined as He peered at the blank canvas He had stretched and prepared for His unparalleled work. He brought red, yellow, and blue, stirring them to create orange, purple, and green. As His finger spread the colors on His paint board to test their capabilities, red began to speak, "I think the entire canvas should be red!" Yellow overheard the audacity of his primary counterpart and shouted, "The painting would be ideal if it were all yellow!" Not to be left out of the debate, blue screamed, "Make it all blue!" Orange, purple, and green chimed in unison, advocating their cause for the painting to be their sole color.

The Artist saw the pride in the colors and replied, "Red, I have great plans for you. You will color the rose, shade the maple leaf, and be the base coat of blood that will provide life." To yellow, the Artist said, "I want you and orange to color the sun as you provide light and heat that will illuminate and warm the entire painting." Staring at blue, He softly spoke, "With you, I want to paint the sky, which will reflect upon all the waters in different hues. Purple will paint the majestic mountains and cover the night." His focus shifted to green, "You will color the grass, the leaves, and the wide array of plants as you comfort the eyes that gaze upon you." The Artist said to all

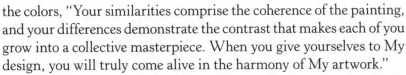

the colors, "Your similarities comprise the coherence of the painting, and your differences demonstrate the contrast that makes each of you grow into a collective masterpiece. When you give yourselves to My design, you will truly come alive in the harmony of My artwork."

The Artist inhaled deeply and slowly exhaled. "Since you the created failed to convince Me The Creator that the painting was all about you, I have forgiven your transgression and have provided a way for you to impact all who see. It's My Brush. When you yield to His saving creativity, He will reveal the ultimate meaning and purpose in Our masterpiece. It is self-sacrificial love. The more you give, the more you receive." The colors saw the truth and justice of the Artist's words, recognizing their unique contributions to the canvas. In response, they surrendered to the Brush who directed them, "Come on, let's go color our world!" "For we are God's masterpiece. He has created us anew in Christ Jesus, so we can do the good things he planned for us long ago" (Ephesians 2:10 NLT).

Sin's Trifecta

Genesis 3

THE first sin was followed by the world's first self-restoration program. It is sin's trifecta: (1) Adam and Eve were *ashamed* because they had been swayed (Genesis 3:7), (2) they *hid* because they were afraid (Genesis 3:12–13), and (3) they *blamed* because they had disobeyed (Genesis 3:12–13). Adam and Eve ate of the forbidden tree of the knowledge of good and evil, and from that point, we humans have determined for ourselves what is right and wrong, a move that has imprisoned us in sin's trifecta (Genesis 3:1–6).

In essence, we take God's gift of life and continually attempt to satisfy our desires by setting ourselves up as gods in our own self-made kingdoms. We trust in our giftedness rather than our godliness. We follow our will rather than surrendering willingly. We rely on our own decisions rather than submitting them to our Creator. However, God the Designer responds by offering us the opportunity to be restored to authenticity (Genesis 3:15, 22).

Have you attempted to satisfy your desires by setting yourself up as god in your own self-made kingdom? Have you trusted in your giftedness rather than His godliness? God the Designer is graciously offering you the opportunity to be restored to authenticity when you surrender to Him. Surrender sin's trifecta and freely receive His forgiveness and restoration today.

Pursuit of Wisdom

1 Corinthians 1:24

EVERYONE wants wisdom, but what is it really, and where do we find it? Wisdom is God's heart combined with street smarts, the vertical intersecting with the horizontal. Wisdom applies our relationship with God to our relationships with others, including our tasks. We were designed to have a heart for wisdom (Proverbs 3:5–6; 22:17–18), to desire wisdom (Proverbs 3:15), and to pursue wisdom with our time, talent, and treasure (Proverbs 4:7).

But where do we find it? Wisdom begins with a humble, malleable, clay-like heart toward God, the author of wisdom (Proverbs 1:7; 11:2; 22:4). Thousands of years ago, Jewish rabbis searched for the ultimate word to describe God. They chose "wisdom." Wisdom resides in a person in whom the vertical perfectly intersects with the horizontal. Christ the Restorer is the wisdom of God (1 Corinthians 1:24). Christ is the authenticity of God (Hebrews 1:3). He is humble in heart (Matthew 11:29). Humility toward Him is the beginning of His wisdom in our lives (Proverbs 11:2).

Foolishness, the antithesis of wisdom, is derived from a proud heart, one that breaks apart the vertical from the horizontal. It begins as wet cement and progressively hardens like cured concrete. A stone heart is foolish. A sand heart is foolish. The two substances added together form a concrete mix that imprisons us in lives filled with pride instead of humility, foolishness instead of wisdom. In our pride, we foolishly pretend that the satisfaction of our desires will occur through the pursuit of more time, talent, and treasure apart from God. The result is a four-walled imprisonment in legalism or license that leaves us unrestored and dissatisfied. That prison gate is unlocked with the cross-shaped Master Key of full surrender to Christ the Restorer.

It's Never Too Late: Five Women's Stories

Hebrews 11:31

THE Gospels show us that sand-hearted sinners were drawn to Jesus more than stone-hearted legalists. Why? A glimpse at Jesus's genealogy gives us a clue. In it we see the stories of five women who were disreputable in the eyes of religious society.

Tamar was a childless widow who had been given to different brothers-in-law after her husband's death, in obedience to Levitical law. After her second husband's death, Tamar disguised herself as a prostitute and tricked her father-in-law into sleeping with her—he had been unwilling to give her to another one of his sons for fear of death (Genesis 38:6–30). After her deception, Tamar conceived and gave birth to twins, Perez and Zerah. Perez continued the family tree of Jesus.

Rahab was a prostitute. She hid Joshua's spies from the townspeople and so was spared by the Israelite army when they conquered Jericho (Joshua 2:1–24). Later, she was commended with these words: "By faith the prostitute Rahab, because she welcomed the spies, was not killed with those who were disobedient" (Hebrews 11:31).

Ruth was a Gentile foreigner from the land of Moab. After her husband and sons died, Naomi journeyed back to Israel, to the town of her youth. In an extraordinary act of devotion, Ruth left her own

country to follow Naomi. In Israel, Ruth met and married Boaz, one of Naomi's relatives. This union allowed Ruth to become the mother of Obed, the grandfather of David, who would become Israel's greatest king (Ruth 1:1–4:22).

Bathsheba betrayed her husband Uriah when she slept with King David. Uriah was killed in battle by David's deceitful plan to dispose of the soldier in his own army, and then David took Bathsheba as his wife. God punished them for this by taking their first child (2 Samuel 11:1–27), but Bathsheba later gave birth to Solomon, who became Israel's king after David and is widely regarded as the wisest man to ever walk the earth.

Mary was the unwed, pregnant, virgin mother of Jesus (Luke 1:35). One can imagine the controversy that surrounded her, an apparently unwed mother-to-be. How the townspeople in her small village must have talked, even after Jesus was born.

Jesus's messy family tree is proof that it is never too late for a sand or stone heart to be transformed into a heart of clay. No religious, stone-hearted formula will magically restore us. Rather, the gate to Restoration Road is unlocked when we humble our hearts, our desires, and our lives to Him (Matthew 11:28).

Rule-Breaking Father

Luke 15

IN Jesus's Parable of the Prodigal Son, the father committed four acts atypical of a Middle Eastern patriarch. First, the father *gave* an unwarranted inheritance. Second, he *ran* to a prodigal son outside the city gates. Third, he *restored* him to authenticity, regardless of the cost. Fourth, he *pleaded* with his elder son who attempted to shame him in front of the whole community.

In the same way, God graciously *gives* us life. He *runs* toward us in spite of our sin. He *restores* us to authenticity to reflect His original design. He *pleads* with us, not only to be restored, but to joyfully help others to do the same.

Hanging in my office is a replica of Rembrandt's painting, *The Prodigal Son Returns*. It was a gift from a friend of mine who purchased it at the museum in St. Petersburg, Russia, where Rembrandt's original hangs. The story did not merely influence my life—it is one I have lived. I too was once lost, unrestored, locked out from the life that reflected the design of the Designer. Happily, the Restorer found me at just the right moment to restore me to authenticity.

Read Luke 15. Ask God to unlock your heart and restore you to authenticity.

The Dirt Road

Jeremiah 29:11–13

A T nine years old, I walked down a dirt road compacted with sand and stone crunched by the horses and buggies that carried people to my home church a century earlier. As I crept inside the church's double doors, I noticed that no one else was in the building—it was just God and me. I walked a few more steps and opened one of the doors to the sanctuary. I remember that the interior was dark due to the dim sunlight that struggled to shine through the stained-glass windows. I slowly walked up the aisle to the altar at the front of the church, and I could not recall a time when I had ever been that close. Now that I was there, I figured I had God's undivided attention, so I thought I would ask Him a question that had been on my heart for quite some time. I knelt down at that wood railing and asked, "God, what do You want me to do with my life?"

Perhaps that moment was my first glimpse at a heart of clay, yet I walked away partially surrendering my heart, attempting to maintain control of my own life. I trusted in myself, rather than fully surrendering to God. My self-restoration program led to an internal battle that would rage for many years.

God told His people through the prophet Jeremiah: "'For I know the plans I have for you,' declares the LORD, 'plans to prosper you and not to harm you, plans to give you hope and a future. Then you will call on me and come and pray to me, and I will listen to you. You will seek me and find me when you seek me with all your heart'" (Jeremiah 29:11–13). Will you seek God and listen to Him with all your heart today?

Indy Storm

Luke 15:20

I ATTENDED my first Indy 500 in 1972, and I didn't miss a race for more than four decades. When I was eight years old, I convinced my parents during the race to allow me to go to the gift shop by myself. I wanted to purchase a blue tie-dyed T-shirt in remembrance of the historic day. I had barely reached the shop when race officials called the race due to a torrential downpour.

The storm presented me with two problems. First, I was lost with no way to communicate with my parents. Second, 400,000 people now stood between us. Step-by-step, tear-by-tear, I walked my way back to my mom and dad. Unfortunately, that's how I saw my relationship with God. I thought that I had to earn my way back to my heavenly Father. It took me about twenty years to understand that God is a God of grace. He chases down lost sinners so that we might have eternal life with Him (Luke 15:20).

Are you attempting to earn your way back to God? Do you see life with Him as depending on your efforts? Step off the treadmill of good works and humbly receive His grace, His undeserved love, His unmerited favor. He will restore your relationship with Him and use you to do the same with others.

God's Response to List-Makers

Matthew 9:16–17

WHEN challenged about rules, regulations, and stipulations, Jesus answered with this word picture: "No one sews a patch of unshrunk cloth on an old garment, for the patch will pull away from the garment, making the tear worse. Neither do people pour new wine into old wineskins. If they do, the skins will burst; the wine will run out and the wineskins will be ruined. No, they pour new wine into new wineskins, and both are preserved" (Matthew 9:16–17).

The old garment and the old wineskin illustrated the Pharisees' mechanical adherence to religious traditions that accentuated their hearts of stone. Jesus was saying that He did not come to patch up the Pharisees' religious system. He came to start an uncontainable revolution. Consequently, Jesus's message of heart transformation was not going to fit into the Pharisees' religious framework. The new patch and the new wine Jesus described alluded to His message of heart transformation.

What rules, regulations, and stipulations have you added to or subtracted from Jesus's message? Have you tried to contain the kingdom of heaven to a certain worship style during one hour on a particular day of the week in the same building? You might be trying to pour new wine into old wine skins. Just like that new cloth and new wine, the revolution within a heart that longs to be restored to authenticity cannot be contained. He invites you to live a life restored to authenticity.

Thermometer or Thermostat?

Romans 12:2

DO you ever ask God what His will for your life is? Often, we wonder about the source of the temperature in our life. We ask ourselves, "Is this desire merely from me or is it from God? How can I know if this is really God's will?" The answer comes from whether we are a thermometer or a thermostat.

First, a thermometer reflects the temperature; a thermostat sets the temperature. Paul urged believers not to be thermometers: "Do not conform to the pattern of this world" (Romans 12:2). Jesus prayed that His disciples would be *in* the world, but not *of* the world, that they would be thermostats, not thermometers (John 17:15–16). Do not merely reflect the temperature of your environment. Instead, set the temperature.

Second, a thermostat sets the temperature because it has been touched by the programmer's hand. Paul compelled believers to be thermostats programmed by the hand of God in Christ: "But be transformed by the renewing of your mind" (Romans 12:2). This renewing of the mind is not only a quiet time with God, but a 24/7 renewing of our thoughts by the Spirit of Christ (2 Corinthians 10:5).

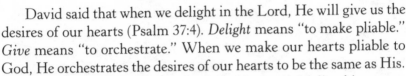

David said that when we delight in the Lord, He will give us the desires of our hearts (Psalm 37:4). *Delight* means "to make pliable." *Give* means "to orchestrate." When we make our hearts pliable to God, He orchestrates the desires of our hearts to be the same as His.

When the world's temperature is fired at you with lies, bitterness, deceit, malice, pride, hypocrisy, coarse language, licentiousness, or laziness, don't reflect it. Rather, renew your mind with the touch of the Programmer's hand, and set the temperature with Christ.

Finally, a thermostat tests and approves the temperature in its environment. Paul summarized: "Then you will be able to test and approve what God's will is" (Romans 12:2). How do you know whether a thought is God's will? First test the temperature and then only approve it if it is consistent with the heart of Christ, the Bible, and the peace of the Holy Spirit within you. If not, set the climate by responding to the touch of the Programmer's hand as your temperature for Christ increases.

The Curio Cabinet

1 Peter 3:15

A S I called my first auction, my voice cut through the public-address system, echoing into the air. On the block was an old curio cabinet. "One hundred dollars. Now one-fifty." Hundreds of bidders watched as Grandpa Russell shouted to stop me from dropping the hammer at too low of a price, "Wait, Mitchell! Is there anything else you can say about this curio that might enhance the bid?"

Conducting my on-the-job training in front of the crowd, he communicated something that radically altered my perspective when he said, "Mitchell, if I can get you convinced, I can get them convinced." After selling the curio cabinet for ten-fold my original bid price, I reflected on Grandpa Russell's words.

God is saying the same thing to us. If we could become convinced of His restorative grace and wisdom, then He could use us to advance His kingdom in others. The apostle Peter wrote: "But in your hearts revere Christ as Lord. Always be prepared to give an answer to everyone who asks you to give the reason for the hope that you have. But do this with gentleness and respect" (1 Peter 3:15). If I can get you convinced, I can get them convinced.

Gold Love

1 Timothy 6:10

WHERE do you turn to satisfy your desires?

As a teenager, I traveled to the nation's premier collector car auction in the middle of the oil patch during its boom of the early 1980s. The clientele reflected that newfound wealth. I attended a party to celebrate the annual auction where gold Rolexes glittered in abundance on the wrists of collectors who jammed the exposition hall that housed 550 of the world's greatest classic cars.

In some ways, this was the beginning of my journey as a workaholic, money addict, and materialist. Like a junkie who attempts to satisfy his desire with his drug of choice, my veins popped, ready for the gold needle that would infuse the obsession of money straight to my heart. Paul revealed: "For the love of money is a root of all kinds of evil. Some people, eager for money, have wandered from the faith and pierced themselves with many griefs" (1 Timothy 6:10).

Have you been pierced with the many griefs caused by an addiction? Surrender your drug of choice to Jesus Christ, the only One who can truly satisfy your desires.

One-of-a-Kind Treasure

1 Corinthians 6:19–20a

DO you ever doubt your value?

In 1985, I brokered the sale of a restored, one-of-a-kind Duesenberg to Tom Monaghan, founder of Domino's Pizza and owner of the world champion Detroit Tigers. He took delivery of his prized possession at home plate in Tiger Stadium in front of thousands of his franchisees. The driver revved the supercharged engine, and it echoed throughout the historic landmark. This was the first car to sell for a documented $1 million cash, and international media pounced on the opportunity to cover the world record price.

Jesus bought you for a world record price, providing His incomparable Spirit to dwell in you. Paul wrote: "Do you not know that your bodies are temples of the Holy Spirit, who is in you, whom you have received from God? You are not your own; you were bought at a price" (1 Corinthians 6:19–20a). Today, live like who you are, a one-of-a-kind treasure of the Divine Collector of souls.

Tradition of the Ring

Exodus 20:6

ON his deathbed, my great-great-grandfather passed down his wedding ring to his sixteen-year-old grandson, my grandfather, who passed it down to me with the same message he had received: "Keep it and pass it on to future generations."

When passing down the Ten Commandments to Moses, God said that He would show love to a thousand generations of those who love Him (Exodus 20:6). The Hebrew word for *generations* is the same word used for *circle* (*dor*), the shape of a ring. Made from precious metal, a ring is symbolic of the abundant value of love. Being circular, a ring is also symbolic of the never-ending value of love. It illustrates God's love that is both abundant and eternal. We will either live inside God's circle of intimacy or we will live outside-in idolatry.

Today, intentionally live inside God's ring of love. Let go of anything that is drawing you outside His circle of trust and experience the intimate connection of your heart with His. Keep it, and pass it on to future generations.

Pride Blocks Restoration Road

Proverbs 20:21

THE prodigal son in Jesus's parable jumped at the chance to live free from the rules of his father; his pride fueled his decision. He survived for a while by his own giftedness and survival skills, but his foolish choices perpetuated a tug of war between pride and humility. Pride won temporarily. With his heart scattered like grains of sand on a beach, the farther he traveled away from home, the more compact his heart became.

The prodigal son had a sand heart, one that required a storm to shape it, and as his resources dwindled, he stood on the verge of a tsunami. It was the natural consequence of the foolish way he had abused his resources in his lack of humility, especially toward his father. Perhaps the prodigal would have reflected on Solomon's warning: "An inheritance claimed too soon will not be blessed at the end" (Proverbs 20:21).

If your sand heart has presented you with a low-pressure system that is about to scatter your resources in the wind, would you consider the prodigal son's example and return to your heavenly Father? He will restore you with a heart of clay.

King Solomon

Proverbs 18:12

HAVE you ever played the fool? King Solomon was the wisest mortal to ever live. Many of his wise sayings are captured in the Book of Proverbs where he had much to say about the destructiveness of being a fool. Solomon's work focused more on the fool than, say, the liar, the cheat, or the murderer. He taught that the fool is the broader category because it represents the condition of a proud heart.

In athletics, parenting, marriage, friendships, work, and ministry, we risk making foolish choices that often carry costly consequences when a wise choice would have improved our life and the lives of those around us. Solomon, arguably the richest, most knowledgeable, most famous, and most powerful person to walk the earth, made many wise and many foolish choices in an effort to discover life's ultimate satisfaction. His reflection on what motivated him is priceless for us today. It was a matter of the heart.

Pride is the antithesis of humility and wisdom, which is to be prized above all else. Consequently, we want to avoid the role of the fool at all costs. Solomon warned: "Before a downfall the heart is haughty, but humility comes before honor" (Proverbs 18:12). Today, ask God to remove any hardness in your heart so that you may avoid playing the fool and its subsequent downfall. He will lift you up.

Five Stages of a Fool

Proverbs 14:15; 26:11; 1:7; 21:24; 30:32

A STUDY of Proverbs shows us five stages of foolish behavior from the Hebrew language. First is the gullible, or *simple*, fool (Proverbs 14:15). The second level of hardening is the *stupid* fool who repeats his gullible behavior (Proverbs 26:11). The third stage is the *stubborn* fool who despises wisdom and discipline (Proverbs 1:7). Fourth is the *scorning* fool, a mocker and destroyer of organizations (Proverbs 21:24; 9:7–8). The fifth and final stage is the hardened *secular* fool who is godless (Proverbs 30:32).

This list represents a cycle of increasing hardness of heart, from *gullible* to *godless*. A good analogy of this pride is cement. When it is poured, it is wet and formable, but afterward it begins a hardening process that cures and turns stone-cold, immoveable, fixed, and unchanging. The gullible fool is still formable, but the godless fool has no hope unless he fully surrenders his foolish heart to the Restorer.

How have you played the fool? Surrender the sand and stone in your heart to the Restorer today.

The Simple Fool

Proverbs 14:15; 28:13

THE first stage of foolishness is the *simple* fool. The simple fool is gullible. Solomon advised: "The simple believe anything, but the prudent give thought to their steps" (Proverbs 14:15). The simple fool is naïve, but still teachable—able to learn from his circumstances, leaving hope for wisdom (Proverbs 19:25; 21:11). If we are ever going to play the fool, we want to do it in stage one so that we will respond to the consequences of our foolishness with repentance and wisdom.

King David's foolishness with Bathsheba might have been simple, but it carried significant consequences. When the prophet Nathan pointed out his sin and rebuked him, David responded with repentance and wisdom. Proverbs says that this kind of fool loves simplemindedness and waywardness. He lacks common sense. He is undiscerning of evil, yet his heart is still wet cement. He has hope for returning to the wisdom of God.

Are you learning from the negative circumstances of your life? Try this little exercise: open your calendar and examine your appointments. Ask God to illuminate any gullible or naive behavior. If He does, confess the pride underneath the foolishness and humbly surrender it to Him. Listen to Solomon's counsel when he says: "Whoever conceals their sins does not prosper, but the one who confesses and renounces them finds mercy" (Proverbs 28:13).

The Stupid Fool

Proverbs 26:11

THE *stupid* fool represents the second stage of a foolish heart. Solomon observed: "As a dog returns to its vomit, so fools repeat their folly" (Proverbs 26:11). The stupid fool repeats his patterns of lashing out in anger (Proverbs 29:11), leading to the disruption of family relationships (Proverbs 10:1). He repeats his wickedness (Proverbs 10:23), deceit (Proverbs 14:8), slander (Proverbs 10:18), and shame (Proverbs 3:35). The stupid fool is a person who has no sense of learning from his actions, no matter how many times he falls.

Solomon also observed the stupid fool is dangerous with money: "Why should fools have money in hand to buy wisdom, when they are not able to understand it?" (Proverbs 17:16). He noticed the stupid fool chases fantasies with his eyes (Proverbs 17:24) until he exhausts all of his resources. The reason for his stupidity is clear: The stupid fool trusts in his own heart. The Book of Proverbs states: "Those who trust in themselves are fools, but those who walk in wisdom are kept safe" (Proverbs 28:26). This self-trust leads to talking rather than listening: "Fools find no pleasure in understanding but delight in airing their own opinions" (Proverbs 18:2). The stupid self-reliant fool is hotheaded and reckless (Proverbs 14:16); he hates knowledge (Proverbs 1:22). Ironically, Solomon himself fell into this trap as his observations are recorded in the Book of Ecclesiastes.

Consider asking a close, trusted friend the following questions regarding your potential arenas of stupidity: Is folly evident in your life? Do you repeat the same destructive behavior? Are you chasing fantasies? In relationships, do you talk more than you listen? If the answer to any of these questions is yes, it's time to consider that you might be trusting in yourself rather than God.

The Stubborn Fool

Proverbs 12:15

THE third stage of foolishness is the *stubborn* fool who is right in his own eyes. Solomon noted: "The way of fools seems right to them, but the wise listen to advice" (Proverbs 12:15). The stubborn fool is so sure of himself that he declines sound advice. He is confounded by wisdom (Proverbs 24:7) and despises it along with discipline (Proverbs 1:7). He is quick to pick and stick: quick to quarrel (Proverbs 12:16), pick a fight (Proverbs 27:3), and stick the blame on someone else (Proverbs 14:9), leaving a trail of relational wreckage. Consequently, he lacks understanding and insight into the perspectives of others (Proverbs 10:21). This pattern destroys relationships. King Saul's heart became hardened to the point of him becoming a stubborn fool (1 Chronicles 19:13–14).

Take Solomon's stubborn fool test. Are you always right? Do you resist advice? Do you despise wisdom and discipline? Is your heart so hard that you show your annoyance immediately, refusing to overlook an insult? Are you characterized by unreconciled relationships, often blaming others for things that go wrong in your life? Do you mock at making amends for your sins? If the answer to any of these questions is yes, then it is time for a heart change.

The Scorning Fool

Proverbs 3:34

THE fourth stage of foolishness is the *scorning* fool. He is a mocker (Proverbs 21:24) who can't even find wisdom (Proverbs 14:6). Consequently, he struggles to separate wise choices from foolish ones, causing dissension in organizations. This is due to the fact that he has ignored all previous rebukes (Proverbs 9:7–8; 13:1). Thus, he must be removed from an organization in order for it to thrive (Proverbs 22:10).

The scorning fool even mocks God (Proverbs 14:9; 19:28). However, God takes direct opposition to the scorner in an effort to bring him back to wisdom: "He mocks proud mockers but shows favor to the humble" (Proverbs 3:34). King Nebuchadnezzar was a scorning fool who eventually responded in humility to God's opposition (Daniel 4).

Is it a challenge for you to separate wise choices from foolish ones? Would anyone at work, home, or play say that you are the cause of organizational dissension? Do you feel like you "kick against the goads" (Acts 26:14)? If so, then you are behaving like a scorning fool. However, it is not too late to soften your heart and turn to Him.

The Secular Fool

Proverbs 30:32

THE final stage of foolishness is the *secular* fool who exalts himself rather than God (Proverbs 30:32). His self-exaltation perpetuates a desire for more manipulative idolatry and disappoints those who have invested in him. The godless fool has hardened his heart with the image of his own handprint impressed so solidly in his inner being that he is unsatisfied by spiritual things (Proverbs 30:22). Consequently, he brings no joy to his earthly father (Proverbs 17:21). Nabal was a godless fool (1 Samuel 25:25) whose state of mind did not work out so well for him; God struck him dead.

Carefully consider your heart. Is there any area inside you in which you have exalted yourself above God? Are you living your life on autopilot, apart from Him? Are your desires truly satisfied in Christ or do you need more and more of your fix of choice to advance your own earthly kingdom at the expense of His? If so, you might be coming dangerously close to playing the secular fool. Surrender your hardened heart to the Restorer today.

Fear Paralyzes, Faith Catalyzes

Joshua 1:9

WHEN I was five years old, I panicked as I peered out the window of our vehicle, while my dad drove across the Mackinac Bridge, one of the world's largest suspension bridges spanning five miles and rising 552 feet above the Straits of Mackinac, connecting the upper and lower peninsulas of Michigan. It didn't help matters that my dad shouted, "You should be scared! Five construction workers died while they were building this!" Seeing my only safe-haven as the floor of the back seat, I crouched down in crash position, closing my eyes until we had crossed. I glanced out the rear window in utter amazement that we had navigated the enormous structure without crashing into the waters.

Fast-forward fifteen years, and I'm behind the wheel of a motorhome with my new wife Susan, my brother, my mom, and my dad, driving toward the bridge. I had dismissed my fear from a decade and a half prior as merely a child's perspective. As we drove closer to the bridge, it appeared larger and larger, looming like something you would see in an action movie. My heart began to beat outside my chest. My breathing was unlike any other time in my life, heavier than our high school basketball practices when we would run seventeens and suicides until we thought we would die. My stomach felt like it was about to heave. I could barely feel my limbs. My fingers were numb.

About that time, I noticed the gusts of wind tossing our RV back and forth. I began to focus on the steep incline of the bridge that looked like it was a ramp to the sky. I could have been diagnosed with gephyrophobia (fear of crossing bridges). Finally, I shouted, "I can't do this! I hate this bridge!" That's when my bride saved the day for me, confidently exclaiming, "Pull over! I'll drive!" Grateful for her bravery, I parked on the shoulder of the road and moved to the passenger's seat, deeply wanting to assume the crash position on the floor of the motorhome until we had crossed.

Fear paralyzes. Faith catalyzes.

In preparing Joshua to lead the Israelites into battle for the Promised Land, God instructed him: "This is my command—be strong and courageous! Do not be afraid or discouraged. For the LORD your God is with you wherever you go" (Joshua 1:9). Fear is the antithesis to faith, trusting in our God who is closer than we realize. Surrender your fear and discouragement to the One who can restore you with strength and courage because He is indeed with you. The God who delivered the Israelites from their enemies will guide you to be a catalyst for Christ amidst any circumstance.

Fear Not

2 Timothy 1:7

THE most frequent command in the Bible is to "Fear not." Fear stems from trusting in ourselves, rather than God. When we operate in fear, at least three things happen: we become weak, we hate what we fear, and we fall apart. Whether inside the lines of athletic competition, in a heated argument, or a marketplace conflict, tight muscles slow us to a screeching halt as we under-perform from how we have been trained and how God designed us to be effective.

The apostle Paul was well acquainted with fear. He experienced fierce governmental and religious backlash as he preached the gospel of Jesus Christ. While imprisoned, Paul reflected on his persecution when he wrote his final letter to his disciple Timothy: "For the Spirit God gave us does not make us timid, but gives us power, love and self-discipline" (2 Timothy 1:7). Fear paralyzes. Faith catalyzes. Faith in Christ leads to the indwelling of His Holy Spirit who transforms our weakness into power, our hate into love, and our brokenness into the Spirit's restorative control. He truly makes us new again, ready to face any conflict or competition in our life, including advancing the cause of Christ in the hearts and lives of those we encounter, regardless of the resistance that surrounds us.

What conflict has paralyzed you in fear? It might be a match-point serve, a crucial free-throw, a speech, a counterpart in a legal battle, a difficult person, boldly sharing Christ with a friend, or even a suspension bridge. Move from fear to faith. When you are weak, hateful, and falling apart, become a catalyst to those around you, rallying them to move toward your common, worthy goal. Memorize the acronym FAITH: Forsaking All I Trust Him. As you deeply inhale and exhale, recite these words to yourself and take your next best step. All the while remember: Fear paralyzes. Faith catalyzes.

God's Calm Amidst the Chaos

Psalm 46:1–9

I N this challenging time of uncertainty and fear, where are you turning for refuge, strength, and help? Each of us has a go-to that we believe will provide us solace. We seek the next deal, a strong balance sheet, an appreciating market account, a profitable income statement, a steady paycheck, a performance recap that moves up and to the right, excellent health, victory in competition, achievement, a social gathering, a sporting event, a concert, a vacation, or even a live church service. However, when it all comes to a screeching halt with very little warning, and circumstances are beyond our control, we risk panic, driven by fear, the most contagious virus of all. If we seek our strength from anything apart from God Himself, we end up worried, anxious, and afraid, feeling insignificant, out of control, insecure, and discontent. The writers of Scripture knew a great deal about the stress of trying times. That's why the psalmist penned: "God is our refuge and strength, an ever-present help in trouble" (Psalm 46:1). As Christ-followers, we want to believe this verse to be true, but when the never-before-seen international storms of life come upon us, we discover whether we truly believe.

The psalmist continued as if he were writing about today's scene of events: "Therefore we will not fear, though the earth give way and the mountains fall into the heart of the sea, though its waters roar and foam and the mountains quake with their surging" (Psalm 46:2–3). Regardless of the circumstances, our Creator offers us continual hope and joy: "There is a river whose streams make glad the city of God, the holy place where the Most High dwells" (Psalm 46:4). Intimacy

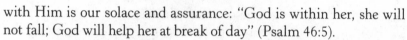

with Him is our solace and assurance: "God is within her, she will not fall; God will help her at break of day" (Psalm 46:5).

The psalmist's words are applicable to our current pandemic: "Nations are in uproar, kingdoms fall; he lifts his voice, the earth melts" (Psalm 46:6). God has not abandoned us. He is close to each one of us, protecting our lives, providing our every breath: "The LORD Almighty is with us; the God of Jacob is our fortress" (Psalm 46:7).

God always wins. He always has the final say. He fulfills every one of His promises. Even in our physical death, God takes us home to be with Him for eternity. No one can fathom His omnipotence: "Come and see what the LORD has done, the desolations he has brought on the earth. He makes wars cease to the ends of the earth. He breaks the bow and shatters the spear; he burns the shields with fire" (Psalm 46:8–9). God will defeat every virus. He will conquer every fear with faith.

Be Still and Know

Psalm 46:10–11

THE Almighty has a message for each one of us: "Be still, and know that I am God; I will be exalted among the nations, I will be exalted in the earth" (Psalm 46:10). In essence, God is saying, "Don't panic. Don't worry. Don't be afraid. Relax, let go, and experience intimacy with Me. You can trust Me. I Am who I say I Am."

Today—more than ever—when we need refuge, strength, and help we must remember: "The LORD Almighty is with us; the God of Jacob is our fortress" (Psalm 46:11). Only God provides security in the storm, clarity piercing the confusion, confidence in spite of the catastrophe, peace during the pandemic, calm amidst the chaos.

This week, pursue intimacy with God by praying specifically for those who are critically ill. Make your muscles move with your prayers by helping someone in need. Share a scarce resource. Make a grocery run for an elderly neighbor. Spend quality time with those you love and connect with family and friends in other communities through a video chat. Our technology-rich society has made face-to-face encounters a rarity. In this season, we can hit the pause button on the busyness of life and experience rich relationships. Play a game, immerse yourself in a novel or biography, watch an inspirational movie, work out, go for a walk, cook a new recipe, write that book God has placed on your heart, read the Bible, listen to a new worship song, or memorize your favorite verse from Psalm 46, reciting it each day, as you experience God's calm amidst the chaos.

The Restoration of Grace

2 Corinthians 8:9

ON the spectrum, the opposite side from sin is God's grace. Grace is the kind of undeserved love and or unmerited favor exhibited in the father who ran to his son outside the city gates in the Parable of the Prodigal Son. God is like that father: even though we break His law, He pursues us with His affection.

Grace flows from the heart of God. In spite of our sin, the Restorer bends the knees of His heart to us in order to engage us, the undeserving, with His love. Paul penned: "For you know the grace of our Lord Jesus Christ, that though he was rich, yet for your sake he became poor, so that you through his poverty might become rich" (2 Corinthians 8:9).

God's radical movement toward us can be remembered in the acronym GRACE: God's Riches At Christ's Expense. Will you accept God's gracious pursuit of you? Pray, "God, thank You for running to me and chasing me down. You have given everything for me. I accept Your free gift of grace."

Moses and God

Exodus 34:8

O N Mount Sinai God revealed to Moses that He was indeed gracious, which is translated from the Hebrew root word, *chanan*, meaning "to bend or stoop to one who is inferior." In spite of our sin, the Creator bends to us, the created, in order to engage us with His love.

Moses' response to the grace of God on Mount Sinai was the only affirmative posture one could take in order to receive unmerited favor. In an act of self-examination and surrender, he not only bent his physical knees, but also submitted to God's glory and presence: "Moses bowed to the ground at once and worshiped" (Exodus 34:8).

The Hebrew word used for *worship* here is *shachah*, the term most frequently translated as *worship* throughout the Old Testament. It means "to bow down." In order to receive grace, we—like Moses— must bow down and humbly receive it from the One who stooped down to us in order to extend His loving offer. Today, bend the knees of your heart, along with the knees of your body in prayer to God. Ask Him to shape your heart to be like His, full of grace.

Walk With God

Exodus 34:9

A FTER being blessed with God's glory on Mount Sinai, Moses spoke to God in a way that showed his heart of confession, repentance, and belief in God's grace: "'Lord,' he said, 'if I have found favor in your eyes, then let the Lord go with us. Although this is a stiff-necked people, forgive our wickedness and our sin, and take us as your inheritance'" (Exodus 34:9).

The word *go* is translated from the Hebrew word, *halak*, which means "walk." In spite of their sin, God graciously walked with the Israelites, just as Jesus walked with His disciples. We learn four important truths from Moses' response to grace. First, Moses examined his heart and surrendered it to God. Second, he confessed his sin. Third, he repented and believed in God's grace. Fourth, he walked with God. All four of Moses' moves toward I AM were empowered by His grace.

Will you humbly walk with God? Ask Him to examine your heart and reveal any area where you are attempting to be the lord of your own life. Agree with God regarding your desires for life apart from Him. Change your perspective of your sin and commit to a new life in Christ. Now, you are ready to take your first steps on a new journey with God.

Sin and Basketball

Proverbs 28:13

THE New Testament writers used several Greek words for sin. However, those most frequently used can be summed up in four predominant terms. Each can be illustrated using a basketball free-throw analogy.

First, missing the mark (*hamartia*) is attempting to make the shot, but missing it. Second, twisting a wrong to make it right (*adikia*) is missing the shot, then going ahead and telling everyone we made it anyway. Third, missing on purpose (*anomia*) is obviously shooting to miss. Finally, leaving good undone (*paraptoma*) is not shooting at all. We step up to the line with the basketball in our hands, knowing what to do, and never release it toward the goal.

How are you approaching your attempts at the line of life? Are you missing the mark, twisting a wrong to make it right, missing on purpose, or leaving good undone? King Solomon taught: "Whoever conceals their sins does not prosper, but the one who confesses and renounces them finds mercy" (Proverbs 28:13). Confess your sins to the Restorer who will lavish you with His undeserved love and make you new again.

Missing the Mark

Romans 3:23; 6:23

DO you ever fall short of what you are trying to accomplish in your relationship with God? *Hamartia*, a Greek word for sin, is missing the mark. In basketball, missing the mark is like attempting to make the shot, but missing it.

Missing the mark describes one aspect of how each of us sins. Using this term for sin, the apostle Paul said: "For all have sinned and fall short of the glory of God" (Romans 3:23). That is why we need God's grace. Paul continued: "For the wages of sin is death, but the gift of God is eternal life in Christ Jesus our Lord" (Romans 6:23). Paul juxtaposed three pairs of terms in this verse: (1) wages and gift, (2) sin and God, and (3) death and eternal life. Let's unpack those terms further.

Wages implies that we earn the results of sin, both by nature and by choice. Consequently, we deserve what comes our way. *Gift*, in contrast, communicates that we merely receive a loving act. *Sin* means that we miss the mark. By contrast, God is the mark that we miss; He is holy—totally apart from sin (Habakkuk 1:13). *Death* is separation from God. On the other hand, *life* is the abundant and uninterrupted spiritual vitality God designed for us to have in Christ, who provides His Spirit to dwell in us.

Left on our own, we cannot right our wrongs. Our falling short earns us separation from a holy God. God's grace in Jesus Christ fills in our sin-gap. In a sense, Jesus rebounds our misses and scores for His kingdom. Have you truly received God's gift of eternal life in Christ?

Twisting the Shot

Romans 1:18; 1 John 1:9

HAVE you ever justified a sin as being acceptable to God? *Adikia*, a Greek word for sin, means twisting a wrong to make it right. This is like missing the shot, then telling everyone that we made it. *Adikia* literally means "no righteousness." John said that all unrighteousness is sin (1 John 5:17), and we must realize the damage we do to the kingdom of God when we justify our unrighteous actions by calling them righteous ones. Onlookers see our hypocrisy much clearer than we think.

Unrighteousness is also translated as *wickedness*. Using this term, Paul said that twisting a wrong to make it right suppresses the truth: "The wrath of God is being revealed from heaven against all the godlessness and wickedness of people, who suppress the truth by their wickedness" (Romans 1:18).

That's why we need grace. The key that unlocks the door to God's grace is *confession*. John wrote: "If we confess our sins, he is faithful and just and will forgive us our sins and purify us from all unrighteousness" (1 John 1:9). *Confession* means "to agree." We see our own sin as God does. When we agree with God that we indeed missed, He forgives us and restores us.

Take a moment to confess your sins to God. Thank Him for His forgiveness and for making you new again.

Missing on Purpose

Romans 4:7

SOMETIMES, even as believers, we go on autopilot apart from God and determine for ourselves what is right and what is wrong. *Anomia* is a Greek word for sin that literally means "no law." It is breaking the law, or committing a transgression, which is stepping over the line. In our basketball illustration, this is missing on purpose, similar to the first sin in the Garden. Adam knew what was wrong, he understood the consequences, and he sinned anyway.

In the face of our intentional sin, the need for God's grace becomes crystal clear. Quoting David who experienced God's grace when he missed on purpose, Paul wrote: "Blessed are those whose transgressions are forgiven, whose sins are covered" (Romans 4:7; cf. Psalm 32:1). The word "transgressions" is also translated from *anomia*. God forgives our purposeful misses with His boundless grace in Christ when we trust in Him (Romans 4:5). This trust leads us to a saving repentance (2 Corinthians 7:10).

Have you been missing on purpose? Do you know what is wrong? Do you understand the consequences, and are you sinning anyway? Trust Christ and repent.

Refusing to Take the Shot

Ephesians 2

Do you feel called to help someone in need, but paralyzed to take the first steps to do so? Oftentimes we sin by leaving good undone. We step up to the line with the basketball in our hands, knowing what to do, and refuse to take the shot. James noted: "If anyone, then, knows the good they ought to do and doesn't do it, it is sin for them" (James 4:17).

When we operate on our own agendas apart from God, we do not execute the good we were designed to do. Paul wrote: "As for you, you were dead in your transgressions and sins" (Ephesians 2:1). *Transgressions* stems from the Greek word *paraptoma*, meaning "to fall away." When presented with an opportunity to do something good, we often fall away from it and do nothing. Jesus gave us an example in His parable about a good Samaritan (Luke 10:25–37).

God's grace in our lives moves us beyond confessing and removing sin. When we experience God's grace, we are then empowered to do good works. In his letter to the Ephesians, Paul wrote: "But because of his great love for us, God, who is rich in mercy, made us alive with Christ even when we were dead in transgressions—it is by grace you have been saved" (Ephesians 2:4–5). By God's grace, through faith in Him, we are made alive in Christ to do all the good works that God prepared in advance for us to do (Ephesians 2:8–10).

Are you leaving good undone? Examine your heart and life, fully surrendering them to God. Confess your sins. Repent and believe in God's grace. Walk with the forgiving God who walks with you.

Locked Boxes

1 Corinthians 6:19–20

HAVE you noticed that the most valuable commodities in the world are locked in boxes? The more valuable the commodity, the more elaborate the box and the lock. I was visiting a customer of mine who lived in a European castle with a bombproof box crafted below ground and secured with an elaborate combination lock. As my anticipation grew, he carefully entered the combination and unlocked the vault door, revealing what was behind it: the world's two most expensive antique secretary desks, purchased for $2 million each and now neatly displayed in his climate-controlled box.

God has placed a box inside each one of us that holds within it a treasure much more precious than those valuable desks. It's the box of the spiritual heart. The Bible tells us that God is the highest bidder for the contents of our inner boxes: "Do you not know that your bodies are temples of the Holy Spirit, who is in you, whom you have received from God? You are not your own; you were bought at a price. Therefore honor God with your bodies" (1 Corinthians 6:19–20). The box of the spiritual heart is either locked and unrestored or unlocked and restored. Pride is the lock on the human heart; humility is the key.

Will you humble yourself to Christ and allow Him to unlock and restore the contents of your heart today?

The Parable of the Pharisee and Tax Collector

Luke 18:9–14

DO you have an inner competitive spirit that wants to be first, right, or at the top of the success ladder? That's pride. It even shows up in our relationship with God. We want to justify His acceptance of us through our religious acts.

In order to humble our hearts, we must continue to surrender our pride. In a great story tucked in the Gospel of Luke, Jesus contrasted the temple prayer of a proud Pharisee with that of a humble tax collector. The respected Pharisee exalted himself while the disrespected tax collector stood at a distance, refused to look up to heaven, and beat his breast—three acts of humility. The tax collector finally made an attempt to put into words the condition of his heart: "God, have mercy on me, a sinner" (Luke 18:13). Jesus said that the tax collector, not the Pharisee, went home justified before God. He summed it up this way: "For all those who exalt themselves will be humbled, and those who humble themselves will be exalted" (Luke 18:14b).

Have you exalted yourself? Bend the knees of your heart to God and with everyone you encounter. Then watch as God's mercy restores your relationships.

Herod and Jesus: Significance

Luke 23:46

DOES your pride lead you to a desire for significance apart from God that has left you feeling insignificant?

There might not have been another human being in Jesus's time whose pride imprisoned him, both figuratively and literally, more than Herod the Great. He proudly held the title of Tetrarch of Judea (a sign of his desire for significance) 2,000 years ago, when Jesus was born. Herod was known as the "King of the Jews," a title he received from the Roman Senate (37–4 BC), but the Jews would not recognize it because of its origin. He lived in his palaces with locked and closed doors, reflective of his heart. In the end, Herod died insignificant in his palace in Jericho in 4 BC. Historians believe he passed away most likely due to a bout with syphilis.

In contrast, Jesus died significant, satisfied in the Restorer's love: "Jesus called out with a loud voice, 'Father, into your hands I commit my spirit.' When he had said this, he breathed his last" (Luke 23:46). Find your significance in the love of Christ and share His love with everyone you see.

Herod and Jesus: Contentment

Luke 23:34

KNOWN for his great building programs, including the rebuilding of the Temple (a sign of his desire for contentment), Herod the Great built his first in a series of palace fortresses three miles southeast of Jesus's birthplace in Bethlehem. However, Herod remained filled with discontent. He killed his favorite of ten wives, three of his sons, and decreed the killing of boys age two and younger after the Magi inquired about the birth of Jesus.

In the end, Herod died discontented.

In contrast, Jesus and His father Joseph were most likely stone masons in Nazareth. They might have worked at a stone amphitheater in Sephora known as the "Ornament of Galilee," only three to four miles away from Herod's familiar grand structures.

Jesus died content, satisfied in the Restorer's peace, forgiving those who were crucifying Him: "Jesus said, 'Father, forgive them, for they do not know what they are doing.' And they divided up his clothes by casting lots" (Luke 23:34).

Discover true contentment in the peace of God found only in Christ. Share that peace by prioritizing reconciled relationships with everyone you encounter.

Herod and Jesus: Security

Luke 23:43

WHAT makes you feel secure? Security is a God-given desire in each of us, but we tend to search for the satisfaction of it in the wrong places, leaving us insecure.

Herod the Great built a series of palace fortresses that were designed to give him safe asylum if forced to flee the country to his homeland of Idumea (a sign of his desire for security). Indicative of his heart, proud and harsh King Herod sought security in his fortresses and locked doors, keeping others out.

In the end, Herod died insecure.

Jesus offered an alternative to the lock of pride and the unrestoration of harshness. He was humble and gentle (Matthew 11:29). He was a liberator who authoritatively freed people, healed them, gave them life, and offered them access to a different kind of power. He sought out others, moving toward them in relationship to uncover the love of the Father in them.

In contrast to Herod, Jesus died secure, satisfied in the Restorer's truth, offering that security to others including the repentant thief on the cross: "Jesus answered him, 'Truly I tell you, today you will be with me in paradise'" (Luke 23:43).

Discover your security in the truth of God in Christ. He is the same yesterday, today, and forever.

Herod and Jesus: Control

John 19:30

Do you have the need to be in control, attempting to manage every desired outcome? This often leads to life feeling out of control. Few have pursued control to the level of King Herod the Great.

Herod's largest fortress was the Herodian, forty-five acres of building constructed on 200 acres of land, the third-largest architectural find in the ancient world. The palace featured four towers, the highest stretching 120 feet into the air, sprawling fifty-five feet in diameter (a sign of his desire for control).

In the end, Herod died out of control. To ensure mourning rather than rejoicing at his death, Herod issued a decree that several prominent Jews be executed at his passing. His sister Salome reversed this edict.

Jesus died in control, satisfied in the Restorer's power to fulfill prophecy (John 19:2).

While on the cross, Jesus did not breathe His last breath until He had finished His purpose, a mark of control discovered in the power of the Restorer: "When he had received the drink, Jesus said, 'It is finished.' With that, he bowed his head and gave up his spirit" (John 19:30).

Discover control from the power of God in Christ who will empower you to advance His kingdom in the hearts of others.

Restoring the Four Chambers of Your Heart: WISE

Proverbs 11:2b; 4:23

JUST as the physical heart is comprised of four chambers, so the spiritual heart is comprised of four chambers remembered in the acronym WISE: *Will, Intellect, Spirit,* and *Emotions.*

The first chamber is the *will,* the chamber of our choices. The second is the *intellect,* or the mind, the chamber of our thoughts. The third is the *spirit,* the lead chamber of our prayers. The fourth chamber is the *emotions,* our feelings.

To understand how they work, imagine filling out a bracket during the NCAA men's basketball tournament. When you look at the two teams playing each game, your intellect tells you which team has the better record. You think that team will win, but the opponent happens to be your alma mater, which is teetering toward a losing record. Your emotions are so favorable toward your former school's team that you really want to select it as the victor. So, you choose with your will to be loyal to your school colors and write its name in the blank. Finally, you pray in your spirit that the outcome will be in your favor.

In order to be restored to authenticity, we must fully surrender all four chambers to the Restorer. We must choose, think, pray, and want to make this surrender. Solomon profoundly stated: "With humility comes wisdom" (Proverbs 11:2b). Genuine humility surrendered vertically toward God will be fleshed out in humility surrendered horizontally toward others. God's subsequent wisdom in Christ will restore our spiritual hearts and our relationships.

Solomon taught: "Above all else, guard your heart, for everything you do flows from it" (Proverbs 4:23). We must guard where we direct our affections. Surrender all your heart to the Restorer today. Choose to, think to, pray to, and want to. He will make you new again.

Restoring Your Will

Luke 22:42

THE *will* is the spiritual heart's chamber of our choices. Nearly every action is preceded by a choice. In order to experience wisdom in our lives, we must surrender our will, or our choices, to God (Proverbs 8:10). In essence, it is the flip of a switch.

Jesus surrendered His will to the Father. Just before His arrest and subsequent crucifixion, Jesus prayed: "Father, if you are willing, take this cup from me; yet not my will, but yours be done" (Luke 22:42). In surrendering His will to the Father, Jesus had the wisdom to accomplish His Father's desires.

God is asking us to flip the switch and choose to make wisdom the measurement of success in our lives. What about you? Will you humbly flip the switch of your heart and choose wisdom? The answer begins when, like Jesus, you choose to bend the knees of your heart to the Father's will.

Restoring Your Intellect

Proverbs 15:33; Matthew 22:37

THE *intellect* is the spiritual heart's chamber of our minds, or our thoughts. In order to unlock the gate to wisdom, we must humble our minds to God. The humbled intellect is a light that illuminates our hearts. King Solomon said: "Wisdom's instruction is to fear of the LORD, and humility comes before honor" (Proverbs 15:33). *The fear of the LORD* is humility toward God. When we humble our intellects to God, we learn wisdom.

Jesus is the Word, or the expression, of the mind of God (John 1:1). Jesus surrendered His mind to the Father (Matthew 22:37). Likewise, Paul said that we should take every thought captive and make it obedient to Christ (2 Corinthians 10:5). This restores us from pretense to authenticity because when we humble our intellects to God, we have the mind of Christ (1 Corinthians 2:16).

Begin filling your intellect with wisdom by reading a chapter of Proverbs each day. God's wisdom will restore your mind.

Restoring Your Spirit

Proverbs 20:27; Luke 23:46

THE *spirit* is the lead heart chamber of our prayers. The Bible refers to the spirit as the lamp of God used to search our innermost beings (Proverbs 20:27). Prayer is the connection of our heart with God's. In essence, it's being online with the Creator. In order to humbly surrender our spirits to the Father, we must pray for wisdom.

Jesus surrendered His spirit to the Father. Each of the Gospel writers recorded Jesus praying alone daily with the Father and living online 24/7 with Him. Luke captured Jesus's last prayer: "Jesus called out with a loud voice, 'Father, into your hands I commit my spirit'" (Luke 23:46).

Follow Jesus's model and become a person who PRAYS: *Praise* your heavenly Father for who He is. *Renew* your mind to be to be focused on His kingdom, rather than your own. *Ask* God for whatever you need to advance His kingdom. *Yield* all unsettled accounts to Him. *Surrender* to be Spirit-led. You will experience His heavenly wisdom in your life.

Restoring Your Emotions

Luke 23:34; 1 Peter 2:23

OUR *emotions* represent the spiritual heart chamber of our feelings. These are the multiple reflectors of the light in us. A simple way to categorize our feelings is: mad, sad, glad, or afraid. In order to fully surrender our hearts to the Father, we must feel like it. We must want to bend our knees to His will. This is a desire that includes an emotive reflection.

Jesus surrendered His emotions to the Father. While being crucified with criminals as Roman soldiers divided up His clothes by casting lots, Jesus prayed: "Father, forgive them, for they do not know what they are doing" (Luke 23:34). Peter, who witnessed this wrote: "When they hurled their insults at him, he did not retaliate; when he suffered, he made no threats. Instead, he entrusted himself to him who judges justly" (1 Peter 2:23). *Entrust* literally means "to hand over."

Are you struggling with a particular set of emotions stemming from a recent offense? Hand over your emotions to God who will restore you to authenticity and use you to bring His restoration to those you encounter.

Yield the Outcomes to God

Joshua 24:23

AT nine years old, I stood in my dad's office supply room in the half-light, in my mind risking eternal salvation for stealing a shiny metal box to hold my rock collection. I hesitated and hedged, but I eventually decided it was worth the risk. I took it. In the days after I stole the box, I tried to justify my actions. I'll never forget the dichotomy of my parents' response during a Sunday lunch when I confessed my hidden sin. Mom was appalled. However, in the other corner my politician dad came through like a champ, saying, "I own the office and everything in it. You're entitled to take whatever you need, including the shiny metal box."

I left the table liking Dad's theology a lot more than Mom's. It was less convicting. However, restoration theology is different. In it, a gracious God pays for our sin in Christ, accepting us as fully loved children when we surrender to Him. Still, something inside each of us attempts to control every outcome in our lives, even if it means taking something that is not ours. Consequently, we need to yield our hearts to God in order to yield the outcomes to Him. Joshua said it this way: "Throw away the foreign gods that are among you and yield your hearts to the LORD" (Joshua 24:23).

In order to yield ourselves to God, we need to ask the Holy Spirit to eliminate any desire for life apart from Him, any sin that separates us from a heart of clay and manifests itself in a foreign god. Each of us must ask Him, "What god am I white-knuckling?" It might be money, an illicit relationship, improper use of the internet, a career,

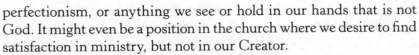

perfectionism, or anything we see or hold in our hands that is not God. It might even be a position in the church where we desire to find satisfaction in ministry, but not in our Creator.

What's your shiny metal box? Are you justifying something that has come between you and God? Surrender it to the Restorer today. Yield your heart to God and then yield the outcomes of every conflict to Him. You will discover intimacy with God is greater than any outcome you try to control.

Restore Your Heart Chart

2 Corinthians 10:5

WE go through life seeing ourselves through one of three lenses: the clouded perspective of others, our own clouded perspective, or the crystal clear 20/20 vision of God. Too often, our thoughts, feelings, choices, and prayers flow from our fallen perspectives that see ourselves in pretense. This is due to our own self-restoration programs that attempt to unlock ourselves from the prison of pride from the outside in.

The Restore Your Heart Chart is a tool for us to see ourselves, not with the clouded perspectives of others, nor from our own clouded perspectives, but from God's authentic, crystal clear perspective.

You can remember it easily. Divide a journal page into five columns: Time, Thoughts, Feelings, Choices, and Prayers. Underneath Time, record the reading of the clock when you encounter a destructive thought. Under Thoughts, write down the destructive idea or image that came to mind. Under Feelings, write your emotions resulting from your destructive thought. Below Choices, write down the choice you made regarding the specific thought and its corresponding emotion. Finally, under Prayers, write, "I can't. You can."

Surrender your thoughts to Christ as the apostle Paul taught: "We demolish arguments and every pretension that sets itself up against the knowledge of God, and we take captive every thought to make it obedient to Christ" (2 Corinthians 10:5).

Experience God's restoration of your heart as you surrender all four chambers to Him.

The Restorer's Water

Jeremiah 2:13

AS a result of the first sin, we have compartmentalized God and dammed the flow of the Holy Spirit in our lives. When we compartmentalize, we create boundaries that did not previously exist in God's design, and we become god in each compartment of our lives. Consequently, through the prophet Jeremiah, God said: "My people have committed two sins: They have forsaken me, the spring of living water, and have dug their own cisterns, broken cisterns that cannot hold water" (Jeremiah 2:13).

A cistern was built to catch and store rainwater by covering a basin of stone with plaster. After years of use, the plaster would crack, causing the cistern to leak. It would no longer hold water. Only clay holds water. That's a picture of a humble heart, surrendered to God.

Jesus Christ provided His Spirit to live through those who fully surrender their hearts and lives to Him (John 7:37–39). God never intended for us to make cisterns. Rather, He designed all of life as an opportunity to release the Holy Spirit in us as we drink from the Spring of Living Water. Flow has always been His design.

Where have you created a cistern? Is it in your body, your finances, your thoughts, your worship, or your relationships? Experience the flow of the Living Water.

The Restorer's Water: Physical

Jeremiah 2:13

A PHYSICAL cistern dams the flow of the Holy Spirit into our bodies, what we eat, what we drink, where we sleep, how we live. God knew fallen mankind's propensity for physical cisterns when He said: "My people have committed two sins: They have forsaken me, the spring of living water, and have dug their own cisterns, broken cisterns that cannot hold water" (Jeremiah 2:13).

Paul said that each of us who fully surrenders his heart to the Restorer becomes the walking temple of the Holy Spirit (1 Corinthians 6:19). That means everyone who locks eyes with us is encountering the Spirit of God.

In light of your body being God's holy temple, begin your day with 3 Ws: *Word*, *Worship*, and *Workout*. Inhale the breath of God through reading the Bible, worshiping Him with music, and exercising each morning. Then exhale His Spirit by humbly quoting the Word, worshiping God with your decisions, and working out your salvation for others to see.

The Restorer's Water: Financial/Will

1 Chronicles 29:11–12

A *FINANCIAL* cistern represents the damming of the will. This hardening of our choices stops the flow of the Holy Spirit in our financial world.

An example of choosing to compartmentalize God from our finances often occurs when we decide to arbitrarily give him ten percent of our gross income. This places God and our finances in a neat and tidy box. However, willfully surrendering our finances is not that simple. God has intended something totally different than neat and tidy boxes that dam the flow of the Holy Spirit in our financial resources. Instead, He calls humble clay hearts to give one hundred percent of our time, talent, and treasure to release the Holy Spirit in our lives.

After receiving more than enough gifts for the construction of the temple, David praised God in front of the entire assembly, saying: "Yours, LORD, is the greatness and the power and the glory and the majesty and the splendor, for everything in heaven and earth is yours. Yours, LORD, is the kingdom; you are exalted as head over all. Wealth and honor come from you; you are the ruler of all things. In your hands are strength and power to exalt and give strength to all" (1 Chronicles 29:11–12).

How could you surrender to release the flow of the Holy Spirit into your financial world?

The Restorer's Water: Mental

2 Corinthians 10:5

WHERE does your mind take you? A *mental* cistern compartmentalizes God from our thoughts. We often seek knowledge to increase our intelligence, in order to make decisions apart from Him.

Thoughts can become a very safe place for a Christian to sin, to lust after someone who is not our spouse or to desire a life we do not have. These destructive mental cisterns will eventually affect our words and our steps. Consequently, we must release the flow of the Holy Spirit in our minds. Paul offered a solution to mental cisterns: "We demolish arguments and every pretension that sets itself up against the knowledge of God, and we take captive every thought to make it obedient to Christ" (2 Corinthians 10:5).

Is your mind thirsty for God? Drink from the flow of the Living Water and memorize 2 Corinthians 10:5 today.

The Restorer's Water: Spiritual

John 7:37–38

D O you limit God to a particular worship style in a specific building during one hour on a certain day, or even a quiet time, a Bible study, or a small group, while you take control of the other 167 hours of your week? If so, you've created a *spiritual* cistern, which compartmentalizes God.

Mankind has been building spiritual cisterns since the first sin, but God desires the Holy Spirit to saturate all of our hearts all 168 hours of the week. Jesus proclaimed: "Let anyone who is thirsty come to me and drink. Whoever believes in me, as Scripture has said, rivers of living water will flow from within them" (John 7:37–38). That stream of living water is His Holy Spirit.

How would your life change if you reclaimed every moment as a spiritual one, constantly drinking from the flow of Living Water?

The Restorer's Water: Social/Emotional

1 John 4:19–21

A SOCIAL cistern contains friends, business associates, spouses, and children to be leveraged for our selfish benefit only.

John offered a different way, one that would allow the flow of the Holy Spirit to all of our relationships. It's called love: "We love because he first loved us. Whoever claims to love God yet hates his brother or sister is a liar. For whoever does not love their brother and sister, whom they have seen, cannot love God, whom they have not seen. And he has given us this command: Anyone who loves God must also love their brother and sister" (1 John 4:19–21). God calls us to the flow of self-sacrificial love.

Reclaim all your thirsty relationships for God with the quenching flow of the Living Water. Solicit a friend to join you in breaking social cisterns. Meet weekly to read the Bible, pray, and serve others in need. You will experience the transformative flow of the Holy Spirit's love.

Don't Forget God

Deuteronomy 8:11a, 17–18

GOD blesses us financially, yet we often forget Him. We tend to measure success and failure in terms of money: our accomplishments and our shortfalls, as well as our profits and our losses. Consequently, we hinder the Holy Spirit's work, putting us at risk of losing everything. However, on our road toward restoration, God calls us to release our financial resources for the advancement of His kingdom.

Have you forgotten God? Read carefully what God said to His people through Moses: "Be careful that you do not forget the LORD your God . . . You may say to yourself, 'My power and the strength of my hands have produced this wealth for me.' But remember the LORD your God, for it is he who gives you the ability to produce wealth, and so confirms his covenant, which he swore to your ancestors, as it is today" (Deuteronomy 8:11a, 17–18).

Today, remember God and surrender your heart to Him, including your financial decisions. He will make you new again.

Outlets

1 Peter 4:10

WHAT is your outlet? At first, you might describe a hobby or a hideaway, if anything at all, but God designed us to have outlets for His restoration to flow to others.

Everything in the Dead Sea dies because it has no outlet. In contrast, the Sea of Galilee brings life because its outlet allows flow. God designed the same for our lives. The apostle Peter wrote: "Each of you should use whatever gift you have received to serve others, as faithful stewards of God's grace in its various forms" (1 Peter 4:10).

When our first of our four daughters was still an only child, I was invited to view our local homeless shelter's new facility. The first person who greeted me was a four-year-old girl playing on the floor. She was the same age as my daughter. For the first time in my life, I realized that a child in the county where I lived could be homeless. After my tour, I went back to my office and wrote a check to the shelter that stretched my sacrificial cardiac muscles. I experienced the flow of the Holy Spirit's water that day.

When our humble clay hearts recognize God as the inlet of our financial resources, we seek ways to help those in need. Today, thank Christ for being your inlet of resources and ask Him for guidance to discover your outlet.

Captive Thoughts

2 Corinthians 10:5

WHAT dominates your thoughts? The apostle Paul penned: "We demolish arguments and every pretension that sets itself up against the knowledge of God, and we take captive every thought to make it obedient to Christ" (2 Corinthians 10:5). Our problem is we try to be god in our own lives.

A humble heart of clay shows us that we must release the Holy Spirit in our minds. If we continue to rely on our own knowledge, we will watch while another cistern begins to crack as the Living Water escapes. *Taking captive every thought* means we identify any destructive idea or image in our minds that flows from a licentious sand or legalistic stone cistern of pride. *Making it obedient to Christ* means we surrender it to Him, experiencing His perspective, His mind, His wisdom. When we identify and surrender destructive thoughts to the Restorer, He will transform our emotions, which tend to follow our beliefs.

In order to release the Holy Spirit's water into the clay chamber of your intellect, read the Bible daily and allow the Word to permeate your thoughts. As you get into the Word, the Word will get into you. You will be empowered to take captive every thought and make it obedient to the Restorer as His Living Water transforms your mind.

Relationships Over Religion

Deuteronomy 6:4–9

THE spiritual was not fashioned for religion, but for relationships. God desires the Holy Spirit to saturate our hearts all 168 hours a week.

"Hear, O Israel: The LORD our God, the LORD is one. Love the LORD your God with all your heart and with all your soul and with all your strength. These commandments that I give you today are to be on your hearts. Impress them on your children. Talk about them when you sit at home and when you walk along the road, when you lie down and when you get up. Tie them as symbols on your hands and bind them on your foreheads. Write them on the door frames of your houses and on your gates" (Deuteronomy 6:4–9).

Today, memorize these verses and recite them twice a day, the pattern of its original audience, a pattern that was maintained for millennia. God will release the Holy Spirit in your spiritual life, as you give Him every moment that encapsulates every act as a spiritual one.

Restored Relationships

Matthew 22:37–39

WHAT is the true purpose of your relationships? We often leverage connections with our friends, business associates, spouses, and children for our benefit only. Jesus bottom-lined the eternal value of relationships when He defined the two greatest commands: "'Love the Lord your God with all your heart and with all your soul and with all your mind.' This is the first and greatest commandment. And the second is like it: 'Love your neighbor as yourself'" (Matthew 22:37–39). We cannot do one without the other. The love of God empowers us to creatively, intentionally, and actively love those around us.

God calls us to self-sacrificial love. Today, find someone in your world with whom you can share part of your time, talent, or treasure to advance the kingdom of Christ. Write a note, meet a need, or give a gift. You will love God through genuinely loving others, bringing His eternal purpose to your relationships.

Reclaiming Relationships

Proverbs 18:24

WHERE do you draw the boundaries for your relationships? Whom do you let in, and whom do you keep out?

Sometimes we draw the lines too loosely. Solomon observed: "One who has unreliable friends soon comes to ruin, but there is a friend who sticks closer than a brother" (Proverbs 18:24). In Hebrew, the phrase "many companions" and the word "ruin" come from the same root. It is a picture of hardening our hearts toward God's design for our relationships. This often occurs when we hang around those who entice us to sin in our areas of weakness.

Other times we draw the lines too tightly, only wanting to be around those who mimic our beliefs, so we feel comfortable. However, Paul continually communicated we should make the most of every opportunity to reach outsiders (Colossians 4:5–6; 1 Corinthians 5:10; 9:22). Otherwise, we risk leveraging every relationship for our selfish benefit.

What would happen if you would surrender your relationships to God's boundaries?

Today, reclaim all of your relationships for advancing the heart of Christ. Search for ways to help your friends experience the Spirit of the Restorer. You might even begin studying the Bible with some of them. Focus on how you can apply your relationship with God to your marketplace encounters. In your conversations with all, be transparent about your journey on Restoration Road. You will discover many people are traveling the same path.

Successful Relationships

Proverbs 15:27

Wʜᴀᴛ'ꜱ your definition of success? Often, we keep score by power, prestige, or profit. Author and speaker John Maxwell defined his measurement of success as: "Those who know me best will love and respect me the most." How would embracing this definition transform your relationships?

Years ago, when I owned an auction business, I decided to make this my benchmark of success. As a recovering workaholic and money addict, I began to prioritize the most sacred relationships that I had neglected, searching for ways I could travel less or even schedule my family to accompany me on business trips. We became the beneficiaries of the Holy Spirit realigning and restoring our relationships to His original design.

Solomon taught: "The greedy bring ruin to their households, but the one who hates bribes will live" (Proverbs 15:27). Is it time for you to start living? Change your definition of success from power, prestige, or profit to one that prioritizes relationships with your family. God will restore them to His original design.

Living Water for Thirsty Souls

John 7:37–39

IS your soul thirsty for God? Jesus said that anyone who fully surrendered to Him would experience the Living Water of the Holy Spirit flowing from his heart: "On the last day, that great day of the feast, Jesus stood and cried out, saying, 'If anyone thirsts, let him come to Me and drink. He who believes in Me, as the Scripture has said, out of his heart will flow rivers of living water.' But this He spoke concerning the Spirit, whom those believing in Him would receive; for the Holy Spirit was not yet given, because Jesus was not yet glorified" (John 7:37–39 NKJV).

Jesus's words were spoken in a loud voice during the last feast of the year, in the temple, where a crowd of hundreds of thousands had gathered. At the Feast of Tabernacles, the priests would lead the people out each day to their source of water, a process they repeated for seven days. They would come through the water gate of the wall surrounding Jerusalem, carrying a gold pitcher of water, and pour it on the altar to commemorate God leading them and providing physical water through the Exodus. Then they would pray for the autumn rains for their crops.

God's answer to those prayers far exceeds physical rain. He pours out Living Water that refreshes thirsty hearts by restoring their foolish desires to wisdom. The Restorer's ripple effect flows to you and me. Today, fully surrender your heart to Him and experience the flow of Living Water.

Restoring Flow

Titus 3:3–7

ARE you attempting to restore yourself from the conse-quences of your sins? Have your efforts left you dissatisfied and unrestored?

Paul described the futility of self-restoration and the hope dis-covered in the only true Restorer: "At one time we too were fool-ish, disobedient, deceived and enslaved by all kinds of passions and pleasures. We lived in malice and envy, being hated and hating one another. But when the kindness and love of God our Savior appeared, he saved us, not because of righteous things we had done, but because of his mercy. He saved us through the washing of rebirth and renewal by the Holy Spirit, whom he poured out on us generously through Jesus Christ our Savior, so that, having been justified by his grace, we might become heirs having the hope of eternal life" (Titus 3:3–7).

Jesus Christ lived, died, was buried, resurrected, ascended into heaven, and provided His Spirit to live through those who fully sur-render their hearts and lives to Him. God never intended for us to restore ourselves by making hardened, cracked cisterns. Rather, He designed all of life as an opportunity to release the Spirit of Christ in us as we drink from the Spring of Living Water. *Flow* has always been the design of the Designer.

Today, surrender your self-restoration attempts to the One who can wash you clean, make you new again, and give you hope.

Satisfaction

John 10:10b

HAS your introspection helped you determine where you have compartmentalized your life with cisterns? Is it the *physical* pursuit, the *willful* drive for *financial* security, the *mental* exercise for more *intellectual* knowledge, the *spiritual* treadmill of good works, or the *socio-emotional* experiment of more surface relationships? Only the flow of the Spirit of Christ will satisfy your thirsty heart.

The Restorer's blood paid the price for our sins. When we fully surrender our hearts to Him, He transforms our lives of black and white to living color by releasing the Holy Spirit in us. The Restorer flows through us and changes a culture thirsting for authenticity, the design of the Designer. Jesus revealed: "I have come that they may have life, and have it to the full" (John 10:10b). He desires to fill everyone with His eternal and abundant life.

Surrender to the flow of His water of life to continually satisfy your thirsty heart, allowing the Spirit of the Restorer in you to bring satisfaction to others who desire to be restored to authenticity.

Foundations

1 Corinthians 3:10–13

AT the executor's request, I visited a New England farmhouse that had been home to an heirless couple. I noticed how the structure leaned in one direction on its foundation. As I entered the foyer, I was surprised to see junk stuffed in boxes spread apart widely enough to form a maze through the various rooms. Below the couple's routine path, I could see through the wood floor to the foundation underneath.

The executor shared that an unfathomable discovery inside this home had generated a plethora of publicity. One million dollars' worth of gold bars had been hidden in the house's foundation. Additionally, in their barn, they had stockpiled thirty rusted antique and classic cars worth millions of dollars, even in their dilapidated state. The wealthy couple had lived like misers since the Great Depression, in fear of another economic collapse.

These powerful images caused me to reflect. With money rather than wisdom as our foundation, we build insecure lives tilted with crooked priorities as our framework, failing to recognize the warning offered in Scripture: "But each one should build with care. For no one can lay any foundation other than the one already laid, which is Jesus Christ. If anyone builds on this foundation using gold, silver, costly stones, wood, hay or straw, their work will be shown for what it is, because the Day will bring it to light. It will be revealed with fire, and the fire will test the quality of each person's work" (1 Corinthians 3:10b–13).

On what foundation have you built your life? Perhaps today is the day that you invite the Restorer to become your foundation and renovate your world.

Desires

Proverbs 2:6; 3:15

DESIRES are not for our gratification, nor their elimination, but for our transformation. They are intended to point us toward desiring God and lead us to restoration, so that we become carriers of this life-altering message. These are desires that can only be satisfied in full surrender to the Restorer.

Amid our travels on Desperation Road to gratify our desires, the Restorer draws us to Himself in order to free us from our addictions that come in many forms: a bottle, a syringe, a plate, a screen, a green rectangle sheet of linen and paper, or even uniquely fashioned flesh. God desires that we surrender these addictions to pursue hearts filled with wisdom so we discover freedom from our enslavement and find transformation in Him.

Solomon offered the location of wisdom's satisfying source: "For the Lord gives wisdom; from his mouth come knowledge and understanding" (Proverbs 2:6). He elaborated, regarding wisdom's value: "She is more precious than rubies; nothing you desire can compare with her" (Proverbs 3:15).

Through the Master Key of full surrender to the Restorer, you will discover wisdom only found on Restoration Road.

God's Will

Psalm 37:4; Romans 12:2

DO you often wonder what God's will is for your life?

King David described the process of knowing the will of the Almighty in a psalm: "Take delight in the LORD and he will give you the desires of your heart" (Psalm 37:4). *Delight, anag* in Hebrew, means "to make one's heart pliable." In essence, it is a surrendered heart, humbled toward God, like clay in the Potter's hands. *Give* is translated from *nathan* in Hebrew, meaning "to orchestrate." Thus, when our hearts become malleable in God's hands, He makes our desires to be like His. This is how we experience God's will in our lives.

Paul said it this way: "Do not conform to the pattern of this world, but be transformed by the renewing of your mind. Then you will be able to test and approve what God's will is—his good, pleasing and perfect will" (Romans 12:2).

Today, offer your heart and mind to God, like clay in the Potter's hands. He will shape your desires to be like His, and you will begin to experience His will for your life.

How Much Is Enough?

Ecclesiastes 5:10

HOW much is enough?

Solomon, the wealthiest person on earth, reflected: "Whoever loves money never has enough; whoever loves wealth is never satisfied with their income. This too is meaningless" (Ecclesiastes 5:10). Money will never satisfy.

During a business trip through Germany, I discovered a proverbial hidden treasure. It was a Horch twelve-cylinder special roadster built in the 1930s, now stored in a small garage across from the owner's flat in a gorgeous German village. As the owner and I were looking at the restored twelve-cylinder power plant under the hood, he shared his philosophy about contentment and money. He was most likely describing why he valued this multimillion-dollar car, yet lived in a modest home.

In his German-accented English, he reflected, "You know, there are two ways to live life. One is to make a lot of money in hopes that you will *someday* be able to enjoy it. The other is to enjoy it as you go. I've chosen the latter." His wisdom got my workaholic attention.

What about you? Have you given your life to earning as much as you can in hopes that you will someday be able to enjoy it? If so, surrender that discontented desire to the Restorer who will give you peace.

Sinful Nature or the Holy Spirit?

Romans 8:5–11

DOES your sinful nature or the Holy Spirit control you?

Paul taught: "Those who live according to the flesh have their minds set on what the flesh desires; but those who live in accordance with the Spirit have their minds set on what the Spirit desires. The mind governed by the flesh is death, but the mind governed by the Spirit is life and peace. The mind governed by the flesh is hostile to God; it does not submit to God's law, nor can it do so. Those who are in the realm of the flesh cannot please God" (Romans 8:5–8).

Paul communicated to those who desired to be restored to authenticity that they were to be controlled by the Spirit of the Restorer: "You, however, are not in the realm of the flesh but are in the realm of the Spirit, if indeed the Spirit of God lives in you. And if anyone does not have the Spirit of Christ, they do not belong to Christ. But if Christ is in you, then even though your body is subject to death because of sin, the Spirit gives life because of righteousness. And if the Spirit of him who raised Jesus from the dead is living in you, he who raised Christ from the dead will also give life to your mortal bodies because of his Spirit who lives in you" (Romans 8:9–11).

Today, surrender to the Holy Spirit, rather than your sinful nature. The result is life and peace.

Power in Weakness

2 Corinthians 12:9–10

WHERE do you find power? It might not reside where you think.

Paul discovered power in humility: "But he said to me, 'My grace is sufficient for you, for my power is made perfect in weakness.' Therefore I will boast all the more gladly about my weaknesses, so that Christ's power may rest on me. That is why, for Christ's sake, I delight in weaknesses, in insults, in hardships, in persecutions, in difficulties. For when I am weak, then I am strong" (2 Corinthians 12:9–10).

This power is the Spirit of the Restorer dwelling in us. The weaker we are in our selfishness, the more He shines through our lives.

Greater power resides in humbly serving others because it frees us from pride's bondage and draws others to Christ in us while we grow in our intimacy with both. The more we give up control, the more we find it. Christ is the power of God (1 Corinthians 1:24), and His complete power is unlocked in our lives through the key of humility.

Today, realize ultimate control rests in the hands of the Restorer and live in freedom. When you are weak, He is strong.

Down Under

Philippians 2:3–5

How do you find wisdom in your personal encounters?

In an effort to fully surrender my business to the Restorer, I developed the mission statement for our company, "Serve God and others," printing it on our brochures discreetly under the postal indicia.

I'll never forget the words of an Australian car collector after he picked up a brochure to read aloud my company's guiding phrase. "You know, before I called you, I noticed this line on your brochures. I realize someone could talk these things and walk a totally different path; however, I felt like it was worth taking a chance to cross the pond for someone who was willing to stand up and be counted."

I learned that day about the power discovered in the Restorer, who calls us to serve Him and others. Paul offered the secret to accomplishing this: "Do nothing out of selfish ambition or empty pride, but in humility consider others more important than yourselves. Each of you should look not only to your own interests, but also to the interests of the others. Let this mind be in you which was also in Christ Jesus" (Philippians 2:3–5 BSB).

When we humble ourselves to God and to the people we meet, we discover the sweet spot where our unselfish interests intersect with God's interest and the interests of others. This is the benchmark to discover wisdom in every encounter.

What Is the Target of Your Success?

Proverbs 17:16

WHAT'S your target of success? For many of us, it's money. We frequently find ourselves working so hard for it that we miss out on our relationships with family, friends, and coworkers.

Placing profit ahead of people is outside God's design for our lives. It's not the money that's evil; rather, it's the desires of our hearts that can be.

Solomon philosophized: "Why should fools have money in hand to buy wisdom, when they are not able to understand it?" (Proverbs 17:16). Money apart from wisdom will never satisfy.

Changing our target of success from money to wisdom unlocks the door to restoration and brings us closer to authenticity, reflecting the design of the Designer.

Today, begin a plan to search for wisdom in every encounter. If you have yet to do so, begin by reading a chapter a day in Proverbs that corresponds with the date of the month. You will read through the thirty-one chapters of Proverbs twelve times over the next year. Each day, select a verse to apply to your calendar. Learn how to connect God's heart with street smarts in all your circumstances.

David's Prayer of Restoration

Psalm 139:23–24; 51:10

IS there any area of your life where you have one foot in and one foot out with God? That's the definition of anxiety, a divided inner being. When our hearts are partially devoted to God, we trust in our giftedness, rather than godliness.

To get both feet in with God requires full surrender of our hearts. We surrender our impurities, our mixed devotions, and relying on our giftedness rather than our godliness (Christ in us). Surrender says to God, "I can't. You can. I can't satisfy my desires with mixed devotions. You can when I am fully devoted to You." In order to do this, we need to pray David's prayer of restoration.

First, we ask God to search our heart for any mixed devotions: "Search me, God, and know my heart; test me and know my anxious thoughts. See if there is any offensive way in me, and lead me in the way everlasting" (Psalm 139:23–24). The way everlasting comes with a pure heart, one that is fully devoted to God.

Second, we ask God to create in us a pure heart: "Create in me a pure heart, O God, and renew a steadfast spirit within me" (Psalm 51:10).

A life restored to authenticity moves us to search our hearts for any mixed devotion, any impurities, and seek renewal for a heart that is fully devoted to restoration in the Father.

Today, pray David's prayer of restoration and watch your anxiety fade.

Sinful Desires

2 Timothy 2:22

SIN is a desire for any life apart from God. It attempts to find significance, contentment, control, and security in everything else, but Him. The more we try to find these apart from God the more insignificant, discontented, out of control, and insecure we become. Our search is right, yet we often look in the wrong places.

Our desires are not for our gratification, not their elimination, but for our transformation. We need to connect our search to the answer of forgiveness and Lordship, found only by grace through faith in the Restorer, Jesus Christ.

Paul described how we find this transformation: "Flee the evil desires of youth and pursue righteousness, faith, love and peace, along with those who call on the Lord out of a pure heart" (2 Timothy 2:22).

When we flee our evil desires that proudly search for satisfaction apart from Christ, we humbly turn with a pure heart to the Restorer where we find true satisfaction. *Righteousness* is what is right in God's sight, which is *truth* that satisfies our desire for *security*. *Faith* is trusting in God rather than in ourselves for *control*, which is *power*. *Love* is self-sacrificial serving where we discover our ultimate *significance*. *Peace* is absence of strife where two become held together as one, satisfying our desire for *contentment*.

Today, focus on the search for your heart's transformation in Christ alone by memorizing Paul's life-changing words.

Life's Wheel

John 3:16; Ephesians 2:14; 1 Corinthians 1:24; John 14:6

IMAGINE life like a wheel.

In our hurriedness, ambition, worry, or anxiety, we attempt to live at the outside of a wheel that seems to move faster and cover more ground as we trust in our giftedness rather than our godliness. This is pride. However, Christ is at the hub of the wheel, drawing each of us to true life in Him.

Each of us wants significance, something that is only found in love so unmerited that it's called grace. Each of us desires contentment. We want our worlds held together. Each of us pursues control, ever increasing the reach of our respective wills. Each of us longs for security, desiring something, anything, to be true all the time. The problem is we search for them at the outside of the wheel, rather than at the hub.

Christ is the answer to our search.

Christ is the grace of God (John 3:16; 2 Corinthians 8:9). Christ is the peace of God (Ephesians 2:14). Christ is the power of God (1 Corinthians 1:24). Christ is the truth of God (John 14:6). When we humble our hearts to Christ, He brings grace, peace, power, and truth to our lives.

Today, humble your heart to Christ. Turn from the outside of the wheel and discover true life at the hub in Him.

Relating the Gospel to Others

Acts 20:24; Ephesians 6:15; Romans 1:16; Ephesians 1:13

HOW do you relate the gospel of Christ to others?

When we fully surrender our desires to Christ, we translate His satisfying restoration to others. The apostle Paul used four nouns to describe the gospel of God's restoration, which we share with others: grace, peace, power, and truth—the satisfaction of our four primary desires.

We were designed to relate restoration to others in this pattern.

We translate restoration to others through the gospel of grace: "However, I consider my life worth nothing to me; my only aim is to finish the race and complete the task the Lord Jesus has given me— the task of testifying to the good news of God's grace" (Acts 20:24).

We translate restoration to others through the gospel of peace: "And with your feet fitted with the readiness that comes from the gospel of peace" (Ephesians 6:15).

We translate restoration to others through the gospel of power: "For I am not ashamed of the gospel, because it is the power of God that brings salvation to everyone who believes: first to the Jew, then to the Gentile" (Romans 1:16).

We translate restoration to others through the gospel of truth: "And you also were included in Christ when you heard the message of truth, the gospel of your salvation. When you believed, you were marked in him with a seal, the promised Holy Spirit" (Ephesians 1:13).

God's design is that we vertically receive the Restorer's grace, peace, power, and truth in order to transfer them horizontally to others. It's a living portrait of the cross. Try it and see!

Restoring the Sand-Hearted

Luke 15:22–24

IN Jesus's trilogy parable captured in Luke 15, the prodigal son exhibited a sand heart, one that was loose and licentious, scattered in the wind. The father satisfied the desires of his sand-hearted younger son through the gift of restoration.

When the younger son returned home, sandals were placed on his feet, which transformed him from a slave back into a son. This illustrated the father satisfying the son's desire for significance translated in the love, or grace, of the patriarch.

Calling for a calf, rather than a goat, implied everyone in the community was invited, not just the family. This noted the father satisfying the younger son's desire for contentment translated into the peace of the father's reconciliation of the son with the community.

The servants scattered to find the father's robe, since it was the best. This symbolized the father satisfying the younger son's desire for security translated in the truth that everything he owned had belonged to the son.

They placed the ring on his son's finger to restore his ability to make business deals, an act that committed the father's resources. This demonstrated the father satisfying the younger son's desire for control translated in the power he had transferred.

These four acts by the father restored his younger son to authenticity, the original design of the Designer.

Are you a sand-hearted younger brother in need of restoration? It's time to come home to your heavenly Father who is waiting for you with open arms.

Restoring the Stone-Hearted

Luke 15:31–32

HAVE you interpreted a relationship with God as a religious set of rules that have left you feeling insignificant, out of control, insecure, and discontented?

In one of the greatest stories ever told, Jesus described an elder son with a stone heart, one that was legalistic, rigid, and immovable. The father offered the same satisfaction of the stone-hearted elder son's desires he had provided in the four images restoring his sand-hearted younger son. Let's examine the text from Luke 15:31–32.

"My son" demonstrates significance translated in the love of the father for his son pictured in sandals covering his elder son's feet.

"You are always with me" reveals control translated in the power of the father noted in the ring that would always be on his elder son's finger.

"Everything I have is yours" illustrates security translated in the truth of the father providing all his son had needed, evidenced in the father's robe draping over his elder heir.

The father's plea: "But we had to celebrate and be glad, because this brother of yours was dead and is alive again; he was lost and is found" points to contentment translated in the father's peace, symbolized by the calf reconciling two lost sons with the community, totally at the father's expense.

The father offered restoration of his elder son's stone heart through the transformation of his desires.

Are you a stone-hearted older brother? Is it time for you to discover the relational clay heart of the Father? Humbly receive His gift of love, power, truth, and peace in Christ.

The Clay Heart of the Father

2 Corinthians 5:18, 20a

WHAT would happen if you surrendered your desires vertically to the Restorer and became significant in the grace of God, content in the peace of God, under control in the power of God, and secure in the truth of God? If you trusted in godliness rather than your giftedness, would you transfer the satisfaction of your desires in the Restorer horizontally to others?

How you answer these questions can bring you one step closer to living with a humble heart of clay. Like the father in Jesus's parable, "The Prodigal Son," who reached out to his two sons, the Restorer offers us grace, peace, power, and truth enabling us to live restored to our authentic condition in an effort to bring authentic restoration to others.

We are not the ones restoring, rather it is Christ in us: "All this is from God, who reconciled us to himself through Christ and gave us the ministry of reconciliation" (2 Corinthians 5:18). "We are therefore Christ's ambassadors, as though God were making his appeal through us" (2 Corinthians 5:20a).

Today, ask Him to use you to bring His restoration to those you encounter.

Good, Bad, or Humble?

Matthew 11:29

OUR goodness can be just as much of a barrier to God as our badness because we often trust in it. Jesus told a parable that became known as "The Prodigal Son." However, Jesus never titled it by that name. Instead, He described two sons, with the climax of the story focusing on the elder son justifying his goodness to the radical grace of the father.

Two thousand years later, those of us with the sand heart of the younger son tend to be loose and *licentious*. Those of us with the stone heart of the elder son are *legalistic* and rigid. When life is good, we thank ourselves. When life is challenging, we blame God. However, those of us with the clay heart of the father have a heart of *love*.

Which heart condition most resembles you?

Jesus called out: "Take my yoke upon you and learn from me, for I am gentle and humble in heart, and you will find rest for your souls" (Matthew 11:29).

Today, humble your heart to your heavenly Father and surrender any sand or stone in your life. He will give you His soft heart of clay.

The Intern, Sales Manager, and Entrepreneur

1 Peter 4:10

AN entrepreneur owned a start-up social networking business. He strategically placed his office in the center of his one hundred employees who could observe his work ethic through the glass panes surrounding his command central. One day, an intern who made wine in her spare time brought him one of her family's best bottles. Her motive was gratitude for the entrepreneur taking a risk to hire her during her last semester of college.

"You are heading up new client management, aren't you?" the entrepreneur inquired.

"Yes sir," the intern answered tentatively.

"How does a promotion sound?" the entrepreneur asked. Assuming the affirmative reply, he continued with issuing his decree, "As of today, you are vice president of marketing. Your salary will triple, you will drive a corporate sport utility, enjoy an expense account, and receive full health benefits. Your first assignment is to recruit a team of fifty sales associates."

His generosity garnered the attention of an onlooking and overhearing sales manager who thought to himself, "Wow, if a cheap bottle of wine gets a six-figure salary and benefits, I wonder what I would get if I gave the boss a week's vacation to the Atlantis?"

After a quick online purchase during his lunch break, the sales manager skipped into the entrepreneur's suite with his $10,000 gift certificate in hand. His eyes beamed as he placed the envelope on his leader's desk waiting for him to open it.

"Wow, thank you so much!" said the grateful business mogul as he pulled the certificate from his envelope for only a matter of seconds. He tossed the gift on his desk and began to walk out of his office to his next appointment. He had barely passed through the threshold of his doorway when the enraged sales manager shouted loudly enough for all to hear.

"Wait a minute!" he screamed. "I saw the intern give you a cheap bottle of homemade Merlot, and you made her vice president of marketing with a six-figure salary and full benefits. I gave you a $10,000 gift certificate to travel to one of the world's finest resorts, and you gave me nothing?" The sales manager pleaded with the entrepreneur who looked him deeply in his eyes and spoke with heart-piercing words.

"The intern gave the gift to me," the chairman replied. "You gave the gift to yourself."

Jesus's disciple Peter offered God's design for gifts: "Each of you should use whatever gift you have received to serve others, as faithful stewards of God's grace in its various forms" (1 Peter 4:10).

Today, live out the heart of the intern.

Giving the Gift to Ourselves

1 Peter 4:11

W E all do it.

A nonprofit corporation CEO offers a favor to a potential donor whom he will ask later for a charitable contribution that will advance his agenda for the organization. He gave the gift to himself.

A busy husband reluctantly adheres to his wife's request to pick up the kids from school only so he might find his reward from her that night. He gave the gift to himself.

A car salesman buys lunch for a prospective new car purchaser. He gave the gift to himself.

A politician serves the homeless for five minutes by filling their plates with food at a local soup kitchen while the television cameras capture the footage. The airing will garner him votes. He gave the gift to himself.

After teaching Jesus's followers to use their gifts to serve others, Peter continued to describe why: "If anyone speaks, they should do so as one who speaks the very words of God. If anyone serves, they should do so with the strength God provides, so that in all things God may be praised through Jesus Christ. To him be the glory and the power for ever and ever. Amen" (1 Peter 4:11).

We either use our gifts to serve others, honoring God, or we use them to glorify ourselves. The condition of our hearts is the determining factor.

Today, examine your gifts and select one to graciously serve someone in need. You will grow in your intimacy with Him.

The Giving Experiment

2 Corinthians 9:11

A RE you eager or reluctant to share your resources? Paul taught: "You will be enriched in every way so that you can be generous on every occasion, and through us your generosity will result in thanksgiving to God" (2 Corinthians 9:11).

God designed us to be *generous* with our gifts of time, talent, and treasure. He wants us to *use* our gifts received vertically to *serve* those horizontally, so that they *connect* vertically with the grace of the Generous One. It's a picture of the cross in action.

Generous and *generate* come from the same Latin word, *genus*, meaning "race or kind." *Generous* means "giving." *Generate* means "multiply." Consequently, *generosity multiplies giving* in the human *race*. God's desire is to multiply our gifts through us to generate generosity in others.

Today, take the giving experiment and generously offer a portion of your time, talent, and treasure to someone. Watch what God does.

Filling the Gap

Psalm 139:1

IS there any area in your life where you are pretending?

Attempting to satisfy our desires apart from God creates the gap of pretense in each one of us. Like a spine that is out of alignment, this gap misaligns our hearts, desires, and three resources of life (time, talent, and treasure), from the outside in, leaving us dissatisfied.

In our postmodern culture, we deconstruct, or peel back, the layers of a person, beginning with the outside working inward, in search of the most valuable word in today's society—authenticity. We can define authenticity as the alignment of our spiritual hearts with our desires and our three resources of life placed in the hands of the Restorer.

When we delve deeper into the aligned life, desires, and heart of a fully surrendered person, authenticity grows in power. In today's culture it is increasingly difficult to find a person without pretense, so it is a surprise when we discover someone who is the same in all places at all times. When we do, we say, "He's the real deal."

David penned: "You have searched me, LORD, and you know me" (Psalm 139:1).

Today, be real and ask God to examine your heart for any area where you have been pretending and surrender it to Him. Be authentic with the One who designed you, and He will fill your gap of pretense.

Favoritism

Jeremiah 29:13

D O you ever show favoritism?

Favoritism is giving the gift to ourselves, and it misses out on intimacy with God (James 2:8–9). It flows from a partially surrendered heart. We show favoritism to those we coach, lead, manage, or serve. We might do so out of fear of losing something we want to keep or hope to gain something we desire to have.

However, God desires full surrender to Him so we treat everyone fairly. When we partially surrender our lives, we are actually surrendering nothing. Surrendering half of our heart is surrendering none. Surrendering some of our desires is surrendering none. Surrendering some of our time, talent, and treasure is, in effect, surrendering none. Partial surrender is nonsurrender because it uses others to serve ourselves. Our Designer knows our motivations and sees what lies behind our actions.

God said that partial surrender is pretense (Jeremiah 3:10). We pretend to surrender to Him when, in fact, we hold back part of our hearts.

God spoke through the prophet Jeremiah: "You will seek me and find me when you seek me with all your heart" (Jeremiah 29:13).

Are you holding back anything from God, showing favoritism to someone in order to keep or gain something? Confess it to the Restorer today.

Posturing Greed

Luke 12:15a

WE must beware of discriminating against the rich in order to help the poor (Exodus 23:3). *This is posturing greed.*

Posturing greed is pretense: helping the poor with a disguised internal jealousy against the rich. We attempt to pursue social justice apart from the loving heart of God. Too often, our hearts for aiding those in need become hardened toward the economically rich, the very ones we ask to help the poor.

This dichotomy arises both inside and outside churches where we pursue helping the poor when we hatefully bash the rich. Posturing greed can take place whenever we seek to help the poor merely to draw attention to our self-serving agendas. We give the gift to ourselves.

Both the rich and the poor need to find Restoration Road. Not all economically rich people are spiritually bankrupt, nor are the poverty-stricken all saints. Whether rich or poor, God focuses on the heart (1 Samuel 16:7)—and He focuses on our hearts as well, as we give to those in need or interrelate with those who are not.

Jesus warned: "Watch out! Be on your guard against all kinds of greed" (Luke 12:15a).

Is there any posturing greed in your heart? Surrender it to the Restorer today. Apply John Wesley's advice, "Earn all you can, save all you can, give all you can."

The "Need" For Greed

Deuteronomy 8:17–18

D O you respond to God's generosity and the needs of others with *greed*? Has your attempt at self-restoration been about what you can gain or protecting what you are afraid to lose? Have you tried to be restored, but your self-ambition has pulled you away from living generously?

If you answer any of these questions yes, consider whether your heart has been hardened toward becoming the kind of generous person God desires you to be.

Think about this—is your generosity reserved only for those who will offer something in return? A nonprofit that will score you points for your business? A hurting relative of a good customer? A church that will put you in leadership? If so, then you give the gift to yourself. Perhaps you think, "Why not? I earned it."

Through Moses, God said: "You may say to yourself, 'My power and the strength of my hands have produced this wealth for me.' But remember the LORD your God, for it is he who gives you the ability to produce wealth, and so confirms his covenant, which he swore to your ancestors, as it is today" (Deuteronomy 8:17–18).

Surrender to the Restorer any thought outside God's design for your life. He will make you new again.

Wisdom Seen

Proverbs 8:11

H OW is wisdom seen in your life?

Wisdom is God's heart intersecting with street smarts. It's a picture of the cross. In order for us to apply our relationship with God to our earthly relationships and tasks, we must humble all four chambers of our spiritual hearts to Him (Proverbs 1:7). Remember the four chambers with the acronym WISE.

The *will* is the chamber of our *choices*. In order to experience wisdom in our lives, we must surrender our wills—our choices—to God. Humbling our wills to Him in order to experience wisdom is a choice (Proverbs 8:10). In essence, it is the flip of a switch.

The *intellect* is the chamber of our *thoughts*. In order to unlock wisdom, we must humble our minds to God (Proverbs 15:33). The humbled intellect is a light that illuminates our hearts. The best way to humble our minds to God is to read the Bible. We can read a chapter each day in Proverbs that corresponds with the date of the month and a chapter each day in the New Testament to complete it in a year.

The *spirit* is the lead chamber of our *prayers*. The Bible refers to the spirit as the lamp of God (Proverbs 20:27). He uses it to search our innermost beings. *Prayer* is the connection of our hearts with God's.

In essence, it is being online with our Creator. In order to humbly surrender our spirits to the Father, we must pray for wisdom before, during, and after our Scripture reading, as well as when we make significant decisions or encounter others during divine appointments.

Emotions represent the chamber of our *feelings*. These are the multiple reflectors of the light in us. In order to fully surrender our emotions to the Father, we must *want* to bend the knees of our hearts. This is a desire that includes an emotive reflection. Solomon passionately shared: "Wisdom is more precious than rubies, and nothing you desire can compare with her" (Proverbs 8:11).

Humble your heart to God and find that wisdom can be seen in your life. Choose it, study it, pray for it, and want it. You will discover that wisdom is a person, and that person is Jesus Christ (1 Corinthians 1:24). He fully surrendered His will, intellect, spirit, and emotions to the Father and dwells in those who fully surrender to Him.

The Heart and the Hand

Deuteronomy 15:7–8

Do you respond to God's generosity and to the needs of others with generosity in kind? What have you done with the three resources of your life when no one was looking that changed the circumstances of someone else? When have you given your time, talent, or treasure to someone who offered nothing in return? Take a moment and write down a few of those things and determine, to the best of your ability, if you did them out of greed or generosity. Was it the real deal or was it your attempt at a self-restoration program?

Greed flows from a hard heart to a tight fist, but generosity flows from a soft heart to an open hand. God's design aligns the heart with our three resources of life. Rather than being *hardhearted* and *tightfisted* with our resources, God's desire is we be *softhearted* and *openhanded*.

"If anyone is poor among your fellow Israelites in any of the towns of the land the LORD your God is giving you, do not be hardhearted or tightfisted toward them. Rather, be openhanded and freely lend them whatever they need" (Deuteronomy 15:7–8).

Today, be softhearted and openhanded.

Possessions and Purpose

Luke 12:15

ARE you locked inside the thought that life consists in the abundance of your possessions? Do you want to accumulate one more car, boat, house, collectible, business, or zero on the end of your investment account?

Jesus warned: "Watch out! Be on your guard against all kinds of greed; life does not consist in an abundance of possessions" (Luke 12:15).

Greed surfaces when we no longer own the stuff, but the stuff owns us. If you're caught in greed's grip, the Restorer can set you free.

As you surrender sacred pieces of your life to Christ, God will shape your career into a ministry that seeks to put people ahead of profit, relationship before remuneration, and ministry above any old greedy marketplace philosophy. When you offer your resources to God, He loosens your grip on money and achievement.

When you open your tight-fisted heart, God blesses your life and makes it possible for you to send those blessings out to help others. A clay heart enables you to see business as a way to generously give back resources to God's kingdom, multiplying His generous heart in others.

While each of us is still a work in progress and far from perfect, we can reflect and see the difference Christ continually makes in us. If there's anything in your life that owns you, surrender it to Him, and He will make you new again.

What's Fair?

Proverbs 3:5–6; 4:11

WHEN it comes to interpersonal conflict, do you struggle to determine what is fair?

Fairness includes straight paths. Solomon taught emerging leaders: "Trust in the Lord with all your heart and lean not on your own understanding; in all your ways submit to him, and he will make your paths straight" (Proverbs 3:5–6).

Solomon also passed along his father's advice, saying: "I instruct you in the way of wisdom and lead you along straight paths" (Proverbs 4:11). *Straight* is translated from the same root as *equity*, pointing toward what is fair. That root can be interpreted "smooth" or "evenly applied," a reference to the fashioning of metal.

Typically, in the course of interpersonal conflict in our lives, we do not evenly apply risk and return between ourselves and the other person involved. Risk is the potential for loss. Return is the gift, gain, or reward. When relational tension arises, we often pile up risk on the other party while we attempt to retain all of the return ourselves. Consequently, our paths become crooked, uneven, and full of greed.

Wisdom's tool for evening our paths is equity, which begins by placing the possibility for risk into God's hands. The antithesis of equity is trusting in our own fallen understanding, which tries to minimize our relational risk, or vulnerability, in a false attempt to maximize our egocentric return.

When encountering conflict with your coworker, spouse, children, parents, or friends, place the risk in God's hands. Trust in Him, and He will make your paths straight.

Restoring Our Time

Ephesians 5:16

I N order to be restored to authenticity, we must surrender our *time*. Paul referred to this as: "Redeeming the time" (Ephesians 5:16 KJV). The NIV translates this phrase, "making the most of every opportunity." Paul had at least two choices for his word *time*: *chronos* and *kairos*. *Chronos* is where we get our English word, chronology, meaning "the clock." *Kairos* means "the right time, or just in time." That is why the NIV translates "redeeming the time" as "making the most of every opportunity."

Both translations imply that in order to surrender our time to the Restorer, we must transition from *chronos* to *kairos*, from following our own selfish agendas on the clock to making the most of every opportunity to meet the needs of others at the right time. We move from trusting in the gift to trusting in the Giver.

Restoring our time means living in the present, which truly is a gift to experience the presence of the Restorer. Some of us are managing our lives backwards from the design God has in store for us. We focus on the past or the future and lock out the present. Consequently, we are so busy accomplishing our selfish tasks that we rarely have time to listen to His still small voice, His whisper (1 Kings 19:12). All we hear is the static of our fallen culture's messages that tells us how to hurry through life on this side.

The key that unlocks His restoration is full surrender of our time to the Restorer. Today, make the most of every opportunity and utilize every encounter to connect others with Christ.

Every Encounter Is a Divine Appointment

Colossians 4:5

DO you often feel interrupted by emails, calls, or people stopping in to see you? The most sacred commodity to each one of us is our time, and we never seem to have enough of it. However, a wise man once said, "Time is the only true democracy." Each of us has the same amount every day.

While surrendering our time to the Restorer does not add any minutes to our day or days to our calendars, it redeems our time to make it more abundant and eternal. Rather than an interruption, we see every encounter with a human being as a divine appointment to discover the Restorer at work. This makes our encounters and our days more productive. We choose more wisely, think more clearly, pray more frequently, and feel more nobly. We need less time to deal with the consequences of our foolish decisions. Time becomes more about developing relationships than giving the gift to ourselves. As a result, we become generous with our time.

Paul taught: "Be wise in the way you act toward outsiders; make the most of every opportunity" (Colossians 4:5).

Take a moment and pull out your calendar. What appointments have you set for the next week? Is it all about busyness or relationships? Are you trusting in the gift of time for your own selfish benefit or are you trusting in the Giver? Today, begin to see every encounter as a divine appointment.

Restoring Our Talent

2 Corinthians 8:9

IN order to be restored to authenticity, we must surrender our *talent*. Talent is our unique identity. From that identity flows our passions. We must discover and develop our unique expression of Christ in us to advance His message of restoration in the lives of each person we encounter. CPAs need to discover how to account with the Restorer. Realtors must uncover how to broker real estate with the Restorer. Attorneys should learn how to practice law with the Restorer.

The key that unlocks this restoration is full surrender of our talent to Christ. He will help us reinvest that talent to bring restoration to others because He is generous: "For you know the grace of our Lord Jesus Christ, that though he was rich, yet for your sake he became poor, so that you through his poverty might become rich" (2 Corinthians 8:9).

A snapshot of our talent is our business cards or the title we use at the end of an email to define who we are and what we do. Look at your business card, and ask yourself this question: "How have I misused for greed what God intended for generosity?"

After you examine the use of your talent, surrender it to the Restorer. Ask Him to make your career a ministry. Underneath the title of your card, write, "Surrendered," and carry it with you as a reminder of your desire for the restoration of your talent.

Two New Hearts

Ezekiel 36:26

I WAS often stone-hearted until I surrendered my heart to God. That led to the restoration of my talent to be used to advance His heart in others.

One example of the Restorer renewing my talent occurred at our Labor Day Weekend kickoff press conference luncheon held at the Auburn Cord Duesenberg Museum. Each year in that historic setting, we offered a preview of the premier vehicles that would cross the auction block. Just prior to walking on stage to take the microphone, I was made aware of a situation that moved my heart. My best friend from elementary school and his wife, who had also been one of our high school classmates, recently gave birth to their daughter who was in need of a heart transplant. She would become the youngest person in the United States to receive a new heart.

Responding to what I believed was a Holy Spirit prompting, I stepped up to the podium and made the crowd aware of the need. As I finished describing her dilemma, I saw a raised hand in my peripheral vision. It was racing legend and heart transplant recipient Carroll Shelby seated next to me offering the first $25,000 toward the infant's operation. Jerry J. Moore matched it, and her funded operation was a success. When I look back at the surrender of my talent to the Restorer, I realize how trusting in the Giver rather than my gifts led to two new hearts that day: mine and the baby girl's.

Through the prophet Ezekiel, God said: "I will give you a new heart and put a new spirit in you; I will remove from you your heart of stone and give you a heart of flesh" (Ezekiel 36:26).

Ask God to give you a new soft heart. He will use your talent to restore the heart of everyone you encounter.

Restoring Our Treasure

Proverbs 17:16

IN order to be restored to authenticity, we must surrender our *treasure*.

We can get one rather obvious indication of how we're managing our treasure by looking at our checking accounts.

Our checkbook registers reveal the costs of our needs: mortgage or rent payments, school tuition, groceries, utilities, gas for our cars, and the balance of expenses for survival.

Our checking accounts also reveal the costs of our wants: new car payments, new boat payments, lake cottage payments, vacations, electronics, and other luxuries that we often prioritize. Consequently, treasure is oftentimes the most difficult of our three resources to give away.

Whether a need or a want, we must seek God in order to reallocate our finances for His kingdom's advancement. Anything else is foolish.

Solomon asked: "Why should fools have money in hand to buy wisdom, when they are not able to understand it?" (Proverbs 17:16).

Today, pray that God would help you prioritize your finances, as you offer all of your assets to advance His kingdom in the hearts of others. Make every payment an act of worship. Your financial life will be restored to its original design.

Tithes and Offerings

Matthew 23:23

IF you were raised in the church, you probably encountered the ongoing debate over tithes and offerings. Tithe means, "tenth." You may ask yourself, "Do I tithe off the gross or the net? Do I have to give to a church, or can I give to another nonprofit? Is it acceptable to spend my treasure on myself, or is that sin?"

In our stone-heartedness, we become diligent about nailing down the specifics of exactly how generous we must be to stay in line with the rules. In our attempt to follow the rules, we remove the heart of God.

Jesus offered the following admonishment to stone hearts: "Woe to you, teachers of the law and Pharisees, you hypocrites! You give a tenth of your spices—mint, dill and cumin. But you have neglected the more important matters of the law—justice, mercy and faithfulness. You should have practiced the latter, without neglecting the former" (Matthew 23:23).

A greedy heart follows the letter of the law and misses the spirit of the law. A generous heart follows the spirit of the law and receives the heart of the Restorer.

Follow the spirit of the law with your treasure and discover Christ's teaching. Ask God where and how He is leading you to give. Then cheerfully and sacrificially share your kingdom investment, flowing from your intimacy with Him (2 Corinthians 9:7).

Pursuing More and Having Less

Proverbs 11:24

H AVING a greedy perspective toward my treasure led to me having less.

Like the prodigal son, money slipped like sand through my fingers. Ironically, when I had less than nothing, I was finally ready to surrender my treasure to the Restorer. This meant that I would have to undertake many humbling face-to-face meetings and telephone conversations with past-due vendors.

Through this process I learned a valuable lesson: never again did I want to be foolish with my treasure. I saw the ripple effect it had on others, and I was ashamed of how poorly it had reflected on the cause of Christ in my personal and business life.

Solomon taught: "One person gives freely, yet gains even more; another withholds unduly, but comes to poverty" (Proverbs 11:24).

Though I had withheld unduly, through a heart change, I was free to trust in the Giver rather than the gifts. I began to see God as my Provider, a belief that restored my treasure to authenticity.

How we steward finances affects people. Wisely valuing our relationships allows us to experience generosity as God restores our treasure.

On the Other Side of Every Expense
Is a Person

Proverbs 11:25

HAVE you ever considered the relationships on the other side of your expenses? If not, take a moment to reflect on the names and faces on the other side of your needs and wants. Have you generously used your resources to serve them, faithfully administering God's grace in its various forms, or have you used others to serve yourself? Do you see any names and faces of those in need with whom you might have neglected to share your gifts? Would you say you have been greedy or generous with your treasure?

Solomon reflected: "A generous person will prosper; whoever refreshes others will be refreshed" (Proverbs 11:25).

Create a treasure restoration plan. Assemble a conservative estimate of your next year's revenue and expenses. Ask God and a wise friend what percentage you should attempt to give, whether calculated from the gross or net. At the same time, pursue wise counsel as to where you should direct those dollars for the highest and best use. Never lose sight of giving generously, with godly wisdom, in both your personal and business dealings. Let every relationship—including customers, vendors, employees, competitors, family, friends, or those you may not know who are in need—reflect the heart of the Giver.

Is There Anything in Your Life That
Needs Restoration?

Matthew 23:25–26

HAVE your self-restoration attempts left you feeling dissatisfied and unrestored? Have you tried a hair transplant, a facelift, or Botox, binging, purging, restricting, over-exercising, or cutting? Have you attempted to fulfill your desire for restoration through a smoke, a toke, a drink, a line, or a pop of a pill? Have you purchased a new car, a new house, a new Rolex, a new diamond necklace, a new vacation, a new academic degree, a new wardrobe, or switched to a new spouse solely to make you feel new on the inside? Have you even sampled religion and its treadmill of good works to discover the rejuvenation of your heart?

It's likely that your dissatisfaction has hardened your heart resulting in foolish choices that continually ding your relationships as well as your time, talent, and treasure.

Unfortunately, most of us turn to ourselves for restoration, attempting to fix up our shortcomings on the outside under the guise that it will change us on the inside. We think if we go somewhere and do something, then we will be somebody. These futile efforts to make ourselves new from the outside in represent two kinds of pride: loose sand-hearted or legalistic stone-hearted arrogance that we can restore ourselves. The former requires a storm to be shaped, the latter a severe tool.

Two thousand years ago, Jesus admonished the Pharisees, noting their attempts at self-restoration from the outside in left them full of pretense: "Woe to you, teachers of the law and Pharisees, you hypocrites! You clean the outside of the cup and dish, but inside they are full of greed and self-indulgence. Blind Pharisee! First clean the inside of the cup and dish, and then the outside also will be clean" (Matthew 23:25–26). In the collector car world, we call this a cosmetic restoration. The surface is touched up just enough to fool everyone that the undercarriage is also new, when in reality it is ready to fall apart. Get the picture? But, there's hope in the Restorer.

Ask God to reveal any self-restoration attempts in your life and confess them today. He will start you on a new journey from the inside out.

Surrender the Old

2 Corinthians 5:17

JUST like a classic car, authentic restoration occurs in three steps. First, we surrender the old. Second, we surrender the pieces. Finally, we surrender the new. Let's talk about the first step, surrendering the old.

When a car collector determines his vehicle needs restoration, he surrenders his old basket case to the restorer, saying, "I can't. You can. I can't restore this old car. You can." The same is true for our unrestored lives. When we recognize our need for restoration and our unsuccessful self-restoration attempts, we must surrender our old lives to Christ our Restorer, saying the big, "I can't. You can." "I can't" indicates repentance. "You can" communicates faith.

The apostle Paul proclaimed to those who were willing to surrender the old: "Therefore, if anyone is in Christ, the new creation has come: the old has gone, the new is here!" (2 Corinthians 5:17).

Do you recognize your need for restoration evidenced by your unsuccessful self-restoration attempts that have left you dissatisfied and unrestored? Whether your heart is characterized by loose sand-hearted or legalistic stone-hearted pride, surrender your old basket case of a life to the Restorer with a soft heart of clay and say, "I can't. You can." He will make you new again.

Surrender the Pieces

1 John 1:9

WHEN he receives a rust bucket, a car restorer's first action is to take it apart, piece-by-piece. Next, the smallest components of the automobile are individually and meticulously restored. The same is true for our personal restoration process. When we surrender our lives to Christ, our Restorer disassembles us, piece-by-piece. Our sins are revealed, followed by our uttering many little, "I can't. You cans." This is confession.

The word *confession* means "to agree with God" that our sins are real. When we confess our sins to God, He forgives us and restores us. The apostle John taught: "If we confess our sins, he is faithful and just and will forgive us our sins and purify us from all unrighteousness" (1 John 1:9). This is why we must confess all of our sins to Him.

Surrender your sins, piece-by-piece. As Christ disassembles your life and reveals your wrongdoings, hand each one over to the Restorer, repeatedly saying, "I can't. You can." He will make you new again, one piece at a time.

Surrender the New

Revelation 21:5b

AFTER the pieces of the collector car are restored, the rolling sculpture is reassembled, reflecting the original design of its designer. It is ready to be used for its intended purpose. The new triumphs and tragedies are both surrendered to the restorer. When a car wins in competition, the restorer receives the glory. However, as the automotive masterpiece is exercised and judged, the paint will fade, the leather will tear, the tires will wear, and the metal will rust, requiring another surrender to the one who makes things new.

When Christ puts the pieces of our lives back together, He uses us for His intended purpose of authenticity, reflecting the original design of our Designer. We discover our ultimate value in being His agents to bring authentic restoration to others, as we surrender our new triumphs and tragedies.

As Christ reassembles the pieces of your life, surrender your new journey to His intended purpose of authenticity, reflecting the unique design of the Designer. Discover your ultimate value in being used by God to bring His authentic restoration to others. On your journey, surrender both the credit for the triumphs as well as the wear and tear of tragedies to Christ your Restorer who said: "I am making everything new!" (Revelation 21:5b).

God's Clay Art

Matthew 11:28

OUR journey toward authenticity unfolds on Restoration Road.

Like every automobile, we began as a clay mold. In the Garden of Eden, God breathed life into the dust to make man in His image. Unfortunately, we all fall short of His original design, proudly pursuing the satisfaction of our desires in self-restoration attempts apart from Him.

When we humble our clay hearts to the Restorer and say, "I can't. You can," He makes us new, authentically reflecting the design of our Designer. As we continue to surrender to Christ, He shapes our clay hearts to be like His. This frees us to experience His renewal and to give all credit to Jesus as His handprints become visible in all our endeavors where we live out His humility with others.

Jesus said: "Come to me, all you who are weary and burdened, and I will give you rest" (Matthew 11:28). His rest is restoration, providing us satisfying new life from the inside out. In Christ, who we are designed to be will determine what we are designed to do, which will determine where we are designed to go.

Humbly bend the knees of your heart to the Restorer Jesus Christ. Surrender your old life, your sins (piece-by-piece), and your new life to the One who makes all things new as you travel Restoration Road.

Cross-Shaped Confession

1 John 1:9; James 5:16

IS there any sin you need to confess? Too often, we hold on to wayward desires, mulling them over in what we believe to be a safe place in our minds. All the while, we die a little inside. However, confession restores us.

Confession agrees with God's perspective of our sins. In our agreement, God restores us vertically with Him and horizontally with others. It's a living picture of the cross.

First, we must confess our sins vertically to God. The apostle John revealed: "If we confess our sins, he is faithful and just and will forgive us our sins and purify us from all unrighteousness" (1 John 1:9). When we confess our sins vertically to the Restorer, He forgives us and restores us.

Second, we must confess our sins horizontally to someone we trust. James taught: "Therefore confess your sins to each other and pray for each other so that you may be healed. The prayer of a righteous person is powerful and effective" (James 5:16). Did you catch that? Horizontal confession heals.

Vertical confession leads to communion: intimacy with God. Horizontal confession leads to community: intimacy with others in Christ. Each represents relationship. Confession helps us to live in the sweet spot where our vertical relationship with God intersects with our horizontal relationships with others. The result is a living portrait of the cross.

Confess to God what you have been holding back from Him. Find a confidant with whom you can share that same sin. You will find restoration.

Living Hope

1 Peter 1:3–5

WHERE do you find hope?
When we surrender our old pattern of desiring life apart from God into the hands of the Restorer, we receive living hope: an inheritance of abundant life now and eternal life in the future.

We see this in Peter's first letter to dispersed believers, searching for hope: "Praise be to the God and Father of our Lord Jesus Christ! In his great mercy he has given us new birth into a living hope through the resurrection of Jesus Christ from the dead, and into an inheritance that can never perish, spoil or fade. This inheritance is kept in heaven for you, who through faith are shielded by God's power until the coming of the salvation that is ready to be revealed in the last time" (1 Peter 1:3–5).

Resurrection, inheritance, and *future salvation* are all terms the Jews used to refer to the last days, or the end times. Peter told them the Messiah had already come. Jesus was God in the flesh. He lived a perfect life and died on a cross, bearing the penalty of the old unrestored life for all who believe. He gave restoration: new life and new hope for all.

In Peter's time, pagan religions preached a much different version of a restored life. Their message for new hope and new life depended upon self-restoration. How true this is for us today. Often, we rely on the words of self-help evangelists and wonder how much has really changed over the last two thousand years. Peter tells us living hope is not based on our works or the works of others, but solely on the hope we have in the Restorer.

Living Hope is only found in Christ. We deserve justice. However, God unleashes mercy so we do not get what we deserve because of our sins. He offers us the opportunity to surrender our old life into the hands of the Restorer and receive what we do not deserve: His amazing grace.

Strongest Steel, Hottest Fire

1 Peter 1:6–7

MY dad always told me, "The strongest steel is made in the hottest fire."

Trials provide us opportunities for strength in Christ. Peter taught: "In all this you greatly rejoice, though now for a little while you may have had to suffer grief in all kinds of trials. These have come so that the proven genuineness of your faith—of greater worth than gold, which perishes even though refined by fire—may result in praise, glory and honor when Jesus Christ is revealed" (1 Peter 1:6–7).

Peter spoke to the early Christians because many of them were losing their physical inheritance when they chose to leave their old lives behind. They had refused to go to the guild meetings at pagan temples and were seen as unprofessional in business. They were criticized for not being family-oriented because they refused to go to the family events that were also held at pagan temples. They were even criticized for being unpatriotic because they would not bow down to Caesar, who called himself divine.

Though we face similar trials today, our faith in Christ will be proved genuine to all. Peter illustrates this with the imagery of a metal refiner. Refinement brings heat to the metal. The hotter the fire, the more the metal's impurities rise to the top. This is the case when trials of our faith come our way, and our impurities rise to the surface. In the refinement process, the deepest impurities ooze out near the end when the fire is at its hottest. In the heat of our trials, the Refiner removes our impurities. He continues the process until He sees His reflection in the metal.

Jesus, the Restorer, is refining us amidst our trials and temptations, ready to remove the impurities rising to the surface so we will be proved genuine and authentic. When He looks at you, who does He see?

The Invisible Becomes Visible

1 Peter 1:8–9

DID you ever play hide and seek, when the adrenaline of the invisible becoming visible could send an electrical current through your body?

Peter wrote: "Though you have not seen him, you love him; and even though you do not see him now, you believe in him and are filled with an inexpressible and glorious joy, for you are receiving the end result of your faith, the salvation of your souls" (1 Peter 1:8–9).

The goal of our faith is the restoration of our hearts. When the Restorer connects with us, His invisible presence in our lives becomes visible through deeds of love unfolding in our lives. These deeds are done because of the inexpressible and glorious joy we have within us that becomes contagious to those around us. When we are restored to authenticity, we reflect a new heart, the heart of the Restorer.

Surrender your deeds of love to Christ, so others will see the Restorer in you. The invisible will become visible.

Restored to Authenticity

1 Corinthians 12:27

A RARE 1908 Auburn touring car had rested peacefully in an old barn for decades, remaining untouched, until one day, a tornado ripped away the barn's roof, leaving the car buried under a pile of rubble. The pieces of the Auburn miraculously survived, but now the car needed to be restored.

The value of this Auburn would be at its greatest when it was restored to its authentic condition. Consequently, the Auburn's owner surrendered his basket case of a car to the Auburn Cord Duesenberg Museum, saying, "I can't restore it. You can. When you do, keep it and use it as a sign for all to see the authentic design of its designer."

For years, the 1908 Auburn sat untouched until a group of volunteers showed up on a mission to restore this work of art to its original authentic state. The first step of the restoring community was to disassemble the vehicle and restore the parts, piece-by-piece. After months of hard work, they reassembled the work of art, and the process was finished. Paint was shiny. Brass was buffed. Leather was stitched perfectly. Tires were new old stock. When the engine fired, the room filled with applause. It was a beautiful sight.

Just like that 1908 Auburn, we need to be restored to authenticity. It begins when we surrender our old basket case of a life to the Restorer who disassembles us, giving us the opportunity to surrender our sins, piece-by-piece, often through a restoring community. Finally, He reassembles us, and we surrender the new: new tragedies and new triumphs where we give all credit to our Designer and Restorer.

Are you part of a restoring community? Paul taught believers: "Now you are the body of Christ, and each one of you is a part of it" (1 Corinthians 12:27). Loving community is where He will make you new again.

Life's Steering Wheel

Jeremiah 29:13

ON May 17, 1996, I lost one of my best friends, Scott Brayton, in a racing accident during practice at the Indianapolis 500. Scott, who just a few days earlier had become the ninth driver to win back-to-back pole positions at the Brickyard with a record run, was driving a teammate's car for about twenty-five laps when a faulty tire on his race car disintegrated. He had just entered turn two and was driving at more than 230 miles per hour. When the tire exploded, the metal rim hit the hot, oily surface of the track and his car slid like it was on ice. His vehicle spun and hit the outside retaining wall at a G-force beyond what the human body could endure.

At the age of thirty-seven, Scott Brayton died.

Regardless of how tightly Scott held onto the steering wheel of his race car, because one of his four tires was bad, he was destined for death. When his car hit the wall, the steering column was broken from the front axle. For me, this represented a picture of the vertical being torn from the horizontal. The same is true for us.

Regardless of how tightly we hold on to the steering wheel of our lives, if we hold back just one of the four chambers of our hearts, then we will break apart the vertical from the horizontal. If we do not

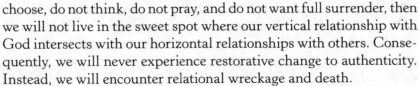

choose, do not think, do not pray, and do not want full surrender, then we will not live in the sweet spot where our vertical relationship with God intersects with our horizontal relationships with others. Consequently, we will never experience restorative change to authenticity. Instead, we will encounter relational wreckage and death.

God taught through the prophet Jeremiah: "You will seek me and find me when you seek me with all your heart" (Jeremiah 29:13). Are you experiencing relational wreckage? Perhaps it is time for you to wave the white flag of full surrender to Christ, wholeheartedly offering Him the steering wheel of your life, and allowing Him to restore the vertical with the horizontal.

A Lost Child

Luke 15:10

WHEN my eldest daughter, Megan, was three years old, she traveled with Susan and me to a collector car auction in Missouri. One morning we walked together about a half-mile from our hotel to a restaurant for breakfast. I gripped her hand tightly as we talked during our morning stroll.

When we arrived at the restaurant, I let go of her hand only for a few seconds to read a menu mounted on a display. When I turned around, she was gone. Panic shot through my body when I realized she wasn't close by. I screamed out her name and I ran. I sprinted up and down the restaurant's large foyer. I burst through the exterior doors and attempted to memorize license plate numbers, makes, and models of cars passing through the parking lot.

In that moment, not one concern regarding self-dignity entered my mind. I just wanted my daughter back, safe. A few minutes later, I found Megan in the women's restroom with an older girl who had taken her to the bathroom. Even though this was the first place I had looked, somehow, I had missed the fact that she was inside a stall. When I found her, I held her in my arms and told her how much I loved her. I felt her breath on my face when I whispered, "Don't ever tell your mother about this."

This is exactly how God feels about any of His lost, or unrestored, children. He searches for lost sheep, lost coins, and lost sons. Jesus said: "In the same way, I tell you, there is rejoicing in the presence of the angels of God over one sinner who repents" (Luke 15:10). Today, read Luke 15 and experience the heart of your loving heavenly Father.

Restoring People

2 Corinthians 5:18

AFTER the Jewish captivity, Nehemiah rebuilt the Jerusalem wall, Zerubbabel rebuilt the temple, and Ezra rebuilt the people.

While God was restoring my company, I realized He had shaped my heart to be like Ezra's. I had a passion to rebuild people. I attempted to place relationships ahead of remuneration, people ahead of profit. The result was deepened community with our customers, vendors, employees, and even our competitors.

As I tried to leverage every opportunity in the marketplace to communicate Christ's message of restoration, I was blessed to engage in conversations with others about the challenges of life and God's desire to restore us to authenticity, the original design of the Designer.

God's design is that we would be His agents of restoration everywhere we go. Paul penned: "All this is from God, who reconciled us to himself through Christ and gave us the ministry of reconciliation" (2 Corinthians 5:18).

Have you given your life to the cause of rebuilding people? It is the most satisfying endeavor on earth. Today, surrender to the One who desires to use you to bring His restoration to others.

Two Minutes

Psalm 27:14

SEVERAL years ago, when I still owned my company, I was unnecessarily delayed at my office, and it frustrated me immensely.

Immediately, I left the facility and began an internal audit. As a recovering perfectionist, I began an exercise that had been beneficial to me. I attempted to quantify the qualitative. I deduced if I could quantify the amount of time that had passed while I had been waiting, then I could let go of the frustration (the qualitative) that had ripped through my heart and body. I looked at my watch and determined how long it had taken for me to get upset due to the delay in my schedule. The answer was: two minutes. That was all it took for me to feel the sense of frustration begin to rise.

Behind the wheel of my sport utility vehicle, I exited my company's parking lot to meet my wife for a long overdue date. I made it about a mile and a half to a bridge on my way home when I encountered four people looking over its edge. Subconsciously, I pulled over and rolled down my window.

"Do you need a cell phone?" I asked.

"No, there's somebody down there," one responded.

"Okay."

"No. No. No." One of the others stepped forward. "A northbound truck just crossed the center line and drove over the bridge. We just called the EMS, and they are on their way."

I tried to take in what they had just said. Meanwhile a friend, who was an officer, arrived and began to look inside the truck that was upside down.

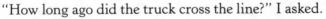

"How long ago did the truck cross the line?" I asked.

"About two minutes ago."

It is difficult to describe the feeling that resonated inside me at that moment. Had I not been delayed, this truck could have hit me, possibly ending my life. Once I recognized everything was under control, I pulled away and headed toward my house.

I sensed God speaking to me, not in an audible voice, but from within my heart. I believed He communicated He was going to use my changed heart, transformed desires, and renewed three resources of my life to become a direct carrier of the message of authentic restoration.

David, who had to wrestle with God's delay in transferring Israel's monarchy from Saul to him, penned: "Wait for the LORD; be strong and take heart and wait for the LORD" (Psalm 27:14). The Hebrew word for wait, *qavah*, carries an active, not passive, connotation. In essence, it is serving God right where we are.

Is it possible God has created an unexpected delay in your life? Whether it's two minutes, two weeks, two months, two years, or even two decades, quantify the qualitative. Measure your wait. Then surrender any frustration to God and serve Him right where you are. He will use you to make others new again.

The Father's Approval

Galatians 4:6

I DISCOVERED that as an adult, when we obey a parent, we assimilate not only their assets, but also their liabilities. Perhaps that is why the Bible calls us to "honor" our parents when we become adults, not to simply just continue to obey them.

The Book of Proverbs gave me a filter to discern, or sift, the wisdom of my heavenly Father from the streets smarts of my earthly father. One proved to reveal divine wisdom, while the other demonstrated political savvy. My pursuit of the Restorer forever shifted my relationship with my dad. While I had placed him on a pedestal as a child, as an adult I learned he was human just like me. Consequently, I could let go of satisfying my desires of *significance*, *contentment*, *control*, and *security* through his approval.

When I came to this realization, it was as if a dam inside me opened wide and released a flow of water that swept me up and took me deeper in my journey with Christ. Instead of seeking my dad's approval, I learned to seek God's wisdom, relying on Him to transform our relationship. Restorative change carried wisdom into my relationship with Dad because I had fully surrendered my heart to the Restorer.

Paul wrote: "Because you are his sons, God sent the Spirit of his Son into our hearts, the Spirit who calls out, 'Abba, Father'" (Galatians 4:6). When we fully surrender our lives to Christ, His Spirit resides in us and calls out "Daddy" to our heavenly Father, our source of wisdom.

Call out to your heavenly Father and ask for wisdom to sift through the earthly advice of others. He will take you deeper in your journey with Him.

ABC Encourager: Aware

Hebrews 10:25

CAN you think of a person who has encouraged you? Now think of someone who discouraged you. Here's the big question. Which one most resembles you?

Encouragement is a catalyst for each of us to journey forward on Restoration Road. *Cor* is Latin for *heart*. Therefore, *encouragement* means "to restore another's heart." Encouragement breathes life into the heart; whereas discouragement sucks the life right out of it.

Chris Schenkel, the Hall of Fame ABC sportscaster, was one of the greatest encouragers in my life. While millions recognized him as an ABC sportscaster, I knew him as an "ABC encourager." His heart beat with three characteristics that restored my heart. He was: (1) Aware, (2) a Builder, and (3) a Comforter.

Chris was aware of people's hearts, desires, and lives. He remembered people's names and details about their lives at a level that I had never seen. He called me weekly to check up on me. He was aware of all that was taking place in my life. He showed up in Scottsdale, Arizona, to surprise me the day before one of our auctions. He was on his way to be inducted into the Sports Broadcaster's Hall of Fame and had received international publicity that week for his well-deserved achievement. He knew I had been struggling. In the back seat of a limousine, he encouraged me in an unthreatening way—a way that only he could—because he was close enough relationally to be aware of my need.

I learned if I was going to encourage others, I needed to assimilate the communication skills that made Chris aware of people's hearts, desires, and lives. First, Chris locked eyes with every person he met. Second, he asked questions that communicated genuine interest and revealed the person's heart, desires, and life. Third, Chris listened intently, often repeating what he had heard. These three traits helped me receive restoration as well as bring it to others.

Scripture records that Jesus was also acutely aware of the people He encountered. He locked eyes with them, asked questions that revealed their hearts, and listened intently. As a result, His encouragement restored them. There is something about encouragement that restores the heart.

Are you an encourager? Are you aware of the hearts, desires, and lives of those around you? The writer of Hebrews told the church to keep "encouraging one another" (Hebrews 10:25). Today, become aware of those around you and breathe life into them as you ask questions and listen intently.

ABC Encourager: Builder

Ephesians 4:29

CHRIS Schenkel, the ABC Encourager, was a builder. I remember many times when he built me up. However, one occasion stands out above all the others. Many years ago, I shared with Chris I had been thinking about moving away from the business. He stopped me in mid-sentence, something he had rarely done.

"No way! This business has been built by you. The customers' relationships are with you. They depend upon you. Right now, they need you more than ever."

Chris built me up when I felt let down. He built me up with words of affirmation. This was a pattern I desired to implement in my own life. I am absolutely amazed at the power of words of affirmation. From children to business leaders, people rarely receive words that build them up. Consequently, when such words flow authentically from our mouths, they enter a person's ears and travel straight to their hearts, bringing restoration.

Jesus was known for building up others—so much so that the people He built up into faith in Him, with the Spirit's power, literally changed the world after His ascension. The apostle Paul was also the recipient of that building up, and he taught that we should do the same: "Do not let any unwholesome talk come out of your mouths, but only what is helpful for building others up according to their needs, that it may benefit those who listen" (Ephesians 4:29). Paul knew there is something about encouragement that restores the heart.

Will you encourage others by building them up with words of affirmation? You will be amazed at what a few words directed toward building up another person can do for your relationship and for their encouragement.

ABC Encourager: Comforter

2 Corinthians 1:3–5

CHRIS Schenkel, the ABC Sportscaster and encourager, not only was *aware* of those he encountered whom he *built* up; he was also a *comforter*. *Comfort* literally means "to call alongside." It comes from the Latin, *com* meaning "together" and *fortis*, which is translated "strong." Consequently, comfort means we come alongside someone in order to invite them to restoration; we strengthen together.

When I had shared with Chris my Holy Spirit prompting to become a direct carrier of the message of restoration toward authenticity, I had expected him to say something similar to what he had said twenty-four months earlier when he articulated how my business needed me. I was wrong. He encouraged me to move forward with the prompting. He comforted me in my most difficult business decision. In essence, he came alongside and strengthened me.

Paul equated encouragement with strengthening and comfort: "But everyone who prophesies speaks to men for their strengthening, encouragement and comfort" (1 Corinthians 14:3). There is something about Christ's encouragement that restores the heart.

Jesus was not only aware of the needs of others and not only built them up with words of affirmation, but He also comforted them by

meeting their needs through restoration. He called the Holy Spirit the "Comforter" (John 14:26 KJV). The psalmist said that God encourages the afflicted (Psalm 10:17). He comforts us in our times of trouble.

Paul described Christ as the source and the flow of comfort when he wrote: "Blessed be the God and Father of our Lord Jesus Christ, the Father of compassion and the God of all comfort, who comforts us in all our troubles, so that we can comfort those in any trouble with the comfort we have received from God. For just as the sufferings of Christ overflow to us, so also through Christ our comfort overflows" (2 Corinthians 1:3–5 BSB). Christ is the inlet, the flow, and the passion for the outlet.

Comfort others by coming alongside them and inviting them to restoration.

The Master ABC Encourager

Hebrews 3:13

SONNY and Cathy Gandee were friends who bought and sold hundreds of muscle cars at our auctions over the years. I had invited them to fly with us to an auction in the southern United States. Just before takeoff from Auburn, I asked Sonny where he got his name.

"My dad. He played for the World Champion Detroit Lions," he responded.

"I think Chris Schenkel was the broadcaster for the game," I offered.

"I think he was. I never got to see my dad play. I would love to have watched a game," Sonny said wishfully.

"Do you want to relive a moment from the world championship?" I inquired as I dialed Chris' number on my cell phone. I knew Chris would remember, but I could not remember if he had actually been the commentator for the game. The ringing stopped and I said, "Chris."

"Mitchell!" Chris responded in his encouraging tone.

"I'm calling in a Citation II sitting at the end of the runway in Auburn ready to go wheels up to this weekend's auction. I'm sitting with Sonny Gandee, the son of Sonny Gandee who played for the world championship Detroit Lions. Did you call that game?"

"Yes, I did!" Chris confirmed.

"Well, Sonny was not fortunate enough to see his dad play. Could you give him a little play-by-play from the world championship

game so he can experience what it was like?" I knew Chris' memory was picture perfect.

"Sure!" Chris obliged.

I handed the phone to Sonny and watched the expression on his face as he listened to Chris, the master ABC encourager. I've never seen that expression on another grown man's face. Chris had breathed life into yet another soul with his classic rewind of an actual play from the world championship.

There is something about encouragement that restores the heart.

You see, it was not merely Chris who encouraged all of us, it was Christ in Chris.

The writer of Hebrews summed up the power of frequent encouragement in this way: "But encourage one another daily, as long as it is called 'Today,' so that none of you may be hardened by sin's deceitfulness" (Hebrews 3:13). As long as we are on this side of the grave, we should be ABC encouragers who bring the Restorer's strength to others.

When you encourage others with a clay heart, you will realize that it is not you, but Christ in you who renews others with encouragement that restores their hearts.

"God, Open or Close the Door"

Psalm 37:4

AFTER years of being in the auction business and never being approached by a prospective buyer for our company, suddenly suitors pursued us when *auction* became the biggest buzzword on the Internet.

I began the due diligence process with an investment banker who was enthusiastic about the prospect of taking our high-profile company public. He made it clear to me that my life-long commitment to the future of our company was paramount to the success of the IPO. I understood what that meant for my family. I wouldn't be around on the weekends.

After months of moving forward with the investment bank, I was prompted to pray a simple prayer, "God, please open the door so wide that I can fall through it or close it so tightly that I can't get it open." That week, the investment banker called me with news that our company needed to be twice its size to conduct an initial public offering. Otherwise we would experience the detriments of being public without the benefits of liquidity and stock appreciation. He thought I might be angry. I thought about my prayer. God had another plan, and I was finally willing to wait on Him.

Not long after this, a large corporation considered acquiring our company in a way that would allow us to achieve all the growth strategies in my vision for the business. As with the previous opportunity, I was told that in moving ahead I was committing my entire future to this endeavor because I was the key leader, the primary revenue generator, and basically the future of the business. Again, I agreed, and again, I prayed that simple prayer.

That same week as my prayer, the prospective purchaser's representative called me with the news the company was being sold to a wealthy investor who had placed all acquisitions on hold. He thought I might be angry. Again, I thought about my prayer. My heart of clay had become patient for what God had in store.

Although I had wanted to spend more time with my family instead of traveling nearly 45 weekends each year, I didn't think it would ever be possible, so with the previous two sale scenarios I was still willing to sacrifice them, a move that was at odds with the genuine desires of my heart. At the same time, I desired to communicate God's message of restoration I had experienced to a culture filled with unrestored people.

God's vision was about to be followed by His provision.

For the first time, someone was willing to acquire our business and let me walk away to pursue the desires of my heart. As I was willing to surrender my business to God, He made a way for me to honor Him through investing in our daughters and bringing His restoration to others. Consequently, I will never forget the prayer that led me to experiencing the desires of my heart.

David penned: "Take delight in the LORD, and he will give you the desires of your heart" (Psalm 37:4). When we make our hearts pliable to God, He orchestrates our desires to be like His.

Are you in the process of making a significant decision? Pray, "God, please open the door so wide that I can fall through it or close it so tightly that I can't get it open." Surrender your heart to Him, and He will give you the desires of your heart.

Community

Psalm 139:23–24

THE value of eBay's publicly traded stock had skyrocketed. Their unprecedented escalation stemmed from their ninety-five percent share in the Internet auction business. In my first meeting with them to discuss their acquisition of our company, I asked, "What keeps a company like Microsoft from flicking you off the map?" I made a gesture at our conference room table as if I were playing caroms. The co-founder answered with a story I will never forget.

A woman who had frequently traded goods on eBay had gone through a bitter divorce that left her penniless. Those who had bought and sold with her noticed her absence from the auction site. They tracked her down, learned of her story, and each pitched in to buy her a computer so she was trading on eBay again.

"In a word, *community,*" he said in answer to my question. I thought back to the parable of the two sons and their father's longing to restore community between them. One of the Bible's deepest values, that of loving others as ourselves, was being lived out in one of the greatest success stories in the history of Wall Street.

Are you living out the radical, limitless love of the father in your world? Are you characterized and known as a forgiver? Would your family and friends refer to you as gracious? Are you experiencing true community? Pray David's refining prayer: "Search me, God, and know my heart; test me and know my anxious thoughts. See if there is any offensive way in me, and lead me in the way everlasting" (Psalm 139:23–24). Communion with Him will lead to community with others.

The Restorative Change Equation

Romans 12:2

A RE you contemplating a job or career change?

Restorative change places the value of the process over the results. When I was discerning what I had believed was God's prompting to become a direct carrier of His message of restoration, I became aware of the following change equation: Dissatisfaction with the present state (DPS) plus awareness of a better state (ABS) plus first steps (FS) equals change. I modified the equation by multiplying all three components by wisdom and leadership (WL) to produce restorative change (RC). Consequently, it looked like this: $(DPS + ABS + FS) WL = RC$.

Dissatisfaction implies something is unmet in our desires. Awareness means we see in our hearts a better way—which is truly the only way—to satisfy those desires. First steps communicate that in our hearts we are choosing, thinking, praying, and wanting to move forward in a God-honoring way with our time, talent, and treasure.

During this time of reflecting, I asked myself a revealing question, one I would like to share with you to discern your own Holy Spirit promptings to make a career shift. "What would I love to do, even if I failed?" In other words, "What process would I absolutely love doing, even if successful results never came?"

I kept coming back to "connecting the culture with Christ the Restorer through communicating the Bible." This became a vision-mission combination for my life. Connecting is leading. My three expressions would be: (1) writing, (2) teaching, and (3) preaching. I planned to communicate in order to connect.

What would you love to do, even if you failed? What process would you absolutely love doing, even if successful results never came? The apostle Paul wrote: "Do not conform to the pattern of this world, but be transformed by the renewing of your mind. Then you will be able to test and approve what God's will is—his good, pleasing and perfect will" (Romans 12:2).

Renew your mind through reading the Word of God, then take first steps toward testing and approving His will for your life.

GATE

1 Corinthians 12:4–6

WHEN it comes to your career, you want to make sure your GATE is unlocked and open for ministry right where you are. You can categorize four key components of your life using the acronym GATE:

G: Gifts
A: Abilities
T: Talents
E: Experiences

Gifts include your spiritual gifts. Abilities are your learned skills. Talents are your unique identity and passions expressed in something you can never remember not doing. Experiences are the complete package of your tragedies and triumphs in life. All four reside in your heart.

Is your GATE unlocked and open for ministry right where you are? Have you thought about how to use your spiritual gifts to serve others within your career? Do your gifts, abilities, talent, and experiences line up in your current role? If you answered yes to these questions, then your GATE is unlocked and open. Now, will you walk through it?

The apostle Paul taught: "There are different kinds of gifts, but the same Spirit distributes them. There are different kinds of service, but the same Lord. There are different kinds of working, but in all of them and in everyone it is the same God at work" (1 Corinthians 12:4–6). God is at work in your life. He designed your GATE to be unlocked and opened for you to serve others.

If your GATE is locked and closed, turn to the One who designed you and ask Him to unlock and open your GATE to serve others right where you are.

LOST And FOUND

Hebrews 12:2

SHORTLY after our sale of our company, I suffered post-business LOST syndrome: Lack Of Stressful Transactions. After the first five consecutive stay-at-home weekends of my life, I began to feel like a failure. I thought there was something wrong with me. I realized these feelings were the result of the absence of deal-making in my life. I felt insignificant, discontent, out of control, and insecure from the pace of my life slowing to what appeared to be a screeching halt. A constant need for the next deal had been removed from my time, talent, and treasure. Consequently, I determined I had nothing to contribute to society. Did I get my spiritual signals crossed?

Like both sons in Jesus's trilogy, I needed to be FOUND: Focus On Understanding New Direction.

In order to be FOUND, the Restorer needed to change my focus. To borrow an illustration from Philip Yancey, life is like a magnifying glass that magnifies the centered object in focus while the surrounding objects remain fuzzy. We focus on either Christ or our circumstances. When we focus on Christ, He becomes magnified, and our circumstances become fuzzy. When we focus on our circumstances, they become magnified, and Christ becomes fuzzy. Unfortunately, I had been focusing on my circumstances and Christ had become fuzzy. Then a friend of mine whom I consider a spiritual giant told me I was headed for the best place in life I could possibly be—sitting at the feet of the Master to learn wisdom and to be restored for a new direction.

The writer of Hebrews reminded his readers to keep "fixing our eyes on Jesus, the pioneer and perfecter of faith. For the joy set before him he endured the cross, scorning its shame, and sat down at the right hand of the throne of God" (Hebrews 12:2).

Are you LOST, focusing on your circumstances, rather than Christ? Perhaps it is time for you to shift your focus to Him and be FOUND.

Authentic Church

1 Peter 2:4–5

WHEN attempting to make my business a ministry, I was deeply impacted by a Bible teacher and local church leader who talked openly about his liabilities. I had listened to every one of his messages for almost seven years. He opened me to the idea of the continual process of restoration—that was authenticity.

Early in my restoration journey, I attended one of his conferences for Christian business owners, and we ended up eating dinner at the same table. I watched as he glanced at our name tags. Next to me sat John Bertrand, skipper of Australia II—the yacht that in 1983 competed for the America's Cup and won, ending 132 years of victories by the New York Yacht Club, the longest winning streak in sports. When the pastor saw my name tag he noticed I was from Auburn, Indiana.

"That's where they have the biggest collector car auction in the world," he said.

I nodded.

Then he asked me, "Mitch, what is it that you do?"

He almost fell out of his chair when I responded, "I do that auction, and you just made my life!"

We both laughed together. We hit it off. The pastor had left his family business to start a church. He had built a student ministry movement inside a church to almost ten times its adult attendance. When he had discerned his own Holy Spirit prompting to create a new movement, he and a group of like-minded friends walked door-to-door asking people if they attended church. If the answer was, "Yes," they thanked the people and moved on. However, when the answer was, "No," they asked, "Why?" The top three responses were:

(1) it's boring, (2) they're always asking for money, and (3) they always end later than scheduled.

In an effort to strategically address the survey responses, the pastor founded a church targeted towards those who did not attend. Each service would be engaging, its leaders would refrain from asking new attendees for money, and each gathering would start and end on time. The first services took place in a movie theater. Today, that church hosts more than 25,000 attendees each weekend and 5,000 during its mid-week services. These mid-week services are populated mostly by believers who fully surrendered their lives to Christ during the weekend gatherings.

One of the most valuable lessons we can learn from this redemptive movement is the power of an authentic church, following the design of the Designer. The apostle Peter wrote: "As you come to him, the living Stone—rejected by humans but chosen by God and precious to him—you also, like living stones, are being built into a spiritual house to be a holy priesthood, offering spiritual sacrifices acceptable to God through Jesus Christ" (1 Peter 2:4–5).

Today, ask the Holy Spirit to align your life with the Living Stone and yield the outcomes to Him.

Speed Bumps

1 Corinthians 3:16

ARE you hindered from becoming active in your local church due to your past sins?

Restoration Road can include a few speed bumps: stone and sand. When I sold my business to pursue my Master's and Doctorate degrees in Theology, the reactions of stone hearts, like the older brother in Jesus's "lost" trilogy, hampered me from continuing on my path toward connecting ministry and marketplace. I received the vibe I had sinned too much to ever consider teaching the Bible in a local church.

The reaction of sand hearts, like the younger brother in Jesus's parable, saw my career change as crazy. I was at the pinnacle of my industry. Many collectors bought and sold classic cars solely on my advice. I have to admit, their argument made sense. However, my prompting had been clear to me.

One customer and friend comforted me with these words, concluding a telephone call where we had discussed my transition, "Mitchell, everyone did business with you, not because of your position, but because of your person." In his own way, he was saying that who I was designed to be determined what I was designed to do and ultimately determined where I was designed to go.

Speaking to a group of believers who had committed many past sins, the apostle Paul wrote: "Don't you know that you yourselves are God's temple and that God's Spirit dwells in your midst" (1 Corinthians 3:16).

Our good works don't make us holy, nor do our sins permanently disqualify us from being used by God. We are holy solely due to the Holy Spirit who lives in us.

Have you been reluctant to get involved in a ministry? Fully surrender anything you are white-knuckling to Christ and experience a clay heart that is malleable in the Restorer's hands. He will use you to draw others to Himself, as you reflect the design of the Designer.

Change

James 1:21b

THE one thing we are guaranteed on our journey is change. Each of us has been locked in pride's prison of pretense, which separates the vertical from the horizontal, our relationship with God from our relationship with others.

It often looks like this. We maintain a legalistic stone heart on Sunday and a licentious sand heart Monday through Saturday. In fact, we often think Sunday stone will restore us from our Saturday sand-hearted sins, but it doesn't work that way with God.

The Master Key that unlocks the gate to Restoration Road has been inside us all along. It is cross-shaped. When we humble our heart to the Restorer, we begin life with a clay heart, one that is malleable in His hands of change. This leads to a humility in horizontal relationships that transforms our desires from foolishness to wisdom.

Jesus's half-brother James wrote: "Humbly accept the word planted in you, which can save you" (James 1:21b).

Today, humbly accept the word of the Restorer planted in you. He will renew you by working from the inside out so those outside will come in. This is the ripple effect of His restoration. He will restore your heart, desires, and life as He restores your communion with Him, your community with others, and uses you to restore your culture.

Confessions of a Recovering Perfectionist

Philippians 1:6b

MY daughter texted me from college after her volleyball practice asking why she was so emotionally linked to her mistakes on the court. Here is what I shared.

"Emotions are a function of expectations, or beliefs. You enjoy the game, and you have trained heavily, so you take a high level of ownership. That torches up your right or wrong, all or nothing mentality. As a result, you personalize every action as if it defines you. The solution is to see it all as a process to improve, rather than an end result."

In marketplace competition, in your home, in ministry, or in your hobby, are you operating from a perfectionist perspective resulting in an unhealthy ownership that is hurting you and those around you?

This perspective will eat us alive until we realize God is not looking for perfection; rather, He is seeking excellence, doing the best with what we have. This shift in mentality allows us to own our mistakes as part of our fallen nature, yet give God the credit for any successes. It frees us from being defined by the outcomes of our efforts. Rather than proving our abilities, we learn to improve them.

Life is a journey. Paul wrote: "He who began a good work in you will carry it on to completion until the day of Christ Jesus" (Philippians 1:6b). Did you catch that? You and I are works in progress, so let's shift our perspectives from perfection to excellence, recognizing we will fall short, but the Restorer will make us new again on Restoration Road.

Be Perfect?

Matthew 5:48; Luke 6:36

ARE you an organized person? Are your DVDs in alphabetical order? Are the clothes in your closet color-coordinated in the different seasons? Are both your house and car spotless? Is your desk free of clutter? Or do you seek all these things yet feel like a failure because you don't measure up to your personal bar of perfection?

Order on the outside flows from a desire on the inside to seek perfection. In fact, the perfectionist's favorite Scripture reads: "Be perfect, therefore, as your heavenly Father is perfect" (Matthew 5:48). However, when we examine the context of this verse and look at its parallel passage in Luke, we discover something quite different: "Be merciful, just as your Father is merciful" (Luke 6:36). Jesus was not teaching we should be flawless; rather, He was communicating we should be complete in our love for others, including our enemies.

Wow! That changes everything! Doesn't it?

Jesus prioritized relationship over religion, excellence over perfection. Excellence features two components: authenticity and wisdom. The perfectionist has a blind spot to the fact that everyone and everything in this life will fall short, except God. Whereas perfectionism implies flawlessness, excellence recognizes (1) authenticity: understanding the truth about our strengths and shortcomings, and (2) wisdom: the intersection of God's righteousness with street smarts, shrewdly doing the best with what we have. When we are authentic and wise, we are equipped to love others, even those who disagree with us.

If you are a perfectionist, try replacing perfection with love. Place a greater value on people than tasks. Begin the journey of a recovering perfectionist. Confess your shortcomings and shrewdly do the best with what you have, demonstrating God's love to everyone you encounter.

Cave of Restoration

1 Samuel 22:2

WHEN I was volunteering full-time as a teaching pastor at a local church, we started a Wednesday night service called Common Ground. Each evening, after we were led in worship music, I would welcome everyone, reminding them of the four hallmarks of our gathering.

First, we had all sinned and desired life apart from God, yet He offered grace in Christ to restore us. Second, I would share our format was relaxed. It was the biggest come-as-you-are party in the city. Third, I would teach the gathering was authentic. It was a safe place to say, "I got it wrong," or even, "I finally got it right." We were to check the pretense at the door. Fourth, I would remind everyone we were going to have fun.

We laughed every night—sometimes to keep from crying, because we included a prayer time. I invited anyone to share a joy that could be multiplied or a burden that could be divided. The stories of death, divorce, disease, debt, and distress were gut-wrenching. Yet the stories of life, reunion, healing, freedom, and peace were invigorating. Sometimes a person shared a need only to have someone else provide for that need by the end of the service. Either an attendee or I would conclude the prayer time by communicating our joys and our burdens to God.

Next, I would teach the Bible with my best effort to make the message relevant to the audience. Usually, I asked the question the text answered and followed it with a real-life story that introduced the topic. I read the selected verses from the Bible, and we walked through the passage line-by-line, as I explained, illustrated, and applied the main themes, often supporting them with other Bible passages. I always

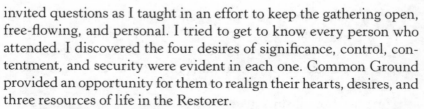

invited questions as I taught in an effort to keep the gathering open, free-flowing, and personal. I tried to get to know every person who attended. I discovered the four desires of significance, control, contentment, and security were evident in each one. Common Ground provided an opportunity for them to realign their hearts, desires, and three resources of life in the Restorer.

A fellow pastor told me once that these Wednesday night gatherings were emblematic of David's community in the Cave of Adullam when he was fleeing from Saul: "All those who were in distress or in debt or discontented gathered around him, and he became their commander. About four hundred men were with him" (1 Samuel 22:2).

Where is your cave of restoration? Who are those in distress, debt, or discontented gathered around you? After you have identified the individuals, reach out to them and take steps to lead each to Restoration Road.

What's Your Story?

Colossians 4:5–6

ONE night, something amazing happened at a worship service where I was about to teach. It was the first in a chain reaction of events that taught me the ripple effect of a restoration story.

A couple sitting next to me stared blankly as I asked them the same question I would ask countless others. During the remainder of the worship songs, I watched as they wrestled with the answer. After the music ended, they approached me and said, "We're ready."

I surprised myself when I asked if they would share their story with those who were in attendance. They agreed, and as everyone gathered, they spoke about their prodigal stories of sand and stone and their attempts at self-restoration, including their struggles with pride. They bravely confessed and humbly surrendered their lives to Christ as their Savior and Lord.

Traveling along Restoration Road is as much about listening as it is about speaking. Our unique stories add value to life as they become teaching parables. God has given each one of us a unique story so we can share His story with others. When we listen to others' stories, they listen to ours.

The apostle Paul wrote: "Be wise in the way you act toward outsiders; make the most of every opportunity. Let your conversation be always full of grace, seasoned with salt, so that you may know how to answer everyone" (Colossians 4:5–6).

Invite God to lead you to someone and ask, "What is your story?" After you listen, articulate how God chased you down to restore your relationship with Him, connecting your story with theirs where it fits. Discover how God will use you to draw another to Himself as you grow in your intimacy with Him.

Listening to Spirit-Promptings

James 1:19

ONE Wednesday night, I was sitting in my church office wrestling with the Holy Spirit prompting that I was supposed to go to that evening's service and ask people to share the trials they had been experiencing. I interpreted this as an indication someone wanted to surrender their life to Christ. The only problem was this meant I would not be preaching a message, a radical idea for a church service.

I decided to go for it. I shared my struggle with the group and was shocked at their response as many hands were raised throughout the room.

I listened to each person's story about tremendous burdens, needs, and the unmistakable longing to be restored to authenticity. I taught from a few Bible passages applicable to their stories and prayed for each one who had been vulnerable enough to share. At the close of the night, I asked once more if there was anyone who wanted to surrender his or her life to the Restorer. No one else raised their hand, so I dismissed the group.

On my way out, a young couple stopped me. They said, "I think we're the people you were talking about at the end."

The young man shared with me their roller-coaster life. He had been a criminal defense attorney who owned a prestigious firm. One day, a client paid him for his services with cocaine. It reignited a casual

usage from his high school days and leveraged an addiction within a matter of months. He lost everything. He and his new bride were forced to return home to live with his mother who had suggested they attend our Wednesday night gathering.

I responded to their questions, eventually asking if they wanted to surrender their lives to the Restorer. She was ready; he was not. I prayed with them as she fully surrendered her heart to Christ as Savior and Lord. We chatted a little, and they were on their way. I would later learn her husband had asked her if she had felt differently as they exited the church. She replied, "All I can tell you is I feel a tremendous peace I've never felt before."

Is the Holy Spirit prompting you to listen to someone's story? James wrote we should be "quick to listen, slow to speak and slow to become angry" (James 1:19). Every time we lock eyes with another human being is a divine appointment to listen.

Today, ask God to guide you to listen to another person's story. You will be amazed by what He does.

Addiction and Surrender

Psalm 145:16

AFTER speaking with the attorney-turned-addict who had repeatedly fought against surrender to Christ, I shared that he was trying to clean himself up as part of his own self-restoration program instead of coming to the Restorer to get cleaned up. He was incarcerated in pride's prison of pretense, and he needed the Master Key of full surrender.

"You're right, Mitch," he replied. "And if that's the case, then I need to do this right now."

He fell to his knees and prayed to God in his broken words, "I can't. You can. I can't free myself from the penalty of my sin. You can. I can't free myself from the power of sin and be lord of my life. You can."

The Restorer was at work, and He was not finished.

The following week his wife returned alone to share her husband had stolen $100, pawned their wedding rings, and went out to buy cocaine in a church parking lot. This time his binge was different. For the first time, he felt guilt and remorse for what he had done. I told her to have him come back the next week and not let this be the deal-breaker for his life. Sometimes, restoration involves taking two steps forward and one step back.

The couple returned a week later, and he shared the story of his binge with the rest of the group. It was the last time he ever used illegal drugs. He later went on to earn his degree in pastoral ministry and volunteered at a local church as a teaching pastor. He also decided to work on reinstating his license to practice law in order to provide legal services as a ministry to people in need.

Only God can truly satisfy our desires when we surrender to Him. David wrote to the Creator: "You open your hand and satisfy the desires of every living thing" (Psalm 145:16).

Are you or is someone you know suffering from an addiction? An addict completely understands the concept of surrender; he is simply misguided on the object of his surrender. Turn to the One who designed you and say, "I can't. You can." He will lead you on a new fulfilling journey down Restoration Road.

The Spirit's Power

1 Corinthians 2:4–5

ONE morning at a restaurant, I invited my waitress to our Wednesday evening gathering at church. She accepted, and, before I left the restaurant, she had asked all of her coworkers to join her.

Neither she nor I realized what God had in store.

That evening, I asked my new believer friend to share his story of cocaine addiction, surrender, and a one-time binge that followed, only for him to feel user's remorse for the first time in his life. My morning's waitress sat in the front row, listening intently to God's peace, purpose, and power this man was now experiencing when she stood up and surprised us all.

She looked up at me intently and said, "I have a cocaine problem, and I want what he has." I asked her if she was ready to fully surrender her life to the Restorer. She said, "Yes." In front of one hundred people, we read the Bible, and she prayed to God for forgiveness and restoration. When the night was over, she had been flooded with names and telephone numbers of others who told her to call them if she were tempted to reuse drugs. With tears in her eyes and mine, we walked downstairs where her two daughters had been enjoying a Bible class to share the news with them. Both girls surrendered their lives to Christ that night.

A few weeks later, we baptized her. She had invited the entire staff from the restaurant to watch as she publicly responded to the Restorer's invitation to live with a clay heart.

The apostle Paul wrote: "My message and my preaching were not with wise and persuasive words, but with a demonstration of the Spirit's power, so that your faith might not rest on human wisdom, but on God's power" (1 Corinthians 2:4–5). When a believer shares their story of restoration, unbelievers are drawn to the Restorer. Will you share your story of restoration with someone today and witness the Spirit's power?

Rest

Matthew 11:28

ARE you attempting a self-restoration program to earn your way to God?

Too often, sand hearts try to become stone hearts to regain their position with their Father, much like the younger brother in Jesus's parable recorded in Luke 15. He had tried to contrive a plan where he would work his way into the family business as a hired hand, thus earning his right to return. Sand hearts often become stone hearts in their process of self-restoration. Sand hearts are weary from their license. Stone hearts are burdened with their legalism.

Jesus said: "Come to me, all you who are weary and burdened, and I will give you rest" (Matthew 11:28). This short verse offers the Master Key that unlocks the gate to Restoration Road.

Rest is synonymous with restoration. In order to receive it, we must humbly come with a heart of clay, one that recognizes its journey through sand and stone, to the humble heart of the Restorer. Humility is the Master Key that unlocks the gate to Restoration Road.

Rather than attempting to clean yourself up to come to Christ, come to Christ and get cleaned up. Bring your heart of sand and stone to the One who will give you rest and make you new again.

The Yoke

Matthew 11:29–30a

I**S** there someone you continually seek for guidance and wisdom? When He walked this earth, Jesus made a transformational invitation to those who would surrender their wills to Him: "Take my yoke upon you and learn from me, for I am gentle and humble in heart, and you will find rest for your souls. For my yoke is easy" (Matthew 11:29–30a).

Take my yoke indicated one would become a disciple of Christ (an idiomatic expression of Jesus's day). Disciple meant "learner." Consequently, a disciple would begin a journey toward wisdom. This required listening through prayer and obedience.

The word *yoke* is often confused with the Greek word used for yoking two animals. However, Jesus's choice of *yoke* was the Greek word *zugos*. This word was used to describe the yoke used by a person carrying buckets of milk or water. The yoke made the load lighter.

Jesus revealing His yoke was easy meant it was not filled with the heavy burden of legalism created by the stone-hearted Pharisees and teachers of the law who had added about 1,500 laws to God's 613 spoken in the first five books of the Old Testament.

Are you willing to take the Restorer's yoke and become His disciple? Jesus Christ is the Master Teacher. When you become His student, He will lead you to wisdom that will transform your life. Take a step by selecting a Gospel and read a chapter each day. You will learn from the Master Teacher.

Paid in Full

Matthew 11:30b

ARE you trying to earn God's forgiveness through acts of self-righteousness? Perhaps you think you will pay Him back for all your wrongdoings.

Jesus said: "My burden is light" (Matthew 11:30b). This meant He covered the cost. Those who surrendered to Him were forgiven.

On the cross, Jesus proclaimed: "It is finished" (John 19:30). The Greek word for the phrase, which was among Jesus's last, is *teleo*. This was the same word written at the top of a Bill of Sale marked, "Paid in Full."

I took part in auctioning nearly 250,000 collector cars, each of which, just like us, had begun life as a clay mold. When they traded hands, each car included a Bill of Sale marked, "Paid in Full."

Christ paid a world-record price for each of us (1 Corinthians 6:20). He offers His restorative forgiveness to all, freeing us from the penalty of self-restoration, the power of self-restoration, and on the other side from the presence of self-restoration, namely sin. He appropriates that forgiveness only to those who humble themselves to Him and come to Him with clay hearts, the authentic design of the Designer, the heart of the Christ, who restores us to authenticity from the inside out.

Offer this prayer to the Restorer: "Thank You for paying a world record price for me. I have sinned against You. I can't pay the penalty of my sin. You can. I can't free myself from the power of sin. You can. I fully surrender my life to You." He will demonstrate your ultimate value as you reflect His design to restore others.

Join the Celebration

Luke 4:18–19

ARE you locked outside the celebration of the kingdom of heaven?

The Restorer holds the Master Key of full surrender to unlock the gate of your heart to Restoration Road. That Master Key is cross-shaped. Full surrender vertically to God leads to humility horizontally toward others.

When Jesus walked the earth, He clarified inside a Nazareth synagogue that His purpose was to restore: "The Spirit of the Lord is on me, because he has anointed me to proclaim good news to the poor. He has sent me to proclaim freedom for the prisoners and recovery of sight for the blind, to set the oppressed free, to proclaim the year of the Lord's favor" (Luke 4:18–19; cf. Isaiah 61:1–2).

Jesus was quoting the prophet Isaiah, who went on to record God's restored ones would rebuild, restore, and renew His kingdom (Isaiah 61:4). They would be priests living at the crossroads of the vertical intersecting with the horizontal; they would be ministers of their God (Isaiah 61:6). With the gates of their hearts unlocked by the Master Key, they would walk Restoration Road to find the celebration of life as they brought that life to others.

When the Restorer unlocks the gate of your heart with His Master Key, He will rebuild your communion with God, restore your community with others, and use you to renew your culture with both. All you need to do is bend the knees of your heart to the Restorer and say, "I can't. You can."

Sinner and Saint

Ephesians 2:8

O NE of my greatest encouragers was Grandpa Russell. I probably shared more stories back and forth with him than I did with any other human being.

At eighty-four years old, Grandpa Russell traveled with Dad and me to the Brickyard for Carburetion Day. While he was entering Dad's motor-coach, Russell was really proud.

"Mitchell, I want you to know I just finished planning my funeral arrangements yesterday, and I ordered a beautiful copper casket," Russell proclaimed.

"I know," I replied. "Your attorney, Uncle Derald, called me." I was joking, setting the stage for him to walk into my funny moment. You see, Russell had suffered from a stroke a few years earlier. This had led to his short-term memory loss. I would always kid him about the benefits that he seemed to leverage from not recalling the past.

"He did?" Russell asked.

"He said you wanted me to use the word saint about you at your funeral," I answered.

"I did?" Russell replied. "I want you to use the word saint at my funeral?"

"Yeah, don't worry I already know how I'm going to use it," I said to Russell as I looked over at Dad. "I'm going to say, 'Russell appreciated the beauty of a woman; he told many racy stories, but compared to his son, Dean, he was a saint.'" I loved hearing Russell burst out laughing, especially if it was at Dad's expense.

Many of us assume God grades on the curve, thinking if we can be less sinful than someone else, maybe He will let us in to His kingdom. That's not the case. God is perfect and holy. Our sin has created a gap (Isaiah 59:2), but God has filled it with the perfect life, death, and resurrection of His Son. All we need to do is surrender to Him by grace through faith.

The apostle Paul wrote: "For it is by grace you have been saved, through faith—and this is not from yourselves, it is the gift of God" (Ephesians 2:8).

Surrender your sin to the One who paid its penalty and become a saint, one who receives the gift of eternal life and is used by God to bring that gift to others.

Mist

James 4:14

SEVERAL years ago, I received a telephone call from my grandfather, Russell, asking me to meet him at the hospital where he would hear the results of his heart tests. I finished my appointment and met him at the heart center. We both waited patiently until the doctor entered the examination room.

"Well, Russell, you have two problems," the doctor said.

"Only two?" Russell replied, referring optimistically as if he were to have only two flaws.

The first problem was congestive heart failure. The second was its affect on his kidneys. That was the beginning of the end.

Over the course of the next few months, we relived many years of stories. I received more joy from those conversations listening to Russell share his life and his legacy than anything else we discussed. Time after time, I observed how he had faced tragedies and triumphs, along with many moments where he had needed restoration. We both commented frequently how quickly time passes.

Jesus's half-brother James penned a picture of the brevity of life: "Why, you do not even know what will happen tomorrow. What is your life? You are a mist that appears for a little while and then vanishes" (James 4:14).

When I think about that picture, I remember exhaling my moist breath on the cold glass of my elementary school bus window, then writing my name in it. God exhales our life into the clay of the ground as the Designer and continues to inhale and exhale through us as the Restorer. We are God's mist. As we walk, He is writing His name in our hearts.

Today, take time to recognize God's identity being written on the mist of your heart.

Tragedies

2 Samuel 14:14

LIFE on this side is full of tragedies. One in particular became a defining moment for my grandfather, Russell, on Restoration Road.

In the 1940s, Russell, a farmer in his mid-twenties, was combining the fields of their family farm with his sixteen-year-old brother Harold at his side. They had planned to be business partners in a couple of years when Harold turned eighteen. As the two of them discussed their future, Harold, who was athletic, jumped off the combine to chase a rabbit that had caught his eye. After a couple of minutes, Harold attempted to jump back on, but slipped when Russell felt his combine run into an obstacle in the field. He got out to look, only to encounter a scene that would be forever embedded in his mind: it was his brother, Harold, twisted in the blades of the combine.

Near death, Harold was whisked to the hospital where he underwent weeks of treatment that restored him to health. When his doctors finally told him that he would be released from the hospital the next day, Harold was excited. He had his softball glove in one hand and a softball in the other as he threw the ball repeatedly into his mitt. "I'm going home tomorrow, Rusty," he said enthusiastically to Russell as the glove popped.

That night, Harold went to sleep without being given his medication to assist in the prevention of blood clots. He never returned home.

When I look back at Russell's life, I realize he had, for decades, carried a major tragedy with him, requiring restoration. While Russell lived his next sixty years on this earth without Harold, only one thing would restore him with his brother, being in Christ.

The wise woman from Tekoa shared the following with King David: "Like water spilled on the ground, which cannot be recovered, so we must die. But that is not what God desires; rather, he devises ways so that a banished person does not remain banished from him" (2 Samuel 14:14).

God is devising ways for you and me to live life in Him.

One day we are all going to return to the ground from which we came. The question remains, "What part of the ground will our hearts resemble: sand, stone, or clay?" The condition of our spiritual hearts at our departure will determine where our hearts travel into the next life: north or south.

The time given to each of us on earth is a gift from the Restorer; our task is to leave a legacy to restore future generations. Keep that life and lose it. Give that life and keep it. Die once; live twice. Live once; die twice. While we travel, there is only one road that travels north. It is called, "Restoration Road."

Pathways

Proverbs 3:5–6

I WILL never forget the time I boarded a plane to Asia. A friend had invited me to speak about sand, stone, and clay in one of the most unexpected places. Fourteen hours later, I stepped off the plane into the humidity of the Philippines. Over the next seven days, I shared my journey on Restoration Road, including how God restored me with a heart of clay.

I traveled with my friend through a gate, down a road, and to the destination of a city dump just outside Metro Manila where more than 14,000 families live in extreme poverty. It was difficult for me to comprehend the images my eyes were burning on my heart as we met the children and their parents who literally lived hand-to-mouth, day-to-day. I encountered even more stories of those who were traveling their own unique journeys on Restoration Road as they were being restored to authenticity.

In that experience, God had taken me from pursuing the rich for my benefit to pursuing the poor for theirs. I learned both ends of the

socioeconomic spectrum are in need of the Restoration Road: rich and poor, whether licentious or legalistic, whether sand or stone.

Restoration Road is a journey we travel our entire lives. Our steps include continual choices, thoughts, prayers, and feelings—to whom or what will we surrender the four chambers of our hearts, our four primary desires, and our three resources of life? We will frequently approach speed bumps of sand or stone on our journeys fully surrendered to and fully aligned with the Restorer.

Every encounter with another human being will offer yet another opportunity to reflect the design of the Designer, our Restorer. Solomon wrote: "Trust in the LORD with all your heart and lean not on your own understanding; in all your ways submit to him, and he will make your paths straight" (Proverbs 3:5–6). Give God all your heart, and He will lead you straight down Restoration Road.

The Restorer's Prayer

Mark 4:1–20

EACH of us travels Restoration Road or Desperation Road. The pathway depends on the condition of our hearts.

Jesus told a parable of seed that was scattered on the road, the rocks, the thorns, and the good soil. In His story, Jesus sowed the seed, which was a picture of the word of God. The substance of the ground was emblematic of the condition of the heart. The path was imagery of a hard heart. The rocks illustrated a shallow heart. The thorns resembled a heart desiring other things. However, the good soil represented a soft, humble heart, one that was cultivated by the Holy Spirit (Mark 4:1–20).

Regardless of where your life has taken you, your story is not finished. In fact, the next step always provides a new beginning. There is one road leading to a life that loves God and loves others. It is the road you and I were designed to seek, the authenticity discovered only on Restoration Road.

You can respond to the Holy Spirit's work in your life by humbling your heart to Him. He will restore you and use you to make others new again.

This week, start and end every day with this prayer:

When my heart is hard help me to sow;
Where my heart is shallow help me to grow;
Whatever my heart's thorns help me to let go;
And the Restorer answers,
"Listen to Me speak, I knock at your door,
Seek Me, find Me, I will give you more.
Loosen your grip, return to Me, I will restore;
When your heart is open, into your life holy rain I will pour."

Simplify

1 Thessalonians 4:11a

A FRIEND of mine experienced the adrenaline rush of driving his Maserati Spyder from a service appointment to his picturesque suburban Texas home where he parked the rolling sculpture in his garage. After making sure his Italian beauty was tucked away, he hopped into his wife's vehicle and headed to their local Einstein Bros. Bagels when tragedy struck. The Maserati caught on fire.

A neighbor who saw the smoke escaping from their garage stretched a nearby garden hose as far as he could to squelch the fire, but the makeshift waterline was too short. As he frantically searched for additional hose, the flames climbed to a plywood attic door in the ceiling that quickly turned to ashes. The resulting explosion blew through the rafters of the house.

In just a few minutes, my friend lost all his personal possessions, including his dog.

Investigators searched for the cause of the sports car's electrical fire.

Walking through the shambles of his home, my friend and his wife came across a sign that, before the inferno, had sat prominently on his desk. It read, "SIMPLIFY." The word had served as a constant reminder to this prodigal son who, years prior, had returned to his heavenly Father after a highly publicized bout with drug and alcohol addiction. If he ever owned wealth again, he never wanted it to own him.

With his mind swirling through the pain of the loss, but thankful none of his family was trapped inside the burning house, my friend trekked through the rubble to his garage in order to take a picture of this sign in front of his burned Maserati. The photo would serve as a new reminder to keep the entire trial in God's perspective.

The apostle Paul wrote: "Make it your ambition to lead a quiet life" (1 Thessalonians 4:11a). In our loud world, we often complicate our lives by over-committing our time, talent, and treasure for our own selfish benefit. God designed something better, a simple life that is quiet enough to experience intimacy with Him as we develop authentic relationships with others.

One year later, my friend and his wife moved in their newly-built home at the same location. On his office wall hangs a photograph. I'm sure you can guess what's inside the frame.

Satisfied Are the Humble

Matthew 5:3

JESUS'S first secret to satisfaction through surrender was: "Blessed are the poor in spirit" (Matthew 5:3a). Restated, Jesus said, "Satisfied are the humble." *Humble* means "to be lower than, or to bend the knees of one's heart." *Humility* and *humanity* come from the same Latin root, *humus*, meaning "from the ground." We call it "down to earth."

The condition of one's heart is determined by the object of its desires. A humble heart desires Christ, above all else. *Poor in spirit* is declaring our moral bankruptcy before a holy God, trusting in Christ's free gift of grace as payment for our sin. Humility says to Christ, "I can't. You can. I can't pay for my sin. You can. I can't be Lord of my life. You can." "I can't" is *repentance*. "You can" is *faith*. Contrast this heart condition with a proud one, which says to God, "I can. You can't." *Pride* means "to be higher than, or to exalt." A proud heart desires self and remains dissatisfied.

Why are the humble satisfied? "For theirs is the kingdom of heaven" (Matthew 5:3b). Jesus, our ultimate example of a humble heart (Matthew 11:29) said that humility was the entrance requirement to the kingdom of heaven (Matthew 18:1–4). This is where we experience God's divine reign, rule, and order, what we were created for.

How are they satisfied? In order to humble our hearts, we must surrender our pride. In a great story tucked in the Gospel of Luke, Jesus contrasted the temple prayer of a proud Pharisee with that of a humble tax collector. The respected Pharisee exalted himself while the disrespected tax collector stood at a distance, refused to look up to heaven, and beat his breast—three acts of humility. The tax collector finally made an attempt to put into words the condition of his heart: "God, have mercy on me, a sinner" (Luke 18:13). Jesus said that the tax collector, not the Pharisee, went home justified before God. He summed it up this way: "For all those who exalts themselves will be humbled, and those who humble themselves will be exalted" (Luke 18:14b).

Take a *poor in spirit* inventory of any pride in your life where you are ruling your own kingdom. It will be manifested in a relationship, a task, or a conflict that is leaving you dissatisfied. Surrender your pride to Christ, saying, "I can't. You can." Live out this humility toward Christ in your relationships where you will experience satisfaction through the surrender of your desires to Him, as you live in the kingdom of heaven where those around you are drawn to Christ in you.

Satisfied Are Those Who Mourn

Matthew 5:4

DO you find yourself guarding your emotions in order to numb the pain? Jesus offered a healing alternative in His second of eight secrets to satisfaction through surrender: "Blessed are those who mourn, for they will be comforted" (Matthew 5:4).

Who are satisfied? "Those who mourn." The Bible records three reasons to mourn: (1) the loss of life, (2) sin—desiring life apart from God, and (3) the lost—those who are not surrendered to Christ. God's people mourned for the loss of life: seventy days for the loss of Jacob (Genesis 50:3) and thirty days for the loss of Aaron (Numbers 20:29) and Moses (Deuteronomy 34:8) among many others. God's people mourned for their sin (1 Samuel 7:2–4). Both Samuel and God mourned for Saul's unrepentant, lost heart (1 Samuel 15:35). David mourned for Absalom's return (2 Samuel 13:37).

Mourning was modeled in the heart and life of Christ. He mourned for the loss of life when Lazarus died. John recorded it succinctly: "Jesus wept" (John 11:35). Jesus mourned for the sin of Jerusalem (Matthew 23:37). While on the cross, He mourned for bearing the sin of the world (Matthew 27:46). Jesus mourned for the lost. When pagan, Roman guards pounded the nails in His hands, Jesus pleaded: "Father, forgive them, for they do not know what they are doing" (Luke 23:34a).

Why are they satisfied? "They will be comforted" (Matthew 5:4). The name for the Holy Spirit, *Comforter*, literally means to call alongside. When we mourn, we release the Holy Spirit both in and out of our hearts. Paul said that this comfort comes only from God who comforts our hearts so that we will comfort others (2 Corinthians 1:3–7). The Old Testament prophet Jeremiah wrote that God turns our mourning into dancing (Jeremiah 31:13). Isaiah communicated that the Spirit of God works through us to comfort all who mourn (Isaiah 61:2). We either release the Holy Spirit and experience satisfaction, or we hold on to our guardedness and experience dissatisfaction.

How are they satisfied? They surrender their guardedness. When we desire to find satisfaction in and of ourselves, we guard our hearts from mourning and thwart the comfort of the Holy Spirit in and out of our lives. However, when we surrender our guardedness, we will release the Holy Spirit in three ways: one for each reason to mourn.

First, we will comfort others when they experience the loss of a loved one. Jesus did so when He encountered Martha at the death of her brother, Lazarus (John 11:31–33). Second, we will repent from our sin and return to God. Jesus told the young woman caught in adultery: "Go now and leave your life of sin" (John 8:11). Third, we will pray for the lost. Before He went to the cross, Jesus prayed for the lost, that they would surrender to Him as Lord and Savior (John 17:20–21).

Read Luke 23 where you will see, while bearing His cross, Jesus mourned for: the loss of life (vv. 29–31), sin (v. 34), and the lost (v. 43). Surrender your guardedness and mourn for: the loss of life, sin, and the lost. You will be satisfied with the comfort of the Holy Spirit Who will comfort others through you, draw you to repent from sin and return to God, and prompt you to pray for the lost.

Satisfied Are the Gentle

Matthew 5:5

HAVE you ever been harsh? Something flawed inside each of us says that we can satisfy our desires by being harsh. Whether at the airline counter or the fast food line, in the checkout isle or the exit lane, on the basketball sidelines or the telephone lines, we believe that harshness will satisfy our desires. Jesus gave us a different way in the third of eight secrets to satisfaction through surrender: "Blessed are the meek, for they will inherit the earth" (Matthew 5:5).

Who are satisfied? The NASB says: "Blessed are the gentle" (Matthew 5:5). Gentleness is power under the Spirit's control. Like a bit in a horse's mouth, the Spirit's residence in our hearts guides us when we are gentle. The Greek word for *gentle* is *praus* from *prautes*. Aristotle defined it as the middle course of being angry, between being angry for no reason and not getting angry at all. Gentleness is getting angry at the right time with the right measure for the right reason.

Jesus described Himself as gentle in heart (Matthew 11:29). The God of the universe is gentle, not harsh. Paul told us that the result of the Holy Spirit's dwelling in us is gentleness (Galatians 5:23). If the Spirit of God is alive in us, then we will be gentle, not harsh, in heart.

Why are they satisfied? "They will inherit the earth" (Matthew 5:5). This is Jewish phraseology for the blessings of God's kingdom, His divine reign, rule, and order on this earth now and in the future. We see this in the Old Testament. Remember the Israelites and their quest to inherit the Promised Land? Canaan, as it was known, was referenced by the Israelites as a type of heaven. Contrasting God's curses for those who are harsh with the blessings for those who are gentle, or meek, David said: "But the meek will inherit the land and enjoy peace and prosperity" (Psalm 37:11). We were designed to be satisfied by the kingdom of heaven, the invisible movement of God's will in our lives. We find satisfaction not through harshness but through gentleness because gentleness restores relationships.

How are they satisfied? They surrender their harshness. We are gentle in heart when we surrender our harshness to God, who satisfies our desires. Today, focus on gentleness in your words and nonverbal cues. You will be satisfied.

How to Be Gentle

Matthew 11:29; Proverbs 15:1; Galatians 6:1; 1 Peter 3:15

GENTLENESS restores three-dimensionally: (1) our relationship with God, (2) our relationships with others, and (3) others' relationships with God.

First, gentleness restores our relationship with God. Jesus said that His gentleness restores our souls (Matthew 11:29). James, the half-brother of Jesus and the pastor of the New Testament church in Jerusalem, said that we should humbly, or gently, receive the word of God planted in our hearts that saves (restores) us with God (James 1:21).

Are you harsh with God in any areas of your life? Perhaps He didn't heal someone in the way or with the timing that you saw fit. Maybe He has allowed suffering in your life you deem unreasonable. Or you don't have the career, spouse, or children you thought He should give you. Whatever the harshness against God might be, surrender it to Him today. Say, "I can't. You can. I can't satisfy my desires through harshness toward You, but You can satisfy my desires when I surrender my harshness to you."

Second, gentleness restores our relationships with others. Jesus taught that our words flow from our hearts (Luke 6:45). When we are harsh in heart, so are our words. When we are gentle in heart, our words are gentle—powerful under the Spirit's control. Solomon observed: "A gentle answer turns away wrath, but a harsh word stirs up anger" (Proverbs 15:1).

Are you harsh with your words in any relationship? Do you even find yourself being harshest with those closest to you? Try

surrendering your harshness for gentleness with your heart and subsequently your words. You will find restoration in your relationships with others.

Third, gentleness restores others' relationships with God. This applies to both the surrendered and the unsurrendered. Paul said that when the surrendered is caught in sin, we should restore him gently, realizing that we could be tempted as well (Galatians 6:1). Peter communicated when we answer the unsurrendered with the reason for the hope that we have in Christ, we should do so gently (1 Peter 3:15).

With whom are you harsh because of their unrestored relationship with God? It might be the self-righteous, conservatives, liberals, or addicts. Are you willing to surrender that harshness to God and them, experiencing gentleness in heart and the inheritance of God's blessings?

Satisfied Are Those Who Hunger and Thirst for Righteousness

Matthew 5:6

Do you desire any life apart from God? That's sin, which leaves a gap between God and us, accompanied by a desire to have it filled (Isaiah 59:2). It's a vicious cycle. We attempt to satisfy our sinful desires apart from God through unrighteousness and then try to fill the resulting gap with our self-righteousness. Consequently, we are left dissatisfied.

Righteousness is important to God who wants us to do what's right more than He wants us to give a tithe or an offering (Proverbs 21:3). However, our best at doing right is like filthy rags in God's sight (Isaiah 64:6). Either we think our desire to fill the gap will be satisfied by our own self-righteousness or we just give up and continue to sin in our unrighteousness. It's as if we are damned if we do and damned if we don't. Jesus gave us an alternative in the fourth secret to satisfaction through surrender saying: "Blessed are those who hunger and thirst for righteousness, for they will be filled" (Matthew 5:6).

Who are satisfied? Jesus proclaimed: "Blessed are those who hunger and thirst for righteousness" (Matthew 5:6a). Righteousness is what is right in God's sight. We find a hunger and thirst for righteousness in the heart of Christ who did not sin but became the payment for our sin, so that in Him we might be the righteousness of God (2 Corinthians 5:21). Just like us, Jesus was tempted in every way, but He did not sin (Hebrews 4:15). He is the only truly righteous one. Jesus's close friend said it this way: "My dear children, I write this to you so that you will not sin. But if anybody does sin, we have an advocate with the Father—Jesus Christ, the Righteous One. He is the atoning sacrifice for our sins, and not only for ours but also for the sins of the whole world" (1 John 2:1–2). Consequently, those who hunger and thirst for righteousness desire Christ, the righteousness of God.

Why are they satisfied? "They will be filled" (Matthew 5:6b). The desire and the resulting gap can only be filled by Christ, who fills everything in every way (Ephesians 1:22–23). The psalmist said that the Lord satisfies the thirsty and fills the hungry with good things (Psalm 107:9). Sin never satisfies, and its resulting gap in our hearts will never be satisfied outside of Christ.

How are they satisfied? They surrender their sin, which comes in two forms: unrighteousness and self-righteousness. Focus on surrendering both today.

How to Find What Is Right in God's Sight

Romans 13:14; Matthew 5:20; 23:27–28, 37

HOW do we do what is right in God's sight?

First, we surrender our unrighteousness. Paul compelled the self-indulged Romans to surrender their unrighteousness to Christ, clothing themselves in His righteousness, not even thinking about how to gratify the desires of their sinful nature (Romans 13:14). We must exchange our unrighteous filthy rags for the righteousness of Christ.

Second, we must surrender our self-righteousness—our self-atonement program to fill the gap left by sin. Jesus said that our righteousness must surpass that of the Pharisees and the teachers of the law to even enter the kingdom of heaven (Matthew 5:20). He challenged the Pharisees to acknowledge their pretense of self-righteousness on the outside while they were unrighteous on the inside (Matthew 23:27–28). Once again, we discover satisfaction through surrender is a heart issue. Jesus pleaded with the self-righteous to surrender to him, but they were not willing (Matthew 23:37). Neither will we, unless we surrender our self-righteous filthy rags, exchanging them for the righteousness of Christ. Surrender says to Christ, "I can't. You can. I can't satisfy my desires. God, in Christ, You can. I can't fill the gap of my sin. God, in Christ, You can."

Surrender your sin and its gap to Christ by letting go of your unrighteousness and your self-righteous attempts to compensate for your desire apart from Him and its resulting chasm. You will be satisfied when you hunger and thirst for Christ.

Left to our sinful nature, we seek satisfaction of our desires in our pride, attempting to be designer and restorer of our own lives. However, in God's kingdom, the pathway up is down, through the door of humility. We find satisfaction through surrender to Christ who brings us into the kingdom of heaven when we say to Him, "I can't. You can."

Satisfied Are the Merciful

Matthew 5:7

WHO has seized an opportunity to wrong you? Do you find yourself believing your desires can be satisfied only through condemnation of that person? Perhaps, you pray for God to bring justice, conviction, and punishment. Too often this is the case in our lives, and we discover that seeking satisfaction of our desires through condemnation of an offender leaves us dissatisfied. In his fifth secret to satisfaction through surrender, Jesus offered us a different way: "Blessed are the merciful, for they will be shown mercy" (Matthew 5:7).

Who are satisfied? Jesus taught: "Blessed are the merciful" (Matthew 5:7a). By definition mercy implies two components: (1) someone is condemned, and (2) someone is forgiven. This takes place in our lives vertically with God and horizontally with others. As sinners, each of us stood condemned vertically with God (Romans 5:16–18). Consequently, when we condemn others horizontally in our relationships, we are dissatisfied (Romans 2:1). In His statement about the kingdom of heaven—God's divine reign, rule, and order in our hearts and lives now and in the future—Jesus portrayed horizontal mercy as evidence of vertical mercy received from God.

The Bible teaches mercy is the desire of Christ's heart (Matthew 9:13, 36; 12:7; John 3:17–18). One of the most powerful images of mercy rests in the story of Jesus and the woman caught in adultery (John 8:1–11). *Mercy* in Latin, *misericordia*, combines two words: *pity*

and *heart*. Mercy flows from the heart cheerfully and only by the gift of the Holy Spirit (Romans 12:8).

Why are they satisfied? "They will be shown mercy" (Matthew 5:7b). They will receive mercy vertically from God. They will be free of condemnation. Paul said that there is no condemnation for those who are in the mercy of Christ (Romans 8:1). The Old Testament prophet Micah said that God delights in giving mercy to those who are condemned (Micah 7:18–10). Recognizing our mercy received vertically from God in Christ frees us to show mercy horizontally to others.

How are they satisfied? They surrender their condemnation—vertically and horizontally (Luke 6:36–37). Jesus said that if we are not characterized and known by administering mercy horizontally to others, then we will not receive mercy from God (Matthew 6:14–15). To do so, we must surrender our condemnation. Surrender says to God, "I can't. You can. I can't satisfy my desires through condemnation of the person who wronged me. You can satisfy my desires through mercy."

By the power of the Holy Spirit, surrender your condemnation of the person who wronged you today. You will be satisfied through mercy.

Satisfied Are the Pure in Heart

Matthew 5:8

WHAT do you add to your devotion to God to satisfy your desires? The equation usually looks like this: (God + _____ = satisfaction). What do you place in your blank? It might be money, sex outside of God's design, porn, risk, a rush, a smoke, a toke, a drink, or a line. It might seem as innocent as attention, affection, acceptance, approval, bigness, an attractive spouse, behaving children, or even religion. In any case, the result is a mixed devotion of the heart. The Bible alludes to these mixed devotions as impurities, or idols, because they compete with our full devotion to God. John said that anyone who does evil has not seen God (3 John 11). In His sixth secret to satisfaction through surrender, Jesus taught a better way: "Blessed are the pure in heart, for they will see God" (Matthew 5:8).

Who are satisfied? The pure in heart. The Bible uses the word *pure* most frequently in reference to precious metal, usually gold. Precious metals must be refined to become pure. This process involves intense heat that brings impurities to the top of the crucible (silver) or the furnace (gold), so the refiner can remove them. The deepest impurities rise last after an intense time of heat. Just like the crucible is used for silver, and the furnace for gold, so God tests our hearts to discover whether they are pure—wholly devoted, or fully surrendered, to Him (Proverbs 17:3). Paul warned us to not be led away from our pure and sincere devotion to Christ (2 Corinthians 11:3).

Our ultimate example of a pure heart is the heart of Christ. The Bible tells us Christ is pure in heart (1 John 3:3; Hebrews 7:26). He demonstrated a fully surrendered heart with unmixed devotion to the Father.

Why are they satisfied? "They will see God" (Matthew 5:8b). The God of the universe will demonstrate His kingdom in their hearts and lives. They will see Christ in themselves. This is illustrated in the molding of silver or gold. The metal refining process continues until the refiner can see his reflection in the metal. Then the metal is fashioned in its useful state. As the refiner of the heart, God removes our impurities until He sees the reflection of Christ (Romans 8:29). When God sees Christ in us, we see God. David noted our desires would be satisfied when we see Him (Psalm 17:15). He communicated God would show Himself pure to the pure in heart, but He would judge those with mixed devotions (2 Samuel 22:27; cf. Psalm 18:26). Addressing those with impurities, God promised to reveal Himself to anyone who would seek Him with a whole heart (Jeremiah 29:13).

How are they satisfied? They surrender their impurities (mixed devotions). Surrender says to God, "I can't. You can. I can't satisfy my desires with mixed devotions. You can satisfy my desires when they are fully devoted to You." In order to do this, we need to follow David's example—(1) ask God to search our heart for any mixed devotions (Psalm 139:23–24), and (2) ask Him to create in us a pure heart (Psalm 51:10).

Ask God to search your heart for any mixed devotion and to renew in you a pure heart—one fully devoted to Him. You will be satisfied through your unmixed devotion to the Creator who will reveal Christ in you.

Satisfied Are the Peacemakers

Matthew 5:9

D O you have unreconciled, relational conflict? Conflict is defined as two objects attempting to occupy the same space at the same time. God designed peace for our relationships (Genesis 1:28). With sin came negative conflict (Genesis 3). Negative conflict includes at least one foolish option. It is internal—our sinful nature and the Spirit are in conflict with each other (Galatians 5:17). It is also external in our relationships. Consequently, when someone wrongs us, we attempt to satisfy our desires through negative conflict. In His seventh secret to satisfaction through surrender, Jesus shared: "Blessed are the peacemakers, for they will be called children of God" (Matthew 5:9).

Who are satisfied? Jesus preached: "Blessed are the peacemakers" (Matthew 5:9a). Internally, peace is a heart condition, flowing from the peaceful relationship of the Godhead—Christ (Colossians 3:15), the Holy Spirit (Galatians 5:22), and the Father (1 Corinthians 14:33). Externally in our relationships, we are commanded by Paul to be peacemakers: "If it is possible, as far as it depends on you, live at peace with everyone" (Romans 12:18). Peace is reconciliation. Forgiveness always precedes reconciliation, but reconciliation does not always follow forgiveness because peace requires two willing hearts. Paul went on to say that we should not attempt to satisfy our desires with negative conflict (revenge), but we should leave room for God (Romans 12:19).

Peace is in the heart of Christ who made our peace with God, allowing us to have peace with others (Ephesians 2:14–22). Internally, we experience vertical peace by the work of Christ. Externally, we can experience horizontal peace in our relationships by the work of Christ.

Why are they satisfied? "They will be called children of God" (Matthew 5:9). A *child* is the "likeness." Faith in Christ makes us children of God (Galatians 3:26–29). His Spirit tells ours that we are God's children (Romans 8:16). As God's children, we are heirs of His kingdom empowered to live in harmony in relationships (Romans 12:16). Therefore, we are satisfied when we exhibit the likeness of Christ in our relationships by exchanging our desire for negative conflict with a desire for making peace. Proverbs tells us that it is better for us to have a little with peace in our relationships than to have a lot with unreconciled conflict (Proverbs 17:1). Peace in relationships allows us to experience the kingdom of God—His divine reign, rule, and order on this earth now and in the future (Romans 14:17).

How are they satisfied? They surrender their conflict. Surrender says to God, "I can't satisfy my desires through negative conflict (revenge) toward the person who wronged me. You can bring peace to the unreconciled conflict in my life." Pray those words to Him today.

How Do We Make Peace?

Philippians 4:7

HOW do we make peace in our interpersonal conflict?

First, we must pray for wisdom—God's heart combined with street smarts. Conflict is why Solomon asked God for wisdom (1 Kings 3:5–9). Internally, when we pray for wisdom, the peace of God guards our hearts like a military fortress in Christ. Paul taught: "And the peace of God, which transcends all understanding, will guard your hearts and your minds in Christ Jesus" (Philippians 4:7). When we have internal peace with God, He makes our enemies live at peace with us (Proverbs 16:7).

Second, we must go make peace. Jesus, the personified wisdom of God, said that when we have unreconciled conflict, we should go make peace and agree (Matthew 18:15–20). *Agree* in Greek is where we get the English word for symphony. Externally, when we have harmony in our relationships, we make a symphony to God. Proverbs tells us that God's wisdom brings peace that satisfies our desires more than negative conflict can (Proverbs 3:15–17).

Identify your conflict. What two objects are attempting to occupy the same space at the same time? First, pray for wisdom and experience the peace of God in Christ. Second, go make peace with your counterpart in the conflict. Live in harmony and make a symphony to God.

Satisfied Are the Persecuted

Matthew 5:10-12

WHEN you are insulted, persecuted, or slandered for your full surrender to Christ, do you endure or give up? The source of the insults might be a spouse, coworker, friend, or foe. In any event, they are threatened by full surrender to Christ because they don't want to surrender something. When this hardship for our faith comes, we often attempt to satisfy our desires by giving up. In His eighth secret to satisfaction, Jesus gave us a different way: "Blessed are those who are persecuted because of righteousness, for theirs is the kingdom of heaven" (Matthew 5:10).

Who are satisfied? Jesus revealed: "Blessed are those who are persecuted because of righteousness" (Matthew 5:10a). Those who are blessed are those who are persecuted for Christ's righteousness, not their own. If we have never been persecuted for our righteousness in Christ—our full surrender to Him—then we might not be fully surrendered. Wholly devoted people boldly advance the kingdom of God through evangelism and discipleship, and at some point, they are persecuted by others (Matthew 10:22; Philippians 1:29; 2 Timothy 3:12).

Enduring persecution flows from the heart of Christ (John 6:27). When Jesus was insulted, He did not retaliate; when He suffered, He made no threats. Instead, He entrusted Himself to God (1 Peter 2:23). Jesus considered it joy to endure the cross, so those who would experience persecution from full surrender to Him would endure (Hebrews 12:2–3). He told His disciples that those who endure persecution to the end will be saved (Matthew 10:22; 24:13–14).

Why are they satisfied? "Theirs is the kingdom of heaven" (Matthew 5:10b). Those who endure persecution for full surrender to Christ possess God's divine reign, rule, and order in their hearts and lives, both now and in the future. Jesus said that those who endure insults, persecution, and slander have a great reward in heaven (Matthew 5:11–12). That reward is praise from God based on our intimacy with Him and our relationships with others (1 Corinthians 4:5). Just as persecution and suffering flow from our connection to Christ, so will our comfort flow from Christ, producing endurance in us (2 Corinthians 1:5–6). Paul said that those who endure will reign with Christ in His kingdom; those who disown Christ will be disowned by Him (2 Timothy 2:12; cf. Matthew 10:32–33).

How are they satisfied? They surrender their persecution. Surrender says to God, "I can't satisfy my desires by giving up. I can't endure the persecution for my full surrender. You can." Today, surrender any persecution for your faith to God. He will give you strength and make you new again.

Endure

1 Corinthians 4:12b–13a

ARE those around you attempting to cause you trouble for your faith in Christ and you feel like giving up? Endure. This condition of the heart results in two behaviors.

First, we must bless those who persecute us, praying for their surrender to Christ (Matthew 5:44). Paul said: "When we are cursed, we bless; when we are persecuted, we endure it; when we are slandered, we answer kindly" (1 Corinthians 4:12b–13a).

Second, we must evangelize others to full surrender. Paul confirmed he had endured persecution for his faith so others would fully surrender their hearts to Christ (2 Timothy 2:10). He went on to tell Timothy to endure hardship and evangelize (2 Timothy 4:5). Jesus commanded His disciples to preach His gospel of full surrender enduring its subsequent hardships to the end (Matthew 24:13–14). Peter said that when we are persecuted for evangelizing others to full surrender to Christ, we are blessed because the Spirit of God rests on us (1 Peter 4:14). He makes us new again. Our desires will be satisfied when we advance Christ's kingdom of full surrender to the point of enduring persecution.

Bless anyone who is persecuting you by praying for their surrender to Christ. Endure and answer kindly. Evangelize others to full surrender in Christ. Experience the Spirit of God restoring your life.

Left to ourselves, we proudly pursue the satisfaction of our desires apart from God, as we attempt to be designer and restorer of our own lives. Jesus taught satisfaction through surrender to Him. He will reign in our lives when we say to Him, "I can't. You can."

Service That Leads to Surrender

Matthew 5:13–14

DO you love good service? Maybe you enjoy being served at your favorite restaurant or resort, but have you ever thought about why? The answer will compel you to serve others. In the Sermon on the Mount, Jesus described service that leads to surrender (Matthew 5:13–16). In essence, Jesus said that who we are to be determines what we are to do, which determines where we are to go. After completing the Beatitudes, which described satisfaction through surrender, like clay in the hands of the potter, Jesus grabbed two more invaluable substances to paint a picture of a disciple—salt and light.

Who is a disciple of Christ designed to be? A servant (Matthew 5:13–14).

Jesus said: "You are the salt of the earth. . . You are the light of the world. . ." (Matthew 5:13–14). His command is not to be salt or to be light. A disciple of Christ already is salt and light, or a servant. Salt and light illustrate the identity of a disciple. Because salt doesn't lose its flavor and light can't be hidden, Jesus's command is not to dilute the salt or hide the light. Only a pretender, a false disciple, would do so.

Salt was mined from the ground and renowned as a valuable commodity in ancient Palestine. Wars were fought over salt. In Old Testament times, salt was used to make covenants and served in the sacrificial system when confessing and repenting of sin and worshiping God. Disciples are servants of the New Covenant, those who confess and repent of their sin and worship God.

From cover to cover, the Scriptures describe light as a metaphor for spiritual life. Jesus described Himself as the light of the world, noting that when we surrender our hearts and lives to Him, we reflect that light (John 8:12). Salt and light are servants to the masses. Servant is the most frequently used title, printed on the business card of biblical characters. Abraham, Isaac, Jacob, Moses, Joshua, Job, and Mary were all referenced as servants. Even Jesus came as a servant (Mark 10:45). He said that anyone who wanted to lead must not lord it over others; rather, he must serve (Luke 22:25–27).

Today, remind yourself, "I am a servant of Christ." Notice how your perspective changes as you encounter others.

The Initiative and Influence of a Disciple

Matthew 5:15–16a

A s a disciple of Christ, what are you designed to do, and where are you designed to go?

Salt brings out flavor. Light illuminates. Servants serve (Matthew 5:15–16a). This is the initiative of a disciple. In Christ, our identity and our initiative are inseparable. God designed us to serve, or to do good works (Ephesians 2:10). These good works are deeds of love, meeting the needs of others. James said that those with authentic faith serve others with deeds of love, and there is no such thing as faith without deeds (James 2:14–17). Paul said that these deeds of love could not be hidden (1 Timothy 5:25). Jesus did not come to be served, but to serve and give His life for others (Mark 10:45).

Why should we serve? Surrender (Matthew 5:16b).

Jesus taught that when we serve, people would see our good deeds and praise our Father in heaven. Salt helps taste and causes thirst. Light helps others see. Service helps others surrender. This is the influence of a disciple. Service leads the lost to surrender (1 Peter 2:12). Service leads the found to surrender (Hebrews 10:24–25). God

designed us to use our gifts to serve others, faithfully administering His grace (1 Peter 4:10–11).

Today, don't look for opportunities to be served; rather, look for opportunities to serve. Be a need-finder. Define the lead (the person in need), the need (the time, talent, and treasure lacking in that person's life), and the deed (the act of service you will do). Look for opportunities to use your gifts in order to lead others to surrender to Christ. Surrender those opportunities and the outcomes to God.

Service leads to surrender because serving illuminates the heart of Christ and draws others to Him. That's why serving satisfies us more than being served (Acts 20:35). Christ in us can't be diluted or hidden when we have truly surrendered our lives to Him. Who we are to be in Christ determines what we are to do in Christ, which determines where we are to go in Christ.

Be Obedient

Matthew 5:17–20

DID your parents ever say, "Do as I say, not as I do"? Our parents knew what was right and yet realized that they would fall short. Aware that we would not only listen to their words, but also watch their behavior, they couched the inevitable disparity in word and deed with "Do as I say, not as I do." In Christ, we have a Lord and Savior who says, "Do as I say, and as I do." His teachings are perfectly aligned with His heart and life. Consequently, He calls the fully surrendered to be obedient from the inside out (Matthew 5:17–20).

Jesus fulfilled the Law and the Prophets (Matthew 5:17–18). Fulfill meant more than "complete." It meant "to clarify the intent of." Jesus fulfilled the Old Testament (the Law and the Prophets) including the three parts of its 613 laws: (1) the ceremonial law, (2) the civil law, and (3) the moral law.

Jesus fulfilled the ceremonial law, the sacrificial system the blood of animals could not satisfy (Hebrews 10:4). Jesus died once and for all for sin (Hebrew 10:10), and there is no longer any need for sacrifice (Hebrews 10:18).

Jesus fulfilled the civil law, also known as the judicial law (John 3:18; 16:11). The civil law brought order to the Israelites leaving Egypt.

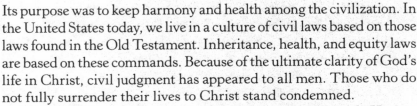

Its purpose was to keep harmony and health among the civilization. In the United States today, we live in a culture of civil laws based on those laws found in the Old Testament. Inheritance, health, and equity laws are based on these commands. Because of the ultimate clarity of God's life in Christ, civil judgment has appeared to all men. Those who do not fully surrender their lives to Christ stand condemned.

Jesus fulfilled the moral law (Hebrews 4:15). Though He was tempted in every way, He did not sin. He kept the Ten Commandments and loved the Father and His neighbors during His entire life on earth. Jesus did not abolish these laws. Jewish teachers said that one abolished the Law by disobeying it (Deuteronomy 27:26). Jesus did not disobey the Law.

Today, in light of Christ fulfilling the law, be obedient to His every prompting. Listen for His still small voice and continually act on His guidance. He will make you new again.

Freedom in Christ

John 19:30

SUPPOSE a man gave his wife a dozen roses for her birthday, but he answered her spoken gratitude by replying, "Oh, I was just doing it out of a sense of duty." How would that make her feel? Unfortunately, we often do the same with God.

The Law and the Prophets testified, or pointed, to Jesus (John 5:39; Luke 24:44). Before He went to the cross, Jesus said He had completed (fulfilled) His mission from the Father (John 17:4). On the cross, He proclaimed: "It is finished" (John 19:30). The Greek word for the phrase meant "paid in full," the same word that appeared at the top of a paid bill of sale 2,000 years ago. Jesus did what the Law was powerless to do—provide righteousness (Galatians 2:21). The purpose of the Law was to point us to Christ so that we might be justified—just as if we had never sinned—through faith in Him (Galatians 3:24; Luke 16:16). Faith in Christ make us no longer under the supervision of the Law (Galatians 3:25).

Now, we must obey Him from the heart to experience inside-out righteousness (Matthew 5:19–20). Obey means "to listen." Jesus said that anyone who would break the least of these commandments and teach others to do the same would be called the least in the kingdom of heaven, but whoever would practice and teach these commands would be called great in the kingdom of heaven. He went on to say that our righteousness must surpass that of the Pharisees and the teachers of

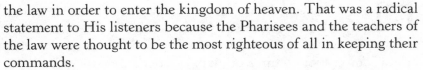

the law in order to enter the kingdom of heaven. That was a radical statement to His listeners because the Pharisees and the teachers of the law were thought to be the most righteous of all in keeping their commands.

Unfortunately, the Pharisees and the teachers of the law practiced outside-in righteousness (Matthew 23:25–28). They thought righteous acts performed mechanically on the outside where others could see justified them before God. This had never been the case. After sinning with Bathsheba, King David lamented God had never been satisfied with burnt offerings, but always attributed His righteousness to a contrite heart (Psalm 51:16–17). Paul taught that in Christ we are the righteousness of God (2 Corinthians 5:21), the living, breathing righteousness of God in the flesh, or actually in the Spirit.

Obedience from the heart occurs from the inside out because it comes from the Spirit of Christ in us (Romans 8:1–4). If we do not have the Spirit of Christ, then we do not belong to Christ (Romans 8:9). We obey and live only by faith—Christ in us (Galatians 2:20). Our ticket to enter the kingdom of heaven is righteousness that comes from another—Christ (Romans 3:21–22).

When tempted to disobey, listen to Christ in you and obey Him from your heart out of love. He fulfilled the law, and He will empower you to obey, experiencing His gracious inside-out righteousness.

Be Anger Free

Matthew 5:21–22

HAVE you ever been angry . . . today? Anger moves us to a physiological response. However, it is possible to be angry and not sin (Ephesians 4:26). Anger is a secondary emotion that follows a combination of three primary emotions: hurt, frustration, or fear. Usually, it works like this. Our emotions are stuck in past hurts; our wills reside in the present, frustrated from unmet expectations; and our minds are focused on the future, afraid of its potential outcomes. The result is a soul (emotions, will, and mind) that is out of alignment. We need Christ to align our angry souls.

In His first of six examples of inside-out righteousness, Jesus taught His disciples to be *free from anger* (Matthew 5:21–26). In each example, Jesus followed a three-fold pattern: (1) He addressed an Old Testament command saying, "You have heard that it was said;" (2) He alluded to the Pharisees' legalistic interpretation; and (3) He clarified the intent, or spirit, of the law, prefacing His fulfillment with, "But I tell you."

The Old Testament command was: "You have heard that it was said to the people long ago, 'You shall not murder'" (Matthew 5:21a). Jesus referred to the sixth of the Ten Commandments (Exodus 20:13). Having the choice of seven words for *murder*, Jesus selected one communicating premeditation and deliberateness, including suicide. The

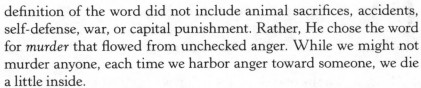

definition of the word did not include animal sacrifices, accidents, self-defense, war, or capital punishment. Rather, He chose the word for *murder* that flowed from unchecked anger. While we might not murder anyone, each time we harbor anger toward someone, we die a little inside.

The legalistic interpretation included: "Anyone who murders will be subject to judgment" (Matthew 5:21b). Jesus alluded to the legalistic interpretation by the Pharisees and the teachers of the law. Translated, "Murderers are to be judged." Once again, the Pharisees and teachers of the law taught outside-in righteousness, which taught that one was made right or wrong with God based on what he did on the outside. However, Jesus painted a different picture.

The Spirit of the Law was: "But I tell you that anyone who is angry with a brother or sister will be subject to judgment" (Matthew 5:22a). The spirit of the Law dealt with the heart because God designed us to live from the inside out. Jesus called His disciples, including us, to a heart condition that desires to be reconciled; not harboring anger toward anyone in our hearts. He taught that unchecked anger and its name-calling had consequences, including hell (Matthew 5:23).

Today, whether you sin against someone or they sin against you pursue the Holy Spirit and be anger free.

Be Quick to Reconcile

Matthew 5:23–26

DO you have any unreconciled interpersonal conflict? Jesus said that we should reconcile, or settle our accounts, quickly, whether we have sinned against someone or someone has sinned against us.

If we are in the middle of a worship service and realize we have sinned against someone, Jesus said to "Go and come." First *go* reconcile, and then *come* and worship (Matthew 5:23–24). If someone sins against us and is taking us to court, whether legal or social, we are to settle the matter quickly because it is likely the unreconciled conflict will only get worse (Matthew 5:25–26).

We are to reconcile and not harbor anger in our hearts because it reflects God's heart to do so. God told Moses that He was slow to anger (Exodus 34:6). Paul revealed Jesus was our peace (Ephesians 2:14), reconciling the world to God so we would reconcile with others in order that they would be reconciled with God (2 Corinthians 5:18–21).

Ask God to help you reconcile conflicts quickly, whether you have sinned against someone or someone has sinned against you. If you have offended someone, go and come. Go and ask the offended person

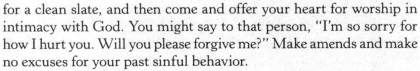

for a clean slate, and then come and offer your heart for worship in intimacy with God. You might say to that person, "I'm so sorry for how I hurt you. Will you please forgive me?" Make amends and make no excuses for your past sinful behavior.

If someone has sinned against you and is taking you to court, whether legal or social, settle the matter quickly so the unreconciled conflict does not get worse (Matthew 5:25–26). Beware of turning off your offender toward you and the heart of Christ by communicating a legalistic, "I forgive you for what you did to me." Rather, initiate reconciliation by asking for forgiveness for your contribution to the fractured relationship. You might ask, "May I seek your forgiveness for the things I've harbored against you because of this situation?" Remember when it comes to forgiveness, behavior often speaks louder than words. Today, be free from unchecked anger and reflect the peaceful heart of Christ in you. He will make you new again.

Be Adultery Free

Matthew 5:27–28

H OW many times have you committed adultery? Jesus said that it might be more than you think. With the invention of Internet pornography, adultery in our world might be at an all-time high. In His second of six examples of inside-out righteousness, Jesus taught his disciples to be *adultery free*.

The Old Testament command was: "You have heard that it was said, 'You shall not commit adultery'" (Matthew 5:27). Jesus referred to the seventh of the Ten Commandments (Exodus 20:14). The Old Testament's penalty for adultery (to alter, or to change, marriage vows) was death of both parties, including an adulterous fiancée (Deuteronomy 22:22–24). Adultery was not considered only a sin against others; it was viewed as a sin against the Creator. After his sin of adultery with Bathsheba, King David said that he had sinned against God (2 Samuel 12:13; Psalm 51:4).

The legalistic interpretation became: "Adultery is a bodily act of sexual intercourse." While this is not mentioned verbatim, it is alluded to by Jesus's context. Outside-in righteousness follows the letter of the law, but misses the spirit of the law. While in this mode,

we seek loopholes that allow us to "keep the letter of the law," while maintaining control of our own lives. "I never had sexual relations with that woman" has potentially become one man's legacy. He chose his words carefully in order to justify his following of the law's letter while falling short of its intent.

The Spirit of the Law revealed: "But I tell you that anyone who looks at a woman lustfully has already committed adultery with her in his heart" (Matthew 5:28). Sin, including adultery, begins when we desire it in our hearts (James 1:14). Jesus was not saying, "Now that you've thought about it, you might as well do it." Rather, He was calling His disciples to be faithful in heart—faithful to God and faithful to their spouses. Jesus said that faithfulness was one of the most important matters of the law (Matthew 23:23).

Today, think of one way you can faithfully pursue your spouse. Write a note, send a text, or make time to be together with no distractions. God can make your marriage new again.

Refocus And Run

Matthew 5:29–30

JESUS offered two tools for His disciples to be faithful in their marriages.

First, refocus your eyes. "If your right eye causes you to stumble, gouge it out and throw it away. It is better for you to lose one part of your body than for your whole body to be thrown into hell" (Matthew 5:29). Jesus referred to the right side of the body because it was considered the most dominant. He was not advocating self-mutilation. Instead, He used a hyperbole, deliberate exaggeration to make a point. In essence, Jesus said that immediate gratification leads to dissatisfaction and death. Sexual temptation enters through the eyes (John 2:15–17), and the eyes are never satisfied (Proverbs 27:20). The more that we see sexual temptation the more we desire it.

Two thousand years ago, the people of Corinth were surrounded with live sexual temptations, not with virtual ones we have available on the Internet today. The apostle Paul told the Corinthians to take every thought captive and make it obedient to Christ (2 Corinthians 10:5).

Second, run. "And if your right hand causes you to stumble, cut it off and throw it away. It is better for you to lose one part of your body than for your whole body to go into hell" (Matthew 5:30). Joseph ran from Potiphar's wife who pursued him to go to bed with her, noting

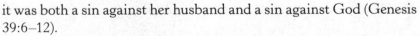

it was both a sin against her husband and a sin against God (Genesis 39:6–12).

Immediate gratification leads to dissatisfaction and death. Sexual temptation enters through our eyes, gets mulled over in our hearts, and is executed through our hands. However, God always provides a way out (1 Corinthians 10:13).

Paul called the Thessalonians to run from sexual immorality (1 Thessalonians 4:3). The Greek word for *sexual immorality* is the same root word for *pornography*. The comprehensive definition of this word includes any sexual gratification outside of marriage. God designed sex to take place between one man and one woman in the context of marital union. This is the only kind of sex that satisfies.

When you are tempted, refocus your eyes and your mind with God's Word and images of your spouse, if you are married, and then run. Surround yourself with photographs of your spouse and family. Men should include a picture of their wife as a little girl, so that they see her as her father saw her, vulnerable and in need of protection.

Fix your eyes on Christ, and always run to Him.

Be Divorce Free

Matthew 5:31–32

HAVE you or anyone in your immediate family been divorced? Divorce means "to go separate ways." A couple cannot divorce unless they have first been married. God designed marriage for the man to leave his family, cleave to his wife, and weave his life with hers (Genesis 2:24). Consequently, God hates divorce (Malachi 2:16). In spite of the Bible's clarity on the issue, the divorce rate is higher among the churched than the unchurched. In His third of six examples of inside-out righteousness, Jesus taught His disciples to be *divorce free*.

Jesus summarized the Old Testament command: "It has been said, 'Anyone who divorces his wife must give her a certificate of divorce'" (Matthew 5:31). Jesus referenced Moses' Law that said: "If a man marries a woman who becomes displeasing to him because he finds something indecent about her, and he writes her a certificate of divorce, gives it to her and sends her from his house" (Deuteronomy 24:1). How one defined "indecent" was the hinge point in the interpretation and application of this verse.

The legalistic interpretation had become: "A husband who gives his wife a certificate of divorce has no obligation to her." Two thousand years ago, two rabbinical schools differed in their interpretation of *indecent*. One held a conservative interpretation, the other one liberal. The conservative interpretation from the School of Shammai defined *indecent* as "adultery." The liberal interpretation from the School of Hillel defined *indecent* as anything displeasing, such as "spoiling a dish," adding an exception for divorce when "finding another fairer than she." Although that sounds flippant, it represents the climate of our culture today. Whether conservative or liberal, the legalistic interpretation of the law removes the man's obligation to his former wife when he issues her a certificate of divorce.

Outside-in righteousness says that what we do warrants a corresponding response from God. Get a legal divorce, and remove any obligation. That's religion, not relationship. It follows the letter of the law, but misses the spirit of the law. Jesus fulfilled the law by clarifying its intent.

Jesus revealed the Spirit of the Law: "But I tell you that anyone who divorces his wife, except for sexual immorality, makes her the victim of adultery, and anyone who marries a divorced woman commits adultery" (Matthew 5:32). The certificate of divorce allowed a woman to remarry, free from obligation to her divorcing husband, so she would not be considered an adulteress. The exception of adultery is not a one-time act to be used as a loophole to exit one's marriage. Rather, it is a continual, unrepentant act; one that is also superseded by forgiveness. Jesus said that Moses permitted divorce only because men's hearts were hard, noting that divorce was outside of God's original design (Matthew 19:8). In essence, Jesus said, "Be committed," which means, "to stay together."

Have you contemplated divorce? Is it time to get help to honor your marriage vows and stay committed to your spouse? Today, ask God to give you and your spouse the strength and endurance to be committed to each other.

God's Unfailing Love

Luke 22:42

INSIDE-OUT righteousness flows from the heart—a heart that is fully surrendered to Christ. This is how His righteousness is applied to us. Commitment is the spirit of the God's law because He is committed—He maintains His love (Exodus 34:7). He will never leave or forsake us (Hebrews 13:5). Christ is the ultimate picture of that commitment. On the way to the cross, He said to the Father, "Not my will, but yours" (Luke 22:42).

In a world where there is so much desire for change in relationships, we can take heart that Jesus is the same yesterday, today, and forever (Hebrews 13:8). We will remain committed to our spouses only through Christ in us. Our commitment to Him is reflected in our commitment to each other. After all, God is searching throughout the earth to strengthen those whose hearts are fully committed to Him (2 Chronicles 16:9).

If you have been divorced, you have not committed the unforgivable sin. In Christ, God will forgive you and restore you. If you are considering leaving your spouse for another person, then turn back to keep your commitment made before God. Most churches will not marry a couple where one party has left his spouse for the other because Jesus was so clear on this issue (Matthew 19:3–12). That relationship is rooted in sin and dishonors God. If you are considering marriage, realize you are about to make a covenant—not merely an agreement—with three parties: you, your fiancé, and Christ.

Today, pray in recognition of your own vulnerability, "God, my commitment is only as strong as your Spirit's commitment in me. I surrender to Your will for my marriage."

Be Falsehood Free

Matthew 5:33–37

HAVE you ever broken your word? You said one thing and did another. Your walk didn't match your talk. In His fourth of six examples of inside-out righteousness, Jesus taught His disciples to be *falsehood free*. He said that a disciple's walk should match their talk.

Jesus shared the Old Testament command: "Again, you have heard that it was said to the people long ago, 'Do not break your oath'" (Matthew 5:33a). The Old Testament repeated the command that an oath made to God must not be broken. A man was bound to keep his word, doing everything he said he would do (Leviticus 19:12; Numbers 30:2; Deuteronomy 23:21). His walk was to match his talk. The ninth of the Ten Commandments simply said that one should not lie (Exodus 20:16).

The legalistic interpretation was: "But fulfil to the Lord the vows you have made" (Matthew 5:33b). Following the letter of the law at the expense of the spirit of the law said, "Keep only your oaths sworn to the Lord." Two thousand years ago, Rabbis taught swearing by things other than God made oaths not binding; thus, providing a loophole to break an oath. People swore by heaven, earth, Jerusalem, and their heads, or lives, so that they could later have a loophole to lie. We do the same today. When our word is doubted, we say, "Swear to God." Sometimes we offer a lesser oath, "Swear on the Bible" or "Swear on a stack of Bibles." While the whole time, we have our fingers crossed.

Jesus reiterated the Spirit of the Law: "But I tell you, do not swear an oath at all . . . All you need to say is simply 'Yes' or 'No'" (Matthew 5:34a, 37a). The spirit of the law is that we would be honest and truthful. Jesus said that experiencing the truth sets us free (John 8:32). Similarly, a businessman said, "When I tell the truth, I don't have to remember what I said." When we have hearts that are truthful, our walk matches our talk. We don't need oaths because our word is our bond.

Inside-out righteousness desires the heart of God. God is truthful (John 3:33; Psalm 31:5). Christ is truth (John 14:6). He referred to the Holy Spirit as the Spirit of truth (John 14:17). It's Christ's Spirit of truth dwelling in us that allows us to discern truth from falsehood (1 John 4:6).

Today, avoid saying, "Swear on the Bible" or "Swear to God." Rather, let your "Yes" be "Yes" and your "No" be "No." This doesn't mean you should be stubborn or immovable. It means that your word is your bond. Your walk matches your talk. Be falsehood free by being truthful, and you won't have to remember what you said. Fully surrender to the Spirit of Christ in you. Only His righteousness is acceptable to God.

Be Retaliation Free

Matthew 5:38–42

HAVE you been harmed by another person? Has someone insulted you, taken something from you, or abused your time? In our humanness, our first inclination is to retaliate by harming the offender in the same way they harmed us. Retaliation means "to repay"—evil for evil. Jesus offered a different way. In His fifth of six examples of inside-out righteousness, Jesus taught His disciples to be *retaliation free*.

Jesus shared the Old Testament command: "You have heard that it was said, 'Eye for eye, and tooth for tooth'" (Matthew 5:38). Old Testament civil laws allowed for equity in judicial matters. If someone took a resource from you, you were to be repaid one-for-one (Exodus 21:24; Leviticus 24:20; Deuteronomy 19:21).

The legalistic interpretation was: "Repay those who harm you." The legalistic interpretation of the law followed the letter of the law and missed the spirit of the law. It said that one should retaliate when harmed. The motto was "When a resource is taken from you, take the same back—one-for-one." We see it today among our children. When bumped on the playground, a child bumps back. We see it in the marketplace. When taken advantage of, a businessman retaliates. We see it in sports. When fouled, an athlete fouls back. We see it in marriages and divorces. When harmed by a spouse, the other harms in return—one-for-one. While retaliation might feel good at the moment, it enslaves us.

Jesus offered the Spirit of the Law: "But I tell you, do not resist an evil person . . . Give to the one who asks you, and do not turn away from the one who wants to borrow from you" (Matthew 5:39a, 42). The word *resist* meant "to take strong opposition against," or "to retaliate." Jesus fulfilled the law by clarifying its intent. The spirit of the law is that we should give generously, or *be gracious* in our hearts. Being gracious does not mean relinquishing one's rights, nor does it prohibit conflict resolution, but it is not repaying evil with evil (Romans 12:17).

Today, focus on being gracious. When harmed by another person, extend the amazing grace God has lavished on you. Only He can make you new again.

Generosity

Matthew 5:39–41

BEING gracious means we are generous with our resources: our *talent*, *treasure*, and *time*.

Generous with our Talent

Jesus taught: "If anyone slaps you on the right cheek, turn to them the other cheek also" (Matthew 5:39). Being struck on the right cheek implied someone slapped you with the back of his right hand. That was a cultural expression for an insult. We use the same imagery today when we say, "That was a backhanded comment." By teaching His disciples to turn the other cheek, Jesus had reiterated an Old Testament principle, "Overlook an insult" (Proverbs 12:16). An insult is designed to attack our *talent*—that unique value of life that God has placed in each one of us. When we ignore the insult, we defuse it by eliminating the insulter's desired reaction. If we retaliate, we play right into their hands.

Generous with our Treasure

Jesus continued: "And if anyone wants to sue you and take your shirt, let them have your coat as well" (Matthew 5:40). Two thousand years ago, a person's interior and exterior clothing was often his only *treasure*, and laws protected him from being wronged or cheated out of it. At the same time, the courts were littered with lawsuits arising from disputes. Rather than sue each other in retaliation, Jesus said that we should be gracious, or generous, with our treasures. Paul

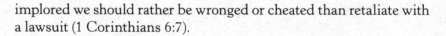

implored we should rather be wronged or cheated than retaliate with a lawsuit (1 Corinthians 6:7).

Generous with our Time

Jesus commanded: "If anyone forces you to go one mile, go with them two miles" (Matthew 5:41). A Roman centurion often interrupted any person at any time for official business. A Persian royal post officer could do the same. The law required the person to carry government goods one mile at their request. Jesus said that when interrupted, one should not retaliate, but go another mile. In essence, He said that we should be generous with our *time*.

Today, be generous with your resources; when harmed, don't retaliate. Be generous with your talent: when insulted, ignore it. Be generous with your treasure: when threatened, wronged, or cheated, don't retaliate with litigation. Be generous with your time: when interrupted, serve beyond the request. In doing so, it won't merely be you; rather, it will be Christ in you.

God Is Gracious

2 Corinthians 8:9

INSIDE-OUT righteousness desires a heart like God's. Our Creator is gracious (Exodus 34:6). He is generous with His resources (Matthew 20:15). Jesus Christ walked this earth and was gracious. When evil people hurled insults at Him, he did not retaliate. Instead, He entrusted himself, or literally handed himself over, to the gracious Father, who judges justly (1 Peter 2:23). Jesus modeled generosity with His resources: "For you know the grace of our Lord Jesus Christ, that though he was rich, yet for your sake he became poor, so that you through his poverty might become rich" (2 Corinthians 8:9).

When we are gracious, we recognize our talent, treasure, and time come from God (Psalm 145:9). His greatest resource is Christ in us, who frees us from the enslavement to retaliation and the weariness of outside-in righteousness. In any situation, He empowers us to hand ourselves over to our gracious God.

Pray, "Thank You, God for Your gracious gift of life You have given me. Thank You for Your amazing gift of Christ who paid a debt He did not owe because I owed a debt I could not pay. Please give me a heart overflowing with grace, Your undeserved love, Your unmerited favor, that I will share with everyone I encounter today."

Be Hate Free

Matthew 5:43–44

D O you hate someone? Is there a person or people group you simply don't love? It might be someone with a different sexual orientation or religion, someone who is addicted, unsaved, rude, late, or disorganized. It could be someone who is introverted or extroverted, rich or poor, conservative or liberal, irreligious or religious, attractive or unattractive. Most likely, it is someone who has wronged you. In our humanness, we make lists. One of them is a list of those we love (those who love us) and a list of those we hate (our enemies). We want to treat others as they treat us.

Jesus offered a different way. In His final illustration of six examples of inside-out righteousness, Jesus taught His disciples to be hate free.

Jesus began with the Old Testament command: "You have heard that it was said, 'Love your neighbor'" (Matthew 5:43a). The command came from the Old Testament Law (Leviticus 19:18). Israelites who were moving from slavery to freedom were commanded by God to not withhold their love from one another, even from someone who wronged them.

The legalistic interpretation was: "Hate your enemy" (Matthew 5:43b). Two thousand years later, the Pharisees and the teachers of the law added a loophole to love. In essence, they said, "Treat others as they

treat you." This axiom followed the letter of the law, but it missed the spirit of the law. It was outside-in righteousness.

We do the same today. If someone mistreats us, we withhold love. If our business competitor criticizes our company to a potential client, we withhold love toward that competitor. If our spouse is rude, we withhold love until he or she repents. If someone disagrees with us, we withhold love. If someone cuts us off on the highway, we withhold love. If someone gossips about us, we withhold love. If a church differs on disputable matters, we withhold love. The problem is that withholding love is hate.

Jesus delivered the Spirit of the Law: "But I tell you, love your enemies and pray for those who persecute you" (Matthew 5:44). The spirit of the law was to love everyone without parameters. God's design was that hate would never flow from one's heart (Leviticus 19:17). Paul said that love fulfills the law (Romans 13:8–10; Galatians 5:13–14).

Ask God to help you love everyone you lock eyes with today, even those who are difficult.

Love and Pray

Matthew 5:44–48

DO you struggle to forgive someone who has wronged you? Jesus offered two ways for His disciples to model the heart of God during interpersonal conflict: love our enemies and pray for those who persecute us (Matthew 5:44).

Jesus fulfilled the law by giving us the ultimate picture of God's heart. He loved His enemies, and He prayed for those who persecuted Him (Luke 23:24). Jesus revealed that these practices flowed from a heart like God's, one that is perfect, meaning complete, or whole (Matthew 5:45, 48). God withholds His love from no one (Psalm 145:9) because God is love (1 John 4:8). Christ is the perfect picture of God's boundless love (Ephesians 3:18; John 1:14).

In Luke's parallel passage to Matthew 5:48, he quoted Jesus as saying: "Be merciful, just as your Father is merciful" (Luke 6:36). Mercy doesn't treat others as they deserve; instead, mercy loves its enemies and prays for its persecutors. The pagan culture in Jesus's day was not merciful (Matthew 5:46–47). Two millennia later, things haven't really changed.

Inside-out righteousness desires a merciful heart like God's. Today, be complete in your love. First, love your neighbor and your enemies. When someone wrongs you, sacrificially serve their needs. Second, pray for those who persecute you. When someone mistreats you, pray for them to be blessed in the same way you want to be blessed by God. It won't be you doing so; rather it will be Christ in you. He will make you new again.

Do Give

Matthew 6:1–2

WHEN we give, we often want to let others see our acts of righteousness in order to be rewarded for our efforts. Our names are placed on buildings, printed in church bulletins, and presented in prominent periodicals. Two thousand years ago, people experienced the same temptation. Jesus offered a different way by exposing the motives of the heart.

In His Sermon on the Mount, Jesus described the be-do-go of full surrender. In essence, He said, "Who you are to be determines what you do, which determines where you go." In Matthew, Chapter 6, Jesus moved from who we are to be to what we are to do. He began with three acts of piety in Judaism: giving to the needy, praying, and fasting. In each, Jesus cut to the heart of the matter, exposing why we do what we do. We either have a selfish motive or a selfless one. With each good deed, He described what not to do, then what to do. Jesus said, "Do give."

Jesus taught: Do not give with the motive to be recognized and honored (Matthew 6:1–2). Acts of righteousness by definition are done as a result of intimacy with the Father and flow from a heart surrendered to Christ (Matthew 5). Doing acts of righteousness to be seen by others is done with an unrighteous motive and not rewarded by God (Matthew 6:1). Jesus preached: "So when you give to the needy, do not announce it with trumpets, as the hypocrites do in the synagogues and on the streets, to be honored by others. Truly I tell you, they have received their reward in full" (Matthew 6:2).

Trumpets were the shape of the giving boxes in the synagogues. The crowd surrounding the giving boxes would know who gave large

sums by the sound of the coins hitting the box. Large coinage made a loud noise when dropped in the boxes. Little coinage made little noise. Motives were often no different inside the synagogues than they were on the streets. Outside Judaism, on the Roman roads, Greeks gave in order to be recognized as significant among their peers.

Check your heart. Are you giving anything in order to be recognized? If so, ask God to remove the motive and give you a pure heart to graciously share with others in need.

Give in Secret and Experience Intimacy With God

Matthew 6:2–4

HISTORIANS believe Jesus might have worked as a stone carpenter on the theatre in Sepphoris, known as the ornament of all Galilee. Consequently, He knew about acting. This was evidenced in His teaching: "So when you give to the needy, do not announce it with trumpets, as the hypocrites do in the synagogues and on the streets, to be honored by others. Truly I tell you, they have received their reward in full" (Matthew 6:2).

Hypocrites were actors. They wore masks on stage, pretending to be one way on the outside, though they were another on the inside. Jesus said that if being seen (on the outside) was a person's motive (inside), then the attention they had received was God's reward in full (a reference to payment in ancient business receipts). There would be no reward of an intimate relationship with God because of selfish motives.

Are you giving to get? Ask the Holy Spirit to identify any area in your life where you are giving to someone in need with the selfish motive to get something in return. It might be time, talent, or treasure you are investing in someone or something in order to receive honor and recognition from your church, friends, relatives, or organization.

Give in secret. Jesus said: "But when you give to the needy, do not let your left hand know what your right hand is doing, so that your giving may be in secret. Then your Father, who sees what is done in secret, will reward you" (Matthew 6:3–4).

Not letting the left hand know what the right hand is doing was hyperbole for giving in secret. Synagogues actually maintained secret giving places for anonymous giving and receiving. Believers were often described as members of Christ's body. The left hand not knowing the right hand's giving activity meant one believer wasn't announcing his gift to another. This does not mean we cannot receive public recognition for our giving. Rather, it means we should not seek selfish recognition and honor or desire attention for our giving. However, when our giving motive is unselfish, our reward is intimacy with God.

Today, give something in secret out of intimacy with your heavenly Father. Don't be motivated to give anything to anyone out of recognition or honor. Rather, give from your gratitude to the One who gave you life. Your reward will be intimacy with Him.

Do Pray

Matthew 6:5–6

WHEN you pray, do you petition God solely for your personal comfort and abundance? Do you ever pray in a public restaurant, hoping people seated nearby you will see you? Do your nighttime prayers sound like broken records saying the same selfish things in the same selfish ways for the same selfish reasons? What would happen if you prayed for what God prayed?

Prayer is being online with God when our hearts are connected with His. In this connection, we upload our requests, and He downloads His presence, shaping our hearts and transforming our desires to be like His (Psalm 37:4). Consequently, God's design is that we would be online with Him 24/7 where we can experience His links with others. Too often, we work offline from God, limiting our encounters with Him to a church building with a particular group of people functioning in a certain style for one hour on one given day of the week.

Jesus taught: Do not pray with the motive to be recognized and honored. "And when you pray, do not be like the hypocrites, for they love to pray standing in the synagogues and on the street corners to be seen by others" (Matthew 6:5). Hypocrites were actors who would not receive the reward of an intimate relationship with God because of their selfish motives.

Jesus continued: Do pray in secret. "But when you pray, go into your room, close the door and pray to your Father, who is unseen. Then your Father, who sees what is done in secret, will reward you" (Matthew 6:6). Jewish homes had only one room with a door—a storage chamber. Jesus used this imagery to describe a secret place where no one but the heavenly Father would see. This does not mean that we cannot pray publicly. Rather, it means that we should not seek selfish recognition and honor when we pray. When our prayer motive is unselfish, our reward is intimacy with God.

Are there any areas in your life where you love to be recognized or honored when you pray? Ask the Holy Spirit to take an inventory of your heart and surrender any impure motives to Him.

No Babbling

Matthew 6:7–8

WHEN you pray, are you seeking a one-for-one benefit from God for your good deeds? Do you frequently offer the same prayer without heartfelt authenticity or thanksgiving?

Jesus cautioned against babbling like pagans who, when they prayed, reminded their deity about their good deeds in order to receive a return favor: "And when you pray, do not keep on babbling like pagans, for they think they will be heard because of their many words" (Matthew 6:7). Sometimes, we do the same with God, reminding Him of all the righteous acts we accomplished in order to receive a one-for-one benefit. Greeks used many names for their deity in order to gain its attention. Oftentimes, we pray publicly using many names for God in order to be seen and heard by others.

Two thousand years ago, rabbis debated the use of fixed prayers, a pattern used by many of us today. They determined these were acceptable only if offered genuinely. Thankfully, Jesus taught us how to pray to the One who knows what we need before we ask Him (Matthew 6:8).

Offer your heart to God. Ask Him for His desires to become evident in your prayers.

Be a Person Who PRAYS

Matthew 6:9–15

JESUS taught each of us how to be a person who PRAYS (Matthew 6:9–15). Prayer is being online with God when our hearts are connected with His. In this connection, we upload our requests, and He downloads His presence, shaping our hearts and transforming our desires to be like His (Psalm 37:4). Consequently, God's design is that we would be online with Him 24/7 where we can experience His links with others. Jesus said: "This, then, is how you should pray" (Matthew 6:9).

Praise. "Our Father in heaven, hallowed be your name" (Matthew 6:9). *Heaven* had three meanings: (1) Where we go when we die, (2) the stars in the sky, and (3) the air in and around us. When we praise our heavenly Father for who He is (holy) and for being as close as the air that is in and around us, He downloads His Person and power that we can share with others.

Renew. "Your kingdom come, your will be done, on earth as it is in heaven" (Matthew 6:10). It was understood that after God's kingdom came, His will would be done on earth as in heaven. Jesus ushered in God's kingdom. As a result, this part of Jesus's prayer calls for a renewing of our minds in order to experience God's kingdom and will in our lives. Paul taught: "Therefore, I urge you, brothers and sisters, in view of God's mercy, to offer your bodies as a living sacrifice, holy and pleasing to God—this is your true and proper worship. Do not conform to the pattern of this world, but be transformed by the renewing of your mind. Then you will be able to test and approve what God's will is—his good, pleasing and perfect will" (Romans 12:1–2). This is a 180-degree turn from our world's standards. Jesus prayed for His Father's will (Matthew 26:39). When we renew our minds to

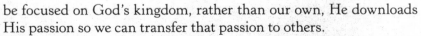

be focused on God's kingdom, rather than our own, He downloads His passion so we can transfer that passion to others.

Ask. "Give us today our daily bread" (Matthew 6:11). This referenced God's provision of manna in the desert for the Israelites. It is an illustration of total dependence on God for our needs to advance His kingdom. When we ask God to meet our needs to advance His kingdom, He downloads His provision that we can share with others.

Yield. "And forgive us our debts, as we also have forgiven our debtors" (Matthew 6:12). C.S. Lewis said that *as* was the most sobering two-letter word in all Scripture because the prayer is for God to forgive us in the same exact manner in which we have forgiven others. For some of us, this is a scary prayer. We have to yield all unsettled accounts to God, radically issuing to others the forgiveness we have received from Him. If we don't, then we really haven't received God's forgiveness (Matthew 6:14–15). When we yield all unsettled relational accounts to God, He downloads His peace that we can experience with others.

Surrender to be Spirit-led. "And lead us not into temptation, but deliver us from the evil one" (Matthew 6:13). The Aramaic sentence structure might indicate, "Let us not sin when tempted," rather than, "Let us not be tempted." This is supported by the fact Scripture tells us that God does not tempt anyone (James 1:13). When we surrender our hearts to be Spirit-led, God downloads His protection to guide us with others.

Thirty-Day Experiment

Romans 12:1–2

COMMIT to a thirty-day experiment, and be a person who unselfishly PRAYS in secret. Go into your own room, get on your knees, if you are physically able, and (1) *praise* your heavenly Father for who He is, (2) *renew* your mind to seek His will for your life, (3) *ask* for His provision of your needs to advance His kingdom, (4) *yield* all unsettled relational accounts to Him, and (5) *surrender* your heart to be Spirit-led. In this pattern, pray specifically for someone who is either skeptical of or seeking God to surrender his or her heart to Him. The kingdom of God will break through your life in a way that only God's intimacy can do. That intimacy will attract others to Christ in you.

Praise God the most where people expect it the least. Praise Him 24/7, including in your work, play, home, and church. Identify any setting where you believe that you are limiting your praise of God. Commit to lifting up God in that setting with your heart, desires, and life so that you worship Him 24/7. When you pray, praise your heavenly Father for Who He is (holy) and for being as close as the air in and around you. God will download His Person and power into your life, empowering you to link the same with others.

Renew your mind 24/7 to refocus your efforts toward the advancement of God's kingdom rather than your own. Memorize

Romans 12:1–2. Recite it to God, praying to Him as you seek the renewal of your mind. God will download His passion, namely His will for your life, and you will link that passion to others.

Ask God 24/7 to supply your needs to advance His kingdom through you and into others. When you pray, ask His Spirit to help you identify and provide any missing resources for you to communicate Christ to those in your life. God will download His provision and equip you to link His provision with others.

Yield all unsettled accounts to Him. Experience the download of God's peace in reconciled relationships.

Surrender your heart to be Spirit-led 24/7. When you are tempted, surrender to the Holy Spirit the bait and your desires that are luring you. When you wake up every morning, pray to God, surrendering your heart to be Spirit-led. God will download His protection and guide you to link His protection with others.

Christ has paid the cost for each of us to become a person who PRAYS, offering us His Spirit who empowers us to be online with God 24/7 (1 Corinthians 6:19–20).

Do Fast

Matthew 6:16–18

DURING trials or times of weighty decisions, do you leverage fasting as a magic wand with God as your object? Do you fast with the motive that others will see your plight and comfort you? Fasting literally means, "to abstain from food or drink;" however, in the Bible it is accompanied with a humble heart toward God (Psalm 35:13). Fasting is an avenue of surrender to God's will for our lives.

Fasting appears in three forms throughout Scripture. First is a *normal* fast (avoiding food). Jesus fasted from food for forty days preparing for His temptation and the inauguration of His preaching (Matthew 4:1–2; Luke 4:1–2). Second is a *partial* fast (avoiding a particular substance or act). Daniel ate no meat, drank no wine, and applied no lotion to his body for three weeks of mourning (Daniel 10:3). Third is an *absolute* fast (avoiding food and water). Esther fasted from food and water for three days during a period of national crisis (Esther 4:16); Paul fasted from food and water for three days after his conversion (Acts 9:9). Jesus taught, "Do fast" (Matthew 6:16–18).

First, do not fast with the motive to be recognized and honored: "When you fast, do not look somber as the hypocrites do, for they disfigure their faces to show others they are fasting. Truly I tell you, they have received their reward in full" (Matthew 6:16). The law had provided for fasting once a year on the Day of Atonement (Leviticus 16:29–34; 23:26–32). The key phrase was "humble your souls" (NASB). By Jesus's time, the pious Pharisees were fasting twice a week (Mondays and Thursdays) because Moses was said to have gone up on Sinai on those days (Luke 18:12). The Pharisees wanted everyone to know they were fasting, so they did not wash or trim their hair, and sometimes they placed ashes on their heads. Abstaining from pleasures such as anointing their heads with oil to prevent dry skin was common, but they still made fasting obvious to the people they encountered. Others pretended to fast by disfiguring their outward appearances. In either case, they had a selfish motive, and there would be no reward of an intimate relationship with God because of their selfish motive.

Second, do fast in secret: "But when you fast, put oil on your head and wash your face, so that it will not be obvious to others that you are fasting, but only to your Father, who is unseen; and your Father, who sees what is done in secret, will reward you" (Matthew 6:17–18). Both anointing one's head and washing one's face, two common acts of daily life in Palestine, were forbidden by the Pharisees during fasting. Jesus did not say that no one can know we are fasting. Rather, He said that fasting should not be done with a selfish motive to be recognized and honored by others. Fasting should be done with a selfless motive to surrender our wills to God. When our fasting motive is unselfish, our reward is intimacy with our heavenly Father, the greatest reward of all.

During your next trial or decision, humbly fast in secret as a support to prayer in an attempt to discover God's will for your life. Ask the Holy Spirit to examine your heart for any selfish motive in using fasting as a tool to manipulate God or others around you. Surrender any impure desires to Him. Fasting has always been about intimacy with God (Isaiah 58:3–12). Jesus taught that when we fast, we are to do so in secret as a support to prayer, surrendering our wills to our heavenly Father.

Do Discover True Satisfaction

Matthew 6:19–33

WOULD a little extra money satisfy any of your desires? Do you want to decrease your liabilities? Perhaps you desire to reduce your mortgage, pay off your car, or eliminate credit card debt. Do you want to increase your assets? Maybe you would like to buy a new car, a new boat, a new house, a new set of golf clubs, a new technological device, or a new piece of jewelry. Money in and of itself is not evil. Owning stuff is not from the devil. The problem occurs when the stuff owns us. Ironically, it isn't money that we desire, rather it is something deeper.

God created us with at least four primary desires. The first desire is *significance*, which came from being created in God's image (Genesis 1:27). The second desire is *contentment* from being blessed by God to be fruitful, multiply, and subdue (bring contentment to) the earth (Genesis 1:28). The third desire is *control* from being empowered by God to rule over the earth (Genesis 1:28). The fourth desire is *security* from being given every seed-bearing plant and fruit-bearing tree (Genesis 1:29–30). These desires flow vertically from the heart of God into each one of our hearts and then horizontally in our relationships with others (Genesis 2:18).

The first sin was pride, man desiring satisfaction of these desires apart from God (Genesis 3:5–6), who had created Adam and Eve with humble hearts. The object of their desires was their Creator who satisfied them. Pride made man the object of his own desires. Now each of us is born with and chooses a proud heart (Genesis 8:21). We trust in our giftedness rather than His godliness.

Money is pride's measurement of our giftedness (time, talent, and treasure). Wisdom is humility's measurement of our godliness (Christ in us). Christ is the image of God (Hebrews 1:3). He is humble in heart (Matthew 11:29), and He is the wisdom of God (1 Corinthians 1:24). Humility is the beginning of His wisdom in our lives (Proverbs 11:2).

Jesus warned his disciples about attempting to satisfy their desires with money, offering wisdom as the alternative. Read Matthew 6:19–33. Ask God to reveal your pursuit to satisfy any desire apart from Him.

Do Discover Significance

Matthew 6:19–21

H AVE you sought significance from money or anything it supposedly promises? This was the first of four desires addressed by Jesus in His Sermon on the Mount.

Pride seeks significance from money. Jesus taught: "Do not store up for yourselves treasures on earth" (Matthew 6:19a). Why do we store up treasures on earth? We do so in order to find significance, which is expressed meaning, purpose, importance, or value. Significance can be encapsulated in attention, acceptance, affection, and approval. Notice the first four letters of significance comprise the word "sign," which says, "Look at me." People might say, "Look at him. He is successful." Others says, "Look at her. She's got it all." We often say to ourselves, "Storing up this stuff really satisfies. I feel significant."

The result is insignificance. "Where moths and vermin destroy, and where thieves break in and steal" (Matthew 6:19b). In the end, the stuff is just that, stuff. The more we pursue it as the satisfaction of our desires, the more we thirst for more. The result is a never-ending cycle of dissatisfaction.

Humility stores up relationships. Jesus continued: "But store up for yourselves treasures in heaven, where moths and vermin do not destroy, and where thieves do not break in and steal" (Matthew 6:20). Relationships are the only treasure that we can store up in heaven because they are eternal. These relationships flow vertically in communion with God and horizontally in community with others.

Our treasures reveal the object of our desires. Jesus elaborated: "For where your treasure is, there your heart will be also" (Matthew

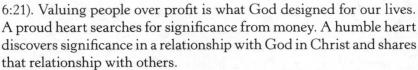

6:21). Valuing people over profit is what God designed for our lives. A proud heart searches for significance from money. A humble heart discovers significance in a relationship with God in Christ and shares that relationship with others.

The result is the love of God in Christ (John 3:16; 1:14). Christ is the love of God, a love so undeserved, a favor so unmerited, it's called grace. Paul wrote: "For you know the grace of our Lord Jesus Christ, that though he was rich, yet for your sake he became poor, so that you through his poverty might become rich" (2 Corinthians 8:9). God humbled Himself in Jesus Christ offering us the satisfaction of our desires when we humble our hearts to Christ. Only He truly satisfies our desires. This frees us to bring His satisfying Spirit to our relationships with a love that sacrificially serves others.

Discover the satisfaction of your desire for significance in the love of Christ and carry that love to others. Initiate conversations with your customers and prospects. Get to know them, asking questions and listening, rather than attempting to sell them a product or service. Do it just for the sake of relationship—storing up treasures in heaven rather than for storing up treasures on earth. With your spouse and family, connect relationally, serving them rather than expecting them to serve you. You will be satisfied. You will be significant. You will be loved. When we humbly center our lives in Christ, we discover His love is greater than our desire for significance.

Do Discover Contentment

Matthew 6:22–23

WHAT makes you content? A walk on the beach? A full bank account? A completed task? We all seek contentment: being in a state or a situation where we are not wanting anything more or anything different. It literally means "held together." The desire for contentment came from being blessed by God to be fruitful, multiply, and subdue (bring contentment) to the earth (Genesis 1:28). This desire flows vertically from the heart of God into each one of our hearts and horizontally in our relationships with others (Genesis 2:18).

Contentment is the second of four desires addressed by Jesus in the Sermon on the Mount. He warned disciples not to seek contentment from money (Matthew 6:22–23). Rather, Jesus taught wisdom for contentment.

Pride seeks contentment from money. "But if your eyes are unhealthy, your whole body will be full of darkness" (Matthew 6:23a). Two thousand years ago, a "bad eye" was a greedy one. It desired something more or something different than the time, talent, and treasure given by God. Paul equated greed with idolatry (Colossians 3:5) because the eyes of the heart are focused on something other than God for contentment.

Today, we often want something more or something different, and we believe money will deliver it. With more money, we can acquire a different car, a different spouse, a different house, a different job, or even a different church.

The result is discontentment. "If then the light within you is darkness, how great is that darkness!" (Matthew 6:23b). Darkness is discontentment. Solomon reflected: "Whoever loves money never has

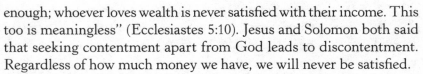

enough; whoever loves wealth is never satisfied with their income. This too is meaningless" (Ecclesiastes 5:10). Jesus and Solomon both said that seeking contentment apart from God leads to discontentment. Regardless of how much money we have, we will never be satisfied.

Humility seeks generosity. "The eye is the lamp of the body. If your eyes are healthy, your whole body will be full of light" (Matthew 6:22). The eye being the lamp of the body references the light that illuminated the heart. The eye allowed its focal point into the body. Two thousand years ago, a good eye meant a generous, content, loyal, and focused eye.

Today, we use the term *good eye* when a batter lets a bad pitch go by. The batter is content enough to let the foolish opportunity pass. When we are content, we don't need something more or something different. We are wise enough to allow life's bad pitches to go by and become generous with our time, talent, and treasure. Rather than focus on our giftedness, we focus on godliness.

The result is the peace of God in Christ. Light is a metaphor in Scripture used for the spiritual vitality of life. Christ is that light (John 8:12). A body full of light is a body full of peace, and Christ is that peace of God who holds us together (Ephesians 2:14). He brings that divine peace into our lives in communion with Him so that we will share it in community with others (John 14:27; 16:33). Christ is our blessing of peace.

Contentment in the Giver, Not the Gifts

1 Timothy 6:6–10; Philippians 4:6–7, 12–13

H OW have you sought contentment apart from God? What shape or size represents the focal point of the eyes of your heart? What has been the result? In our pride, we seek contentment apart from Him, and the result is discontentment.

Warning against the pursuit of money for contentment, Paul taught: "But godliness with contentment is great gain. For we brought nothing into the world, and we can take nothing out of it. But if we have food and clothing, we will be content with that. Those who want to get rich fall into temptation and a trap and into many foolish and harmful desires that plunge people into ruin and destruction. For the love of money is a root of all kinds of evil. Some people, eager for money, have wandered from the faith and pierced themselves with many griefs" (1 Timothy 6:6–10). Have you been pierced with many griefs of discontentment from trusting in your giftedness for the satisfaction of your desires?

In his letter to the church at Philippi, Paul penned that the peace that passes all understanding comes from a content (thankful) heart

surrendered to Christ in prayer (Philippians 4:6–7). He went on to say that the secret of contentment was that he could do all things through Christ who gave him strength (Philippians 4:12–13). He discovered contentment in the Giver, not the gifts.

Be generous with your time, talent, and treasure. Be content enough in Christ to give to someone in need. Spend extra time with your spouse or children, allowing them to set the agenda. Invest your talent into a coworker. Give some of your treasure to a neighbor in need. Be content in the peace of God in Christ, the focal point of the eyes of your heart.

When life is centered in Christ, we discover His peace is greater than our desire for contentment.

Do Discover Control

Matthew 6:24

DO you desire money for the control that it brings? Control literally means "to roll against." It is the extension of our will over another person or object. We attempt to control others, our own lives, or even God. The desire for control came from man being empowered by God to rule over the earth, and to use that control to humbly serve Him (Genesis 1:28).

In the Sermon on the Mount, Jesus warned His disciples about attempting to satisfy their desires with money. He offered wisdom as an alternative. The third desire He addressed was control (Matthew 6:24).

Pride seeks control by serving money. "No one can serve two masters" (Matthew 6:24a). Jesus knew our desire for control would be abused in a dualistic lifestyle where we would attempt to selfishly control others in an attempt to control our own lives. Bob Dylan said, "Everybody's going to serve somebody."

The result is a life that is out of control. "Either you will hate the one and love the other, or you will be devoted to the one and despise the other" (Matthew 6:24b). Serving two masters is serving one. It is an attempt to serve our selfish desires (Romans 8:5–8). At some point the two interests collide, leaving us with a choice of which master to serve. The question is, "Who or what has ultimate control of our lives, God or money?" What controls us affects how we try to control others.

Humility seeks to serve God. "You cannot serve both God and money" (Matthew 6:24c). We flesh this out by humbly serving others rather than controlling them. In doing so, our unselfish desires are satisfied as well as the desires of God and the person served (Philippians 2:3–5).

The result is the power of God in Christ (1 Corinthians 1:24; 2 Corinthians 12:9–10). Great power resides in humbly serving others because it frees us from pride's bondage to money and draws others to Christ in us while we grow in our intimacy with both. The more we give up control, the more we find it residing in us. Christ is the power of God (1 Corinthians 1:24), and His complete power is unlocked in our lives through the key of humility (2 Corinthians 12:9). This power is the Spirit of Christ dwelling in us (Romans 8:9–11).

How have you sought control apart from God? Are you trying to serve two masters? When presented with a choice of serving God or money, choose God because serving two masters is serving one. Humbly serve every person you encounter. You can serve their interests while at the same time serving your unselfish interests, as well as God's. It will not merely be you who is serving; rather, it will be Christ in you (1 Peter 4:10–11).

Do Discover Security, Part 1

Matthew 6:25–32

A BUSINESS mentor of mine told me he was spending so much time worrying about money he decided to make an appointment on his calendar to worry for twenty minutes and get it out of the way. He deemed the exercise such a waste of time, he never worried again.

Do you worry about money? Are you seeking financial security? How much money would it take for you to have it? Security means we don't have to worry. We can trust in one resource to be true all of the time. This desire for security came from God providing man every seed-bearing plant and every fruit-bearing tree (Genesis 1:29). This is the fourth desire Jesus addressed to be fulfilled by wisdom in the Sermon on the Mount (Matthew 6:25–34).

Pride seeks security from money. "Therefore I tell you, do not worry about your life" (Matthew 6:25a). When our hearts are hard, we focus on our own selfish desires, seeing money as the ticket to the doorway of security. We desire to be financially secure so our needs will always be met. This leads us to a life of worry because we fear not having enough. Deep inside our hearts, we are not merely trusting in money for security, we are trusting in ourselves—our ability to earn, keep, and grow the stockpile of cash.

The result is insecurity. "Can any one of you by worrying add a single hour to your life?" (Matthew 6:27). The more we pursue the satisfaction of our desire for security apart from God, the more insecure we become. Insecurity is worrying that our resource will not remain true. Worry is literally a divided mind, or heart. We trust in

God a little and in ourselves a lot. We think by doing so we will add security to our lives.

We were created to function by trust; however, sometimes we have trust in the wrong object—that which is temporary, rather than that which is eternal. Jesus summed it up as having "little faith" (Matthew 6:30). Paul called it walking by sight—having faith in what we see around us, rather than believing in who is in us (2 Corinthians 4:18; 5:7). When we worry, we trust in the gifts rather than the Giver, in our giftedness rather than Christ's godliness.

Our insecurity perpetuates the need to prove our resources are true. Consequently, we find ourselves leveraging our time, talent, and treasure toward those ends. This occurs most frequently where our self-trust is highest: in tasks where we are skilled or in relationships where we are most familiar. The outcome is a never-ending cycle of trusting in our giftedness to prove our security, and the outcome is further insecurity. Jesus commanded us to stop the cycle of insecurity, saying: "So do not worry" (Matthew 6:31a). Worrying is for the proud who do not trust God; the humble trust that God knows their needs (Matthew 6:32).

How have you sought security apart from God? Where do you go and what do you pursue in order to feel secure? What has been the result?

In our pride, we seek security apart from God, and the result is insecurity. However, when life is centered in Christ, we discover His truth is greater than our desire for security.

Do Discover Security, Part 2

Matthew 6:33–34

H UMILITY seeks first God's kingdom and His righteousness. "But seek first his kingdom and his righteousness" (Matthew 6:33a). God's kingdom is His divine reign, rule, and order in the hearts and lives of people on this earth now and in the future. It is the effective reach of His will. God's righteousness is what is right in His sight. The two intersect to form wisdom: God's righteousness combined with streets smarts (the shrewd reach of God's will into our tasks and relationships).

Wisdom is not a principle; it is a person. Christ the wisdom of God came as the Righteous One (1 John 2:1) to inaugurate the renewal of God's kingdom (Mark 1:15). When we humble our hearts to Him, we experience the security of God's kingdom and righteousness in our lives. Solomon, the pinnacle of wisdom, said that the fear of the Lord (humility) was the ticket to the doorway of security (Proverbs 14:26). This humility seeks to prioritize God's will in our tasks and our relationships.

The result is the truth of God in Christ. "And all these things will be given to you as well. Therefore do not worry about tomorrow, for tomorrow will worry about itself. Each day has enough trouble of its own" (Matthew 6:33b–34). *These things* represent our needs. God satisfies our desire for security with the truth of God in Christ (John 14:6). He is the resource of wisdom that will never run dry.

Solomon reflected: "Wisdom is a shelter as money is a shelter, but the advantage of knowledge is this: Wisdom preserves those who

have it" (Ecclesiastes 7:12). That extra hour of life we were seeking by worrying is infinitely found in wisdom. The psalmists added that the person who humbly trusts God will have no fear, and his heart will be secure (Psalm 112:7–8).

Do two things: (1) don't worry, and (2) seek first God's kingdom and His righteousness. First, make an appointment with yourself to worry for 20 minutes. Write down everything that worries you. After you experience the silliness of this exercise, commit to not worrying again about financial security by trusting in money. Second, pray. Humbly trust God with all of your concerns by seeking first His will for your life.

Make your muscles move with your prayers by working wisely. Seek God's wisdom, allowing money to be a byproduct of relationships. Seek intimacy with your customers, vendors, employees, employers, family, and friends as you seek intimacy with God. Read the chapter of Proverbs corresponding to each day of the month, applying this wisdom to your tasks and relationships, including your finances. You will become secure, as you trust in godliness rather than your giftedness. It won't be you doing so; it will be Christ in you.

Condemning, Careless, or Connected?

Matthew 7:1–12

HAVE you ever struggled with how you should go to others with the gospel of full surrender to Christ?

When a person is caught in their sin, desiring life apart from God, we tend to go to them in one of two extremes: we are either condemning or careless. These responses are rooted in the two expressions of a proud heart: (1) stone (condemning), or (2) sand (careless). In the Sermon on the Mount, Jesus described the heart and mannerisms of an effective carrier of His gospel message.

Jesus conveyed that we should not go to the world either condemningly or carelessly; rather, we should go connectedly with the Spirit of God in total humility, and with a heart of clay (Matthew 7:1–12). Consequently, every encounter with another person is a three-way call. When we are connected with God and connected with others, then they are connected with God. Whereas pride brings static on the line, humility offers a clear connection.

Let's examine more closely what Jesus said about a condemning heart.

We are not to approach others condemningly with a hard heart of stone (Matthew 7:1–5). Jesus commanded: "Do not judge" (Matthew

7:1a). Jesus was communicating that we should not condemn because we will in turn be condemned by God and others (Matthew 7:2; cf. Luke 6:37–38). Paul said when we condemn others we pass judgment on ourselves because we do the same things (Romans 2:1). Jesus indicated that the judgment of God was predicated on how we flesh out His heart with others (Matthew 5:7). A hard heart of stone condemns out of judgment and legalism. A heart of stone often pretends to connect with God, while disconnecting with others. A heart of stone requires a severe tool to be shaped.

Today, surrender your stone heart to the One who makes things new. He will give you a heart of clay, one that is malleable in His hands and use you to bring His message of restoration to others.

"Me, Too"

Matthew 7:3–5

J ESUS linked a condemning heart with the eyes, or one's perspective. Borrowing an illustration from His construction days, He revealed the antidote to a condemning heart was to take the plank out of our own eye so that we can see clearly enough to help someone with the speck in his (Matthew 7:3–5).

The plank in our own eye is our personal sin of pride, and it leaves a blind spot (Ephesians 4:18). Jesus referred to a person with this blind spot as a hypocrite, or an actor, one with a mask, a pretender. Paul told the Galatians to go restore someone caught in sin with total humility as if they were capable of committing the same mistake, no acting, no masks, no pretending (Galatians 6:1).

Someone who has truly received God's forgiving grace simply cannot condemn another person.

Jesus, the Author of grace, did not condemn the woman caught in adultery: "Jesus straightened up and asked her, 'Woman, where

are they? Has no one condemned you?' 'No one, sir,' she said. 'Then neither do I condemn you,' Jesus declared. 'Go now and leave your life of sin'" (John 8:10–11).

One of my mentors owned a landfill outside an upscale southeastern community. We traveled throughout the United States together searching for collector cars to add to his collection. On one trip, he was telling me how challenging it had been for him to receive zoning approval for his landfill, something every community needs, but no community seems to want. I will never forget what he told me. He said, "Mitchell, everybody thinks garbage stinks, except his own." In many ways Jesus was saying the same thing, the plank in our eye is believing that our own sin garbage does not really stink.

One tool we can use to recognize and remove the plank in our own eye lies in two simple words: "Me, too." Before we go to anyone caught in sin, we need to be able to look inside our hearts and say, "Me, too."

Don't Be Careless When Handling Pearls

Matthew 7:6

HAVE you been careless in the way you approach others with the gospel message of restoration?

We often see careless words played out this way. A believing woman is married to an unbelieving husband. Over time, their marriage gets dinged and corroded, resulting from two people with totally different hearts being united in matrimony. The believing woman begins to seek counsel from her believing friends and their husbands. That group begins to go carelessly, one after another, loosely handling the gospel pearls of wisdom with her unbelieving husband. Not once do they attempt to discern the wisdom appropriate for the level of hardheartedness in the unbelieving spouse. Going carelessly with a heart of sand often confuses the person we want to bring to Christ and leaves a disconnect with them.

A heart of sand is careless because it is loose. A heart of sand often pretends to connect with others, while disconnecting with God. A heart of sand requires a storm to be malleable.

Jesus taught that we are not to approach others carelessly with a loose heart of sand: "Do not give dogs what is sacred; do not throw your pearls to pigs. If you do, they may trample them under their feet, and turn and tear you to pieces" (Matthew 7:6). The Master Teacher warned of a kind of pride that is careless and loose with the gospel

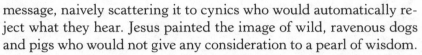

message, naively scattering it to cynics who would automatically re-ject what they hear. Jesus painted the image of wild, ravenous dogs and pigs who would not give any consideration to a pearl of wisdom.

This is why Jesus taught in parables. He was careful with his words. He discerned the wisdom appropriate for the level of hard-heartedness among his listeners. Jesus pointed out that cynical hearts were already hard, so if He merely presented truth, it would auto-matically be rejected. However, He knew if He would share a story, then people would leave thinking about the details of the story, and from that, could perhaps discover the truth of the story in an un-threatening fashion. The truth concealed could be the truth revealed through a story. Two thousand years ago, a Rabbi would teach a para-ble and then explain it more fully to those who would call themselves his disciples.

Discern the level of hardheartedness of your audience and care-fully place the pearls of restoration in front of them. Rather than merely presenting facts, seek to understand, then wisely lead others to the Restorer.

Discerning the Heart

Proverbs 9:7–9

WHEN you communicate the gospel message of restoration, do you first give thought to the heart condition of your audience? For example, Proverbs teaches of the dilemma that occurs when we attempt to argue with a fool (Proverbs 26:4–5). When doing so, we just can't win.

Solomon taught that when attempting to connect with others, we must discern the wisdom appropriate for the level of hardheartedness: "Whoever corrects a mocker invites insults; whoever rebukes the wicked incurs abuse. Do not rebuke mockers or they will hate you; rebuke the wise and they will love you. Instruct the wise and they will be wiser still; teach the righteous and they will add to their learning" (Proverbs 9:7–9).

The apostle Paul agreed, teaching we should be wise with outsiders, discerning the wisdom appropriate for their level of hardheartedness (Colossians 4:5–6). In order to do this, we need one ear toward heaven and one ear toward the ground.

Jesus warned the hardhearted Pharisees of carelessly speaking against the Holy Spirit (Matthew 12:34–37). In contrast, Jesus was careful with His words with Nicodemus (John 3:1–21). Jesus discerned the wisdom appropriate for the level of hardheartedness with the rich young ruler. He listened to His heavenly Father as He listened to His audience.

Today, direct one ear to heaven and one ear toward the ground in order to discern your audience's level of hardheartedness. Ask the Holy Spirit to direct you to listen more than you speak, and when you open your mouth, to give you the wise words to say.

Every Encounter Is a Three-Way Call:
Connection One

Matthew 7:7–11

JESUS said we should not go to a lost and hurting world either condemningly with a hard heart of stone or carelessly with a loose heart of sand; rather, we should go connectedly with the Spirit of God in total humility, and with a soft heart of clay (Matthew 7:1–12). That makes every encounter with another person a three-way call. When we are connected with God and connected with others, then they are connected with God. Whereas pride brings static on the line, humility offers a clear connection.

Jesus described the three connections in a manner that resembles a three-way call today:

Connection One: ASK God.
Connection Two: Ask others.
Connection Three: Others ask God into their lives.

Let's look at the first connection.

Jesus taught we should go to others with a heart of humility first connected with God. Whereas a stone heart tells condemningly, and a sand heart tells carelessly, a clay heart asks connectedly.

Jesus commanded us to ASK: Ask, Seek, and Knock. He described a progressive intensity of humility in prayer, one's heart connected with God's. He promised if we ask humbly, we will receive; if we seek (making our muscles move with our prayers), we will find; and if we knock persistently, the door will be opened (Matthew 7:7–11).

You might ask, "Receive what? Find what? Open what door?"

In Luke's parallel passage, we discover that the answer is not what, but who: "Your father in heaven [will] give the Holy Spirit to those

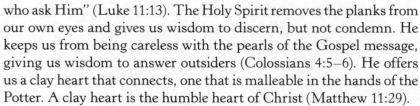

who ask Him" (Luke 11:13). The Holy Spirit removes the planks from our own eyes and gives us wisdom to discern, but not condemn. He keeps us from being careless with the pearls of the Gospel message, giving us wisdom to answer outsiders (Colossians 4:5–6). He offers us a clay heart that connects, one that is malleable in the hands of the Potter. A clay heart is the humble heart of Christ (Matthew 11:29).

We must first ask the Holy Spirit into our lives and then ask Him for wisdom regarding each encounter.

Ask the Holy Spirit for wisdom for your every encounter, seeing any supposed interruption as a divine appointment to connect first with God.

Every Encounter Is a Three-Way Call:
Connection Two

Matthew 7:12

LET'S examine how to ask others to connect with God.
Jesus summed up the Sermon on the Mount with the main
horizontal theme: "So in everything, do to others what you would
have them do to you, for this sums up the Law and the Prophets"
(Matthew 7:12). When we do to others what we would have them do
to us, we connect with them. In essence, Jesus said if we ask others
about their needs, then we will be better equipped to meet them in
order to connect others with God.

We will never know how to serve anyone in the way they need
to be served unless we humbly ask and listen. Solomon taught that
anyone who answers before listening is foolish (Proverbs 18:13). A
humble clay heart connects with both God and others.

I have developed a few simple questions to connect with others.
To date, these have never resulted in push back from those who were
unrestored.

First, I often ask, "What is your church or spiritual background?"

Next, I inquire, "Will you please tell me your story?"

After asking this question, which often generates descriptions of
tragedy and triumph in another person's life, I ask, "Where is God
in all that for you?"

Then I ask this penetrating, unthreatening question, "In terms
of the God thing, would you describe yourself as skeptic, seeker, or
surrendered?" Someone who is unrestored will usually attempt to
choose between skeptic and seeker.

Will you commit today to asking these questions and discover
more about those in spiritual need God has placed around you?

Every Encounter Is a Three-Way Call: Connection Three

Matthew 7:12

WHEN we ask God for guidance (Connection One) and ask questions of others (Connection Two), the Holy Spirit connects others with God (Connection Three).

Describing Connection Three, Jesus commanded: "So in everything, do to others what you would have them do to you, for this sums up the Law and the Prophets" (Matthew 7:12). The Law and the Prophets were designed to connect others with God. Jesus described this humility toward God and others as the greatest commandments (Matthew 22:37–40), and Paul said the entire law was summed up in one command: "Love your neighbor as yourself" (Galatians 5:14). He told the Romans that love fulfilled the law (Romans 13:9–10). Jesus's half-brother James agreed (James 2:8).

The apostle Peter clarified the importance of others asking God into their lives: "But in your hearts set apart Christ as Lord. Always be prepared to give an answer to everyone who asks you to give the reason for the hope that you have. But do this with gentleness and respect" (1 Peter 3:15).

On a hot Middle Eastern day, Jesus provided the ultimate picture of a three-way call when He connected with the heart of the Father and with the woman at the well, who then also connected with God. He was not condemning. He was not careless. He was connected, and

He asked. Consequently, she asked the Restorer into her life (John 4:1–54).

I have prayed with scores of people to surrender their lives to Christ. Every single one was asked. I usually phrase the question this way, "Would you like to draw a line in the sand, put a stake in the ground, and fully surrender your heart and life to Christ as Savior and Lord?" Then I ask each to pray a simple prayer to God, "I can't. You can. I can't free myself from the penalty of my sin. In Christ, You can. I can't free myself from the power of my sin. In Christ, You can. I fully surrender my heart and life to You as Savior to free me from the penalty and Lord to free me from the power of my sin. Please forgive me and restore me."

Trade your condemning heart of stone or your careless heart of sand for a soft heart of clay that is connected with God and others. Ask the Holy Spirit to take the plank out of your own eye so you can clearly see the speck in others' eyes. Ask Him for wisdom to answer outsiders. Ask others how you can serve them. Listen. In everything, act with Christ's heart of humility, and His Spirit will connect them with God.

Every encounter is a three-way call. Whereas pride causes static on the line, humility offers a clear connection.

The Gate, the Road, the Destination

Matthew 7:13–14

SUSAN and I were returning from our annual anniversary week of rejuvenating in the sun at Atlantis in the Bahamas. We sat and talked in the Nassau Airport awaiting the boarding announcement for our return flight home. When our flight number was called, we quickly grabbed our bags and merged into the line to enter a secured area leading to the tarmac. We followed the flow of foot traffic through the gate, down the jetway, and onto the plane where the only two vacancies on the small jet matched the seat assignments on our boarding passes. I wondered how everyone had boarded so quickly because we had immediately responded to the first boarding call. Then I noticed something was not right.

Having traveled more than two million miles by air, I was sensing a vibe of American Airlines blue rather than Delta Airlines blue. When I looked at the logo on the flight attendant's badge, I knew we had a problem. Instead of a letter from the Greek alphabet pinned to his shirt, I saw two adjoining A's flanked by wings. If my eyes were deceiving me, my ears were not.

At that moment, I heard the final pre-takeoff announcement over the plane's tin-can public address system: "Ladies and gentlemen, please stow your luggage under your seats or in the overhead bins as we prepare for an on-time departure to Miami." We were going to Cincinnati.

Susan and I grabbed our bags, sprinted off the plane, up the jetway, and through the gate. We ran through the airport hallway like Usain "Lightning" Bolt, searching for our airplane's gate, worried we would miss our flight. Suddenly, we were stopped by a team of uniformed, armed airport staffers. We learned in a post-9/11 world, airport security guards do not appreciate two travelers who board a plane and then immediately run off it.

We were searched in more ways than I care to remember. The security personnel, apathetic to the fact we might miss our flight, combed through every crevice in our carry-on bags. The more I pleaded we were risking having our flight take off without us, the more they found a new zipper to open in our duffle bags. Finally, the guards finished their search, and we were set free. We ran past several gates with our eyes scanning ahead. Finally, we entered through the correct gate, sprinted down the right jetway, and boarded the flight that would arrive at our scheduled destination.

Two different gates led to two different roads, which led to two different destinations.

We approach life with God through one of two gates, traveling one of two roads, leading to one of two destinations. One is religious, traveling from the outside in. The other is relational, traveling from the inside out.

In the Sermon on the Mount, Jesus described the two gates, the two roads, and the two destinations: "Enter through the narrow gate. For wide is the gate and broad is the road that leads to destruction, and many enter through it. But small is the gate and narrow the road that leads to life, and only a few find it" (Matthew 7:13–14).

Which road are you traveling?

The Wide Gate

Matthew 7:13

WE approach life with God through one of two gates, traveling one of two roads, leading to one of two destinations. One is religious, traveling from the outside in. The other is relational, traveling from the inside out.

The first gate is wide (Matthew 7:13). Jesus referenced the Pharisees' outside-in righteousness, using an analogy of wide city gates typical of the day. They had taken God's covenant community through a wide gate of rules, adding 1,500 of them to the 613 Old Testament laws. Paul said that they had created a righteousness of their own, not one that came from God (Romans 10:1–3).

The road is broad. Two thousand years ago, the main road traveling in and out of city walls spanned about twenty-four feet wide, an image familiar to Jesus's audience. The broad road most likely referred to the sinful nature. When we trust in our own man-made righteousness, we end up trusting in our own sinful nature for success. We fluctuate between legalism and license, based on our personal preferences, leaving us disconnected from intimacy with God. Paul said that those who are controlled by the sinful nature cannot please God (Romans 8:5–8).

The destination is destruction. The wide gate and broad road lead to death. Jesus revealed the Pharisees' outside-in righteousness actually closed the gates to the kingdom of heaven to others and even themselves (Matthew 23:13–14). The result was no life abundant and no life eternal.

Many are entering through it. The many are the proud in heart, both the legalistic and the licentious (Matthew 7:1–6). Our natural state, by birth and by choice, travels through the wide gate, down the wide road, and to the destination of destruction (Genesis 8:21). Pride is the lock on the human heart.

Are you one of the many traveling through the wide gate of outside-in righteousness, down the broad road led by the sinful nature, arriving at the destination of destruction? If so, confess it to God today. He will lead you through a new gate, down a different road leading to life.

The Narrow Gate

Matthew 7:14

JESUS taught the second gate is narrow (Matthew 7:14).

Narrow meant only one gate led to life. Jesus described inside-out righteousness, one that looks within to find His Spirit. Christ is that Gate (John 10:7–9). Jesus told the Pharisees that the kingdom of God was within them, or in their midst (Luke 17:21). Describing the two gates to the Israelites who were entering the Promised Land, God said through Moses that the narrow gate was in their mouths and in their hearts (Deuteronomy 30:14). Referencing this passage, Paul told the Romans that the narrow gate within was where they find Christ (Romans 10:4–13). He called this the mystery of the gospel, "Christ in you, the hope of glory" (Colossians 1:27).

The road is also narrow. Jesus's hearers would have been very familiar with the images here. Two thousand years ago, cities had narrow roads to private entrances where people could enter and exit the city walls. These entrances spanned only six feet wide. Here Jesus was describing the personal relationship with His Spirit. Paul described

this as the road that led to life (Romans 8:9–11). Again, Christ is that Road (John 14:6).

The destination is life. The Greek word for *life* is *zoe*, which means abundant and eternal life. Jesus said that we find life with God when we enter His narrow gate (John 10:10). Christ is that Destination of Life (John 14:6).

Few find it. And the few who do are the humble in heart (Matthew 5:3; 18:3). The key to the narrow gate of Christ is humility. He holds the key (Revelation 3:7) because He is humble in heart (Matthew 11:29). His half-brother James said that we should humbly receive the word of God planted in us that can save us (James 1:21).

Today, choose life (Deuteronomy 30:19). Humbly go through the narrow gate, down the road with the Holy Spirit. It is a matter of the heart, and the only way to experience life with God.

Living in Front of Two Gates

Matthew 7:13–14

"ENTER through the narrow gate. For wide is the gate and broad is the road that leads to destruction, and many enter through it. But small is the gate and narrow the road that leads to life, and only a few find it" (Matthew 7:13–14).

Two people read the Bible. One goes through the narrow gate, one through the wide gate. One softens his heart to Christ in order to build up others, while the other hardens his heart to be puffed up with knowledge.

Two people go to church. One goes through the narrow gate, one through the wide gate. One softens his heart to Christ's mercy while the other hardens his heart hoping that others will see his religiosity.

Two people pray. One goes through the narrow gate, one through the wide gate. One softens his heart to Christ's Lordship while the other hardens his heart in an attempt to manipulate the Savior.

Two people give. One goes through the narrow gate, one through the wide gate. One softens his heart to Christ's generosity while the other hardens his heart, desiring attention and recognition for his gift.

Choose life. Go through the narrow gate of Christ, not the wide gate of religion (legalism or license). Travel down the road led by the Spirit, not the road blinded by your sinful nature. Enjoy the destination of life abundant and life eternal with God over the destination of destruction. Pride is the lock on your heart. Humility is the key.

Go With Discretion: Discern

Matthew 7:15–20

HAVE you ever entrusted yourself to a mentor who wanted you to be more oriented toward man-made rules than relationships? Rather than base his advice on the teaching of Christ and the counsel of the Bible, he developed his own personal potpourri of teachings. Describing two trees, Jesus addressed this dichotomy in the Sermon on the Mount when He taught His disciples how to *go* to their teachers and leaders (Matthew 7:15–23).

Discern. The fruit is determined by the root (Matthew 7:15–20). Jesus warned His audience to watch out for false prophets who led others away from God (Matthew 7:15; cf. Deuteronomy 13:1–18). Many had surfaced on the scene during Jesus's day. They pretended to be good on the outside, but they were evil on the inside.

Jesus said that false prophets could be recognized by their fruit, or what their lives produced (Matthew 7:16, 20). Disciples of Christ humbly led people to God (Proverbs 11:20). False prophets led others away from God. Being fruitful in multiplying the heart of God in others was the Creator's original idea (Genesis 1:28). Jesus communicated that the fruit was determined by the root (Psalm 1). The root is either the *sinful nature* or the *Spirit of Christ*.

Paul taught that the *fruit of the sinful nature* were obvious: "sexual immorality, impurity and debauchery; idolatry and witchcraft; hatred, discord, jealousy, fits of rage, selfish ambition, dissensions, factions and envy; drunkenness, orgies, and the like" (Galatians 5:19b–21a). However, the *fruit of the Spirit of Christ* is: "love, joy, peace, patience, kindness, goodness, faithfulness, gentleness, and self-control" (Galatians 5:22b–23a).

Conduct a fruit inspection. Ask, "Am I a false prophet, or do I have one in my life?" Do you have a mentor sowing hatred over love, rage over joy, or discord over peace? Rather than being *condemning* (viewing him as all bad for one spoiled fruit) or *careless* (viewing him as all good despite a bushel of spoiled fruit), be *discerning*. Separate the outside from the inside and examine his fruit—what he produces in his life—recognizing that his fruit is determined by his root.

Go With Discretion: Disciple

Matthew 7:21–23

JESUS taught His disciples to discern and disciple. First, they were to discern their mentors, noting that their roots determined their fruit (Matthew 7:15–20). Second, His disciples were called to disciple others who would multiply the fruit of the kingdom (Matthew 7:21–23).

Disciple. Intimacy with the Root produces His fruit (Matthew 7:21–23). Jesus preached that only those who do the will of His Father will enter the kingdom of heaven (Matthew 7:21). On judgment day, He will tell false prophets plainly, "I never knew you" (Matthew 7:23). *Know* meant "to experience intimately." The one who does the will of God is the one who has intimacy with Him. We find intimacy with God in Christ (John 15:1–7). He is the Root (Revelation 5:5; 22:16). The fruit He produces includes seeds that produce more fruit when they are planted in fertile soil. Thus, the fruit is another disciple who discerns and disciples with the heart of Christ.

Discern and disciple. Discerning the fruit of one's life is determined by the root. The root of sinful nature produces hatred, rage, and discord. The root of the Spirit produces love, joy, and peace. Disciple another fruit-bearer, recognizing intimacy with the Root produces His fruit. In order to do this, nourish your roots by reading the same passage in the Bible each day for a week; serving those who are scheduled in your agenda, as well as those who aren't; and praying for every detail in your life. Then you will be energized to nourish the roots of another. Ask God who you should meet with once a week to disciple through reading the Bible, praying, and serving. God will use you to make disciples who make disciples.

Go Wisely: Wise Builder

Matthew 7:24–29

ON what foundation do you make every choice, capture every thought, process every feeling, or offer every prayer? Jesus painted the picture of a foundation upon which His disciples could build their hearts and lives. Jesus summarized it as building one's house on the rock (Matthew 7:24–29). He closed the greatest speech ever given with a comparison of two builders—one wise, one foolish; two foundations—one solid, one shifting; and two fates—one eternal, one temporary.

The foundation of the wise builder was the solid rock of Jesus Christ including His righteousness and message of heart transformation. Jesus taught that whoever heard His words and put them into practice was like the man who built his house on the foundation of the rock (Matthew 7:24; cf. James 1:22–25).

The fate of the wise builder was eternity. Though the storms of life came, the house did not fall because its foundation was on the rock (Matthew 7:25). Everyone in Palestine knew a house had to be built on the rock (thirty feet below grade) because storms washed out the veins of sand underlying the topography. Jesus used a construction analogy to describe the wisdom of His teachings compared to the foolishness of the Pharisees. Jesus's words might have alluded to the Jerusalem Temple, which was often referred to as *the house on the rock.*

The foundation of the rock is wisdom: God's righteousness combined with street smarts. Every foundation has a vertical and horizontal component. Wisdom resides in the sweet spot where the vertical (God's righteousness) intersects with the horizontal (street smarts). Jesus Christ is the ultimate embodiment of the vertical (fully God) intersecting with the horizontal (fully man). The wise builder hears Jesus's words (vertically) and does them (horizontally).

The Jews' ultimate name for God was Wisdom. Paul defined the wisdom of God, not as a principle, but as a person—Christ (1 Corinthians 1:24). He went on to define Christ as the only foundation (1 Corinthians 3:11). This was not a new idea. Proverbs, the book of wisdom, described the preincarnate Christ as the wisdom of God (Proverbs 8:22–31). Solomon elaborated that a successful house is built on the foundation of wisdom (Proverbs 24:3). Christ's message of heart transformation is the foundation for a wise life. Jesus told Peter that He would build His church on the rock (Matthew 16:18). Peter knew Jesus was referring to Himself, and we would build our lives on His (1 Peter 2:4–5).

Has a storm of life revealed your foundation? If so, what is it?

Go Wisely: Foolish Builder

Matthew 7:24–29

THE foundation of the foolish builder was the shifting sand of man-made righteousness. The foolish builder heard Jesus's words and ignored them (Matthew 7:26). The Pharisees had hijacked God's Temple forcing their 1,500 rules and regulations on His people for their own profit. Thus, the foolish builder heard Jesus's words of heart transformation and did not put them into practice, choosing religion over a relationship with God.

The fate of the foolish builder was temporary. The storms of life came and the house fell with a loud crash because its foundation was built on the shifting sand of man-made righteousness (Matthew 7:27). In 70 AD, the Jewish Temple in Jerusalem (*the house on the rock*) fell with a loud crash. Many believe that Jesus had predicted this demise (Matthew 24:2). The body of each believer is the temple of the Spirit of Christ (1 Corinthians 6:19). The advancement of the kingdom of God occurs through His Spirit breaking through each living temple whose heart fully surrenders to Christ.

Each of us is a builder—either wise or foolish. Each of us builds his life on something—either the solid rock of Christ or the shifting sand of man-made righteousness. Each of us builds a destiny—either eternal or temporary.

Build your life on the Rock. Fully surrender your heart to Him. Choose His will (Luke 22:42). Capture every thought, and make it obedient to Him (2 Corinthians 10:5). Cast all your anxiety on Him because He cares for you (1 Peter 5:7). Pray in His name (Philippians 4:6–7; John 14:13–14).

When we make every choice, capture every thought, process every feeling, and offer every prayer to Christ, we wisely build on His solid foundation that is eternal. Anything else is foolish, shifting, and temporary.

An Audience of One

Luke 15:10; Colossians 3:17

THE first time I taught the Bible on a Sunday morning—at my good friend's church where he pastored—was a defining marker for me in my restoration process. He had invited me to preach, since he would be traveling back to his California hometown for his birthday. I jumped at the chance to communicate what God had done with my life up to that point, and there was no better text to describe my journey than the parable of the father who had two sons. I still remember this like it was yesterday.

A pastor had told me that when I preached I should picture an audience of one in the balcony applauding his approval. That person is Christ the Restorer who taught: "There is rejoicing in the presence of the angels of God over one sinner who repents" (Luke 15:10).

At the conclusion of the sermon, a young woman walked down the aisle to pray with me. She humbled her heart to Christ as Savior and Lord, freeing her from the prison of pride and pretense. I pictured a thunderous applause in heaven. God's vision had been followed by His provision. He was using me while on my own journey to bring His restoration to others.

That's exactly what He wants to do with you. Commit to live your life for an audience of One. The apostle Paul penned: "And whatever you do, whether in word or deed, do it all in the name of the Lord Jesus, giving thanks to God the Father through him" (Colossians 3:17).

Whether you work or play, do it all for an audience of One.

Surrender for an Audience of One

1 Samuel 13:14

H OW have you considered living for an audience of One? Unfortunately, most of us live for the wrong audience of one. We either live solely for ourselves or unhealthily for another person, all at the expense of living for God. One of the Bible's most prominent characters was King David whose chronicles demonstrate for us what it means to live for an audience of One.

David fully surrendered his heart for an audience of One. Samuel, the prophet, priest, and judge of all Israel, spoke a sobering truth to its first earthly monarch, King Saul: "But now your kingdom will not endure; the LORD has sought out a man after his own heart" (1 Samuel 13:14a). The man after God's own heart was David, a shepherd, poet, and musician who would become Israel's warrior and king. Much of the Old Testament is devoted to the man whose lineage would lead to the Messiah.

Heart in Hebrew is *leb* or *lebab*. It is our entire inner being, our will, intellect, spirit, and emotions. We can remember the four chambers of the spiritual heart with the acronym WISE. David chose God's heart with his will. He meditated on God's heart with his mind, or his intellect. He prayed for God's heart with his spirit. He wanted God's heart with his emotions.

David fully surrendered his heart and his desires to God. He described the process of knowing God's heart in a psalm: "Take delight in the LORD, and he will give you the desires of your heart" (Psalm

37:4). *Delight, anag* in Hebrew, means "to make one's heart pliable." In essence, it is a surrendered heart, humble toward God like clay in the Potter's hands. *Give* is translated from *nathan* in Hebrew, meaning "to orchestrate." *Desires* represent the beat of the heart. They connect our hearts with our lives: time, talent, and treasure. Thus, when our hearts become malleable to God's hands, He makes our desires to be like His. This is how we experience God's will in our lives.

David modeled this process by praying to God for a fully surrendered heart: "Teach me your way, LORD, that I may rely on your faithfulness; give me an undivided heart, that I may fear your name. I will praise you, Lord my God, with all my heart; I will glorify your name forever" (Psalm 86:11–12). Notice how all four chambers of the heart are referenced in these two verses: *teach* leads with the mind; *will walk* is primarily a matter of the will; *fear* includes the emotions; *praise* leads with the spirit, not to mention the entire petition is prayer of full surrender. Whereas an undivided heart is one that is fully surrendered to the Divine, a divided heart is partially surrendered, indicating a mixed devotion, or impurity, inside our inner being.

Today, pray Psalm 86:11–12 aloud to God. He will make you new again.

Examine and Surrender

Psalm 139:23–24

A WELL-KNOWN illustration of David's heart for God lies in his refining prayer for his Lord to examine and help him surrender any offensive way inside his heart: "Search me, God, and know my heart; test me and know my anxious thoughts. See if there is any offensive way in me, and lead me in the way everlasting" (Psalm 139:23–24).

One offensive way that through the Holy Spirit David examined and surrendered is one that we face today, a heart set on riches: "Though your riches increase, do not set your heart on them" (Psalm 62:10b). Full surrender of our hearts and desires to God is a dynamic process that features the Holy Spirit's refining components of *examine* and *surrender*. This is how He shapes our hearts and desires to be like His, clarifying His will for our lives.

Surrender your heart and desires for an audience of One. Memorize David's refining prayer (Psalm 139:23–24). Request the Holy Spirit would examine your heart and help you surrender any offensive way manifested from a mixed devotion, or a divided heart. It might be a heart set on riches, selfish pleasure, perfectionism, or even religion all at the expense of a relationship with God. Choose His heart. Meditate on His heart. Pray for His heart. Want His heart. When you do, He will shape your heart and desires to be like His, clarifying His will for your life.

Battle for an Audience of One

1 Samuel 17:45–47

DAVID battled for an audience of one. As a young shepherd boy, David came onto the scene of a winner-take-all battle between a designated member of the Israelites and Goliath, the chosen warrior for the Philistines. Abhorred by the gall of the giant Goliath's defaming comments toward the God of Israel, a confident David rushed to battle for his Creator. "David said to the Philistine, 'You come against me with sword and spear and javelin, but I come against you in the name of the LORD Almighty, the God of the armies of Israel, whom you have defied. This day the LORD will deliver you into my hands, and I'll strike you down and cut off your head. This very day I will give the carcasses of the Philistine army to the birds and the wild animals, and the whole world will know that there is a God in Israel. All those gathered here will know that it is not by sword or spear that the LORD saves; for the battle is the LORD's, and he will give all of you into our hands'" (1 Samuel 17:45–47).

David's perspective of victory shifted from *we* to *He*. Rather than battling for his own causes, David fought for God's. His heartfelt words recorded in a psalm reflected his perspective that gave God all of the credit for victory: "With God we will gain the victory, and he will trample down our enemies" (Psalm 60:12; cf. 108:13). In order to be victorious for an audience of one, we must shift our perspective of success from *we* to *He*, transitioning from battling for our own selfish causes to fighting for God's, namely the advancement of His kingdom in the hearts and lives of people. This shift in perspective will flow to our words. Rather than saying, "Look what we did!" we will find ourselves proclaiming, "Look what He did!"

Victorious means God *delivers* and *sustains* us in our spiritual battles. This was the pattern in David's life. He penned regarding God's deliverance: "To the One who gives victory to kings, who delivers his servant David" (Psalm 144:10a). David was free to give credit to His deliverer: "O Sovereign LORD, my strong deliverer, who shields my head in the day of battle" (Psalm 140:7). David wrote regarding God's sustenance: "You make your saving help my shield, and your right hand sustains me; your help has made me great" (Psalm 18:35). When our perspectives shift from *we* to *He*, we become victorious for an audience of One Who *delivers* and *sustains* us in our spiritual battles.

Today, battle for an audience of One. Change your perspective of victory from *we* to *He*. Let your measurement of success transition from a dependence on meeting your selfish agenda to the advancement of God's kingdom in the hearts and lives of others. God will grow His kingdom in you as you experience His deliverance and sustenance, freeing you to give Him the credit for victory. Your words will change from, "Look what we did!" to "Look what He did!"

Strengthen for an Audience of One

1 Samuel 30:6

ARE you in need of restoration by the only One who can provide it?

David was strengthened for an audience of One. In the backdrop of David's pre-monarch raids, his men had lost their wives and children to the captivity of a nomadic enemy who had ransacked their camp while they were away. Scripture records: "David was greatly distressed because the men were talking of stoning him; each one was bitter in spirit because of his sons and daughters. But David found strength in the LORD his God" (1 Samuel 30:6). David found strength in and for an audience of One.

Strength is not merely a divine attribute, rather it is the Person of God. David said in his psalm: "I love you, O LORD, my strength" (Psalm 18:1). In order to be strengthened by and for an audience of One, we need not seek something from God; instead, we must seek God Himself. It has been said that rather than seek His hands, we should seek His face. This means in place of seeking what God can do for us, we seek who He is.

David vividly illustrated how God *lifts* us from the old and *gifts* us with the new: "He lifted me out of the slimy pit, out of the mud and mire; he set my feet on a rock and gave me a firm place to stand" (Psalm 40:2). God lifted David from his old struggles and gifted him with new life. David described God's imminent proximity to those in need of strength along with His desire to save them: "The LORD is close to the brokenhearted and saves those who are crushed in spirit"

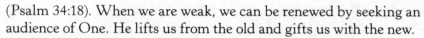

(Psalm 34:18). When we are weak, we can be renewed by seeking an audience of One. He lifts us from the old and gifts us with the new.

Today, be strengthened for an audience of One. In your weakness, renew your strength in the Person of God Who *lifts* and *gifts*. Seek His face by surrendering your old struggles and receiving a new heart shaped like His, bringing new life.

Worship for an Audience of One

2 Samuel 6:14, 21–22

DAVID worshiped for an audience of One. When the ark of the Lord was restored to David's possession, he worshiped God publicly: "Wearing a linen ephod, David was dancing before the LORD with all his might" (2 Samuel 6:14). David's wife, Michal, the daughter of King Saul, was mortified at David's transparency. David's response gave insight into his heart of worship: "David said to Michal, 'It was before the LORD, who chose me rather than your father or anyone from his house when he appointed me ruler over the LORD's people Israel—I will celebrate before the LORD. I will become even more undignified than this, and I will be humiliated in my own eyes. But by these slave girls you spoke of, I will be held in honor'" (2 Samuel 6:21–22).

In his psalm, David depicted his philosophy of a 24/7 worship: "I will exalt you, my God the King; I will praise your name for ever and ever. Every day I will praise you and extol your name for ever and ever. Great is the LORD and most worthy of praise; his greatness no one can fathom" (Psalm 145:1–3). He went on to say: "My mouth will speak in praise of the LORD. Let every creature praise his holy name for ever and ever" (Psalm 145:21).

In order to worship for an audience of One, we must worship God the most where others expect it the least—our work. Too often, we limit our worship to one selected style, taking place in one explicit building on one particular day during one specific hour of the week. Our praising of God has always been designed to take place beyond a worship service, encompassing all 168 hours a week. This includes our work. In fact, the Hebrew word *abad* can be translated *work* or *worship* (Numbers 4:39).

When we worship God 24/7, we are blessed with the awareness of His presence.

Today, worship for an audience of One. Worship God 24/7. Worship God the most where people expect it the least, at work. Go public with your worship of God by revealing His heart in all of your tasks and relationships. He will bless you with the awareness of His presence.

Repent for an Audience of One

2 Samuel 12:13

H AVE you sinned today? If so, it's time to return your heart
to God.

David repented for an audience of One. In essence, David repented as boldly as he sinned. After the prophet Nathan confronted David regarding his sin with Bathsheba, including orchestrating the death of her husband Uriah the Hittite, David's first words uttered his concern for his broken fellowship with God: "Then David said to Nathan, 'I have sinned against the LORD'" (2 Samuel 12:13a). When we sin against God, we must repent as boldly as we sin, focusing on our restored fellowship with God. The Old Testament's word for *repent*, is *return*, one of the most frequently used verbs by the writers of the Bible's first 39 books. When we sin, we turn our hearts away from God. Repentance means we return our hearts to Him.

When we repent, we are *contrite* toward God and *forgiven* by God. In his psalm repenting of his sin with Bathsheba, David communicated his contrition toward a Holy God: "Against you, you only, have I sinned and done what is evil in your sight; so you are right in your verdict and justified when you judge" (Psalm 51:4). *Contrite, dakah* in Hebrew, means "broken," or "sore." In Latin, it literally is translated, "to rub together" which is defined as "worn," or "bruised." To be contrite, we exhibit a godly sorrow for our sins, one that leads to repentance (2 Corinthians 7:10). David's genuine repentance was evidenced in his request for God to give him a pure heart, one with unmixed devotion: "Create in me a pure heart, O God, and renew a steadfast spirit within me" (Psalm 51:10). He went on to paint a picture of God's desired sacrifices for sin, which featured a *contrite* heart: "My sacrifice, O God, is a broken spirit; a broken and contrite heart you, God, will not despise" (Psalm 51:17).

David rested in the peace that his repentance flowing from a contrite heart resulted in the fact that he had been forgiven: "Blessed is the one whose transgressions are forgiven, whose sins are covered. Blessed is the one whose sin the LORD does not count against them and in whose spirit is no deceit" (Psalm 32:1–2). In other words, there is no pretense in us when we genuinely *repent* with a *contrite* heart as we stand forgiven.

David noted that God does not seek a one-for-one punishment of our sins: "He does not treat us as our sins deserve or repay us according to our iniquities" (Psalm 103:10). He continued by describing the peace of mind available to us in the truth that God does not recount our sins against us when we stand forgiven: "As far as the east is from the west, so far has he removed our transgressions from us" (Psalm 103:12).

Today, repent for an audience of One. Repent with a *contrite* heart and return to God in order to be *forgiven*. Thank God for the truth that He does not seek a one-for-one punishment for your sins and that standing forgiven means that He will not recount your sins against you.

God Is Our Provider: Win Little by Little

Proverbs 16:3

SOMETHING inside each one of us wants to earn all our resources up front, taking them in all at once, rather than over the long haul. That's the way many of us would design it, if we were the sole provider.

An examination of Proverbs offers wisdom for the vertical and horizontal lines of the flow of resources. The vertical represents the *Ups* and *Downs*. The horizontal represents the *Ins* and *Outs*. Since resources originate by coming into our lives, God gives us the *Ins, Outs, Ups, and Downs of Resources in Wisdom's Ten Ws: Ten Characteristics of a Wise and Generous Heart.*

First, we win little by little (Proverbs 13:11; 30:8–9).

Solomon advised: "Commit to the LORD whatever you do, and he will establish your plans" (Proverbs 16:3). He was communicating that *God is our Provider*. Abraham gave this name (*Yahweh Yireh*) to the mountaintop where God had provided the sacrificial ram in place of his son Isaac (Genesis 22:14).

Solomon said that it is wise and generous to win our resources little by little. He observed: "Dishonest money dwindles away, but whoever gathers money little by little makes it grow" (Proverbs 13:11). God has designed that we take in our time, talent, and treasure little by little.

We take in our time little by little, or moment by moment. None of us can live in the past or the future, only in the present, which comes to us second by second.

We take in our talent little by little, or a piece at a time. None of us was born with the superior polished talent we exhibit in our careers. Rather, our talent was learned skill by skill and built little by little.

We take in our treasure little by little at fair market increments. For example, the stock market frowns on IPOs that line the pockets of its operators with exorbitant amounts of cash. Rarely does anyone purchase an asset and immediately resell it for ten times that amount. Few ever receive their entire lifetime wages at the beginning of their careers.

Regarding resources, Solomon warned: "Keep falsehood and lies far from me; give me neither poverty nor riches, but give me only my daily bread. Otherwise, I may have too much and disown you and say, 'Who is the LORD?' Or I may become poor and steal, and so dishonor the name of my God" (Proverbs 30:8–9). When we win our resources little by little, we trust God as our Provider, relying on Him for the volume.

God Is Our Provider: Work

Proverbs 10:4–5

DOES work energize or drain you? In order to honor God as our Provider, we must worship Him in our work. The Hebrew word, *abad*, is actually translated, "work" or "worship" (Numbers 4:39). God designed work to be worship, as if we were laboring for Him (Colossians 3:17, 23). Praising God has always been designed to take place beyond a worship service, encompassing all 168 hours a week, including our work. In the second characteristic of a wise and generous heart, Solomon noted we should *work* in order for resources to come in as God intended.

God wants us to work hard. Solomon advised: "Lazy hands make for poverty, but diligent hands bring wealth" (Proverbs 10:4). Hard work usually brings a profit; however, we cannot rely on hard work alone.

God wants us to work smart. Solomon continued: "He who gathers crops in summer is a prudent son, but he who sleeps during harvest is a disgraceful son" (Proverbs 10:5). Our modern day translation is "Make hay while the sun shines."

When we work hard and smart with a wise and generous heart, we honor God as we serve others.

Whether you are a student, an athlete, a business owner, a volunteer, or an employee earning minimum wage, work hard and smart. Solomon taught: "Do you see someone skilled in their work? They will serve before kings; they will not serve before officials of low rank" (Proverbs 22:29). God will use your efforts to honor Him to reveal to you that He is indeed your Provider. You will be free to trust in Him for the ins of your resources.

God Is Our Provider: Weigh Relationships
Greater Than Remuneration

Proverbs 11:24–26

WHEN you earn money, do your actions demonstrate that you most value people or profit?

In the third characteristic of a wise and generous heart, Solomon noted we should *weigh relationships greater than remuneration* in order for resources to come in as God intended.

Solomon witnessed how generosity multiplied wealth, yet greed perpetuated scarcity: "One person gives freely, yet gains even more; another withholds unduly, but comes to poverty" (Proverbs 11:24). The king elaborated on the secret why: "A generous person will prosper; whoever refreshes others will be refreshed" (Proverbs 11:25).

Solomon was communicating that a generous person values people more than profit. Consequently, when we are generous, we are fair in our pricing. Solomon taught: "People curse the one who hoards grain, but they pray God's blessing on the one who is willing to sell" (Proverbs 11:26). The only reason someone hoards grain is that he is asking more than the market price; he weighs remuneration over relationship.

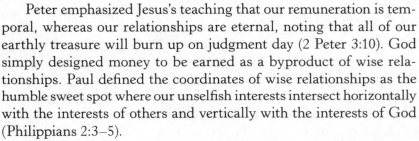

Peter emphasized Jesus's teaching that our remuneration is temporal, whereas our relationships are eternal, noting that all of our earthly treasure will burn up on judgment day (2 Peter 3:10). God simply designed money to be earned as a byproduct of wise relationships. Paul defined the coordinates of wise relationships as the humble sweet spot where our unselfish interests intersect horizontally with the interests of others and vertically with the interests of God (Philippians 2:3–5).

When resources come into your life, do you recognize God as your Provider? Do you win your resources little by little? Do you work both hard and smart? Do you weigh relationships greater than remuneration? Begin to focus on these objectives in order to grow in wisdom and generosity. He will continue to renew your resources as you honor Him with how you earn your income.

God Is Our Passion: Waive in Three Directions
(Give to God)

Proverbs 16:6; 3:9–10

WHEN we live and give with a wise and generous heart, we send money out in a fashion that says to the world, "God is our Passion." Solomon taught: "Through love and faithfulness sin is atoned for; through the fear of the LORD evil is avoided" (Proverbs 16:6). *Love, faithfulness,* and *the fear of the Lord* represent a passion for God. Consequently, we *waive,* or *give, in three directions,* to: *God, the poor,* and *our children.* Let's look at giving to God.

Solomon commanded: "Honor the LORD with your wealth, with the firstfruits of all your crops; then your barns will be filled to over-flowing, and your vats will brim over with new wine" (Proverbs 3:9–10). The *firstfruits* referred to the *source,* or the *gross.* Unfortunately, most of us want to give from our leftovers. The result is usually giving little to God. We can give to God by supporting our local churches in the form of a tithe or an offering.

Tithe is defined as a *tenth.* Tithing is a longstanding pattern modeled by wise leaders whose lives are chronicled in the Bible. They gave a tenth of their income to the advancement of God's kingdom in the hearts and lives of others. Jesus appeared to uphold the concept of tithing in His teaching (Matthew 23:23). However, this was a beginning, not an ending.

Offering is a gift beyond a tenth of our gross income. It flows from our fully surrendered generous hearts that see God as our Passion. God confronted His people with partially surrendered greedy hearts through the prophet Malachi: "'Will a mere mortal rob God? Yet

you rob me. But you ask, "How are we robbing you?" In tithes and offerings. You are under a curse—your whole nation—because you are robbing me. Bring the whole tithe into the storehouse, that there may be food in my house. Test me in this,' says the LORD Almighty, 'and see if I will not throw open the floodgates of heaven and pour out so much blessing that there will not be room enough to store it'" (Malachi 3:8–10). Too often, we are reluctant to test God for His blessing because we do not trust Him for replenishment.

God's original design for the Israelites was for them to be generous, giving in excess of ten percent of their gross income. In addition to the tithe, the Israelites rested their land every seven years; cancelled debts every seven years (as well as the Year of Jubilee every seventh seven-year period); gave during their *Three Great Feasts*; and gave through gleaning laws. Additionally, they gave an offering for the construction of the Tabernacle "from everyone whose heart prompts them to give" (Exodus 25:2), to such a level of abundance the Israelites were told to stop because they had given "more than enough" (Exodus 36:3–7). Their total annual giving averaged twenty to thirty percent of their annual income.

When we send our resources out with a wise and generous heart, we communicate God is our passion. This week, try giving to a cause that advances Christ's kingdom. It might be your church, a youth ministry, or a homeless shelter. Give a portion of your time, talent, or treasure and experience the passion of God.

God Is Our Passion: Waive in Three Directions
(Give to the Poor)

Proverbs 14:31; 19:17; 21:13; 28:27

WHAT percentage of your time, talent, or treasure do you give to those in need?

Solomon communicated that whether or not we give to the poor depends on our passion for God: "Whoever oppresses the poor shows contempt for their Maker, but whoever is kind to the needy honors God" (Proverbs 14:31). He went on to say that God rewards those who give to the poor: "Whoever is kind to the poor lends to the LORD, and he will reward them for what they have done" (Proverbs 19:17). This reward is, most likely, intimacy with God.

When we waive our resources to the poor, we demonstrate that God is our passion, and we grow in our relationship with Him. Conversely, ignoring the poor hinders intimacy with God. Solomon continued: "Whoever shuts their ears to the cry of the poor will also cry out and not be answered" (Proverbs 21:13).

Barriers to our intimacy with God bring many problems into our lives. Solomon summarized: "Those who give to the poor will lack nothing, but those who close their eyes to them receive many curses" (Proverbs 28:27).

Would you like to grow in your intimacy with God? Give to someone in need. This week, find a person who could benefit from a portion of your time, talent, or treasure, and waive it on to him or her. You will honor God as your passion.

God Is Our Passion: Waive in Three Directions
(Give to Our Children)

Proverbs 13:22; 17:2; 20:21

HAVE you given any thought to preparing a will? Most of us don't think much about this necessary task, assuming it can be done later when we are old, to pass along our wealth to the next generation. Now, here's a deeper question, and the answer might sting a bit. How often do you intentionally invest wisdom into your children? When asked what he would share if he could tell all of Athens one thing, Aristotle was quoted as saying, "Why do you scratch and crawl and look under every stone for money, yet spend so little time with your children to whom you will give it all in the end?"

When we exhibit a wise and generous heart, we give a spiritual and, sometimes, financial inheritance to our children. Solomon offered: "A good person leaves an inheritance for their children's children, but a sinner's wealth is stored up for the righteous" (Proverbs 13:22). The inheritance of wisdom is paramount, which is why Solomon said: "A prudent servant will rule over a disgraceful son and will share the inheritance as one of the family" (Proverbs 17:2).

A financial inheritance unaccompanied with a wise spiritual inheritance will destroy most children. Solomon said: "An inheritance claimed too soon will not be blessed at the end" (Proverbs 20:21).

This week, spend time with your children to whom you will give everything when you die. Choose a verse in Proverbs to discuss with them. Ask for their insights, as you waive your resources to the next generation.

God Is Our Passion: Ward-Off Debt

Proverbs 22:26–27

D O your liabilities outweigh your assets?

When we are wise and generous in heart, we *ward-off debt*, the fifth of Solomon's characteristics. Borrowing is not prohibited in Scriptures. We are merely reminded we will have to repay the debt. However, surety—borrowing more than our means to repay—is to be avoided as if it were the plague. The *Thirty Sayings of the Wise* include instruction regarding the risk of surety: "Do not be one who shakes hands in pledge or puts up security for debts; if you lack the means to pay, your very bed will be snatched from under you" (Proverbs 22:26–27).

Today, consumer debt is at an all-time high, credit card debt reaches five digits for most households, and surety is primarily responsible for economic turmoil throughout the world.

Is it time for you to develop a plan to pay what you owe? Seek wise counsel from a financial advisor and consider the 10-10-80 plan. Give God ten percent of your gross income through a tithe to your local church. Save ten percent of your gross earnings. Live off the remaining eighty percent. Your first step toward savings might be to pay your highest interest rate debt first. If you are paying eighteen percent interest on a credit card, and you pay it off, you just earned eighteen percent on your investment.

Ward-off debt and discover the freedom God has in store for you as you make Him your passion.

God Is Our Passion: Waste Not

Proverbs 27:23–24

DO you spend more than you earn? Too often, this is the case with many of us.

When we are wise and generous in heart, we wisely spend less money than we net in order to *waste not*. This occurs when we closely monitor the relationships responsible for our income as well as our expenses. Solomon recorded: "Be sure you know the condition of your flocks, give careful attention to your herds; for riches do not endure forever, and a crown is not secure for all generations" (Proverbs 27:23–24).

How well do you know the condition of your flocks? This week, when you encounter your staff, customers, or vendors, engage them relationally. Discover their needs and desires, asking questions about their lives, rather than merely business. Listen to their answers and connect their hearts with your organization's vision, mission, values, objectives, goals, and strategies.

In all things, give careful attention to your relationships in order to waste not your resources, spending less than you net. Demonstrate that God is your passion in the manner in which your resources flow out. He will expand your heart with wisdom.

God Is Our Passion: Withhold Not

Proverbs 3:27–28

ARE you withholding payment from someone you owe?
When we are wise and generous in heart, we do not delay payment from a vendor when it is due in order to *withhold not*. Solomon admonished: "Do not withhold good from those to whom it is due, when it is in your power to act" (Proverbs 3:27). The king elaborated: "Do not say to your neighbor, 'Come back tomorrow and I'll give it to you'—when you already have it with you" (Proverbs 3:28).

Unfortunately, we too often utter the proverbial, "The check is in the mail." Rather than make promises we cannot keep or delay payment to take advantage of using someone else's money, we should be quick to pay what we owe. This can paint a powerful picture of God as our Passion.

Perhaps, you have perceived paying your vendors late as a shrewd business practice. Try paying them as soon as you owe them and discover their response. At a time when I had no other choice but to pay cash up front to contract vendors to whom I owed past due accounts, I learned how eager they were to continue our relationship and provide excellent service. At the same time, I paid them a portion of the overdue balance I owed until it was paid in full. This led to me paying every vendor early from that time forward.

Demonstrate God as your passion when your resources go out. Waive your resources wisely and generously by giving three directions to: God, the poor, and your children. Ward-off debt in your life, both borrowing and surety. Waste not by spending less than your net income. Withhold not by paying what you owe when it is due. You will honor God as you honor others.

God Is Our Purpose: Walk Worthily

Proverbs 19:21

DOES your walk match your talk?

Solomon advocated that we demonstrate God as our Purpose when our resources go up. The author of Proverbs clarified the purposes of God: "The LORD works out everything to its proper end—even the wicked for a day of disaster" (Proverbs 16:4). God has a purpose for our resources before we get them. When our resources build up, it is important we seek God to discover His reason for blessing us.

In order to be wise and generous, we must *walk worthily* of the resources God purposefully built up in our storehouses. This means our walk matches our talk. Consequently, we: *steward, save,* and are *shrewd and harmless* with our resources.

What does it mean to be a steward of our resources? When we walk worthily, we recognize God owns all the resources, and we merely steward our wealth for His purpose. Solomon penned: "Many are the plans in a person's heart, but it is the LORD's purpose that prevails" (Proverbs 19:21). God's primary purpose is to advance His kingdom in the hearts and lives of people.

After Solomon's father David had collected the funds for the Temple that would glorify God, he prayed: "Yours, LORD, is the greatness and the power and the glory and the majesty and the splendor, for everything in heaven and earth is yours. Yours, LORD, is the kingdom; you are exalted as head over all" (1 Chronicles 29:11).

King David saw himself as a steward. His legacy was a man after God's own heart, one that God honored as part of the lineage of the Messiah.

Consider your legacy. Are you walking worthily of the resources God has given you by stewarding them for His kingdom? First, be

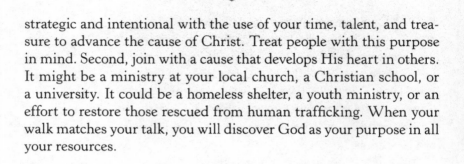

strategic and intentional with the use of your time, talent, and treasure to advance the cause of Christ. Treat people with this purpose in mind. Second, join with a cause that develops His heart in others. It might be a ministry at your local church, a Christian school, or a university. It could be a homeless shelter, a youth ministry, or an effort to restore those rescued from human trafficking. When your walk matches your talk, you will discover God as your purpose in all your resources.

Walk Worthily: Save and Be Shrewd, Yet Harmless

Matthew 10:16

D O you have an intended purpose for your savings account? When our resources build up, it is important we seek God to discover His purpose for them. Let's look at what it means to save and be shrewd, yet harmless.

When we walk worthily, we save. Solomon observed: "The wise stores up choice food and olive oil, but fools gulp theirs down" (Proverbs 21:20). Too often, we devour our resources via the foolish use of credit cards and consumer debt. As believers, we espouse a worldview that acknowledges we live in a fallen world, yet we leave little or no margin in our budgets through saving.

When we walk worthily, we are also shrewd and harmless with our resources. Solomon cautioned: "Ill-gotten treasures have no lasting value, but righteousness delivers from death" (Proverbs 10:2). In essence, he said that when our resources go up, it should be only from walking worthily, including being shrewd and harmless with others. At the same time, we must seek God's shrewd and harmless purposes for our wealth.

Jesus illustrated the risks embedded in the marketplace, along with His desire for wisdom to endure them, when He said to His disciples: "I am sending you out like sheep among wolves. Therefore be as shrewd as snakes and as innocent as doves" (Matthew 10:16).

This week, examine your savings. Do you have enough resources to cover two to six months of living expenses should your current income cease? If not, is today the day you start a savings plan, setting aside ten percent of your income for your future, including a kingdom purpose, as you are shrewd, yet harmless, in your dealings with others? After all, Solomon taught: "If you have to choose between a good reputation and great wealth, choose a good reputation" (Proverbs 22:1 GNT).

God Is Our Purpose: Worship Not

Proverbs 8:10–11

Do you ever find yourself idolizing wealth?

In order to demonstrate God as our Purpose when our resources increase beyond our commitments, we must be careful to *worship not* our wealth, rooting out any hint of greed. *Greed* is worshipping our possessions. Paul called it *idolatry* (Colossians 3:5). Solomon confirmed wisdom is more valuable than any temporary resource: "Choose my instruction instead of silver, knowledge rather than choice gold, for wisdom is more precious than rubies, and nothing you desire can compare with her" (Proverbs 8:10–11).

Solomon conveyed that we were designed to worship God: "The name of the LORD is a fortified tower; the righteous run to it and are safe" (Proverbs 18:10). Unfortunately, as our resources escalate, we risk seeking security from our wealth, rather than God. Solomon communicated: "The wealth of the rich is their fortified city; they imagine it a wall too high to scale" (Proverbs 18:11).

Financial resources provide no security at our judgment. The king warned: "Wealth is worthless in the day of wrath, but righteousness

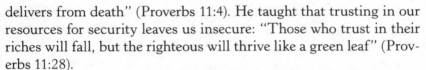

delivers from death" (Proverbs 11:4). He taught that trusting in our resources for security leaves us insecure: "Those who trust in their riches will fall, but the righteous will thrive like a green leaf" (Proverbs 11:28).

Jesus warned against greed: "Watch out! Be on your guard against all kinds of greed; life does not consist in an abundance of possessions" (Luke 12:15). When our resources go up, we must not worship our wealth.

Remember, money is pride's measurement of our giftedness. Wisdom is humility's measurement of our godliness. When your resources build up, discover God as your Purpose. Walk worthily of wisdom and generosity by beginning to steward, save, and be shrewd and harmless with your wealth. Above all, worship not by rooting out any hint of greed or idolatry of wealth. God will give you eternal meaning for your resources.

God Is Our Protector: Worry Not

Proverbs 23:4–5

DO you worry about money when your banks accounts are drained?

When our resources go down, we can act wisely and generously by authentically trusting in God for His protection. Solomon wrote: "When the LORD takes pleasure in anyone's way, he causes their enemies to make peace with them" (Proverbs 16:7). In other words, *God is our Protector*.

In order to see God as our Protector when our resources go down, we must *worry not*. *The Thirty Sayings of the Wise* inform us of the brevity of wealth: "Do not wear yourself out to get rich; do not trust your own cleverness. Cast but a glance at riches, and they are gone, for they will surely sprout wings and fly off to the sky like an eagle" (Proverbs 23:4–5). Jesus said that we could not add a single hour to our lives by worrying (Matthew 6:27).

When your resources appear to be over-extended, trust in God as your Protector. Worry not. Whenever you sense anxiety creeping into your heart, pray. Ask the Holy Spirit to help you move from fear to faith in God as your ultimate source of security.

When we are wise and generous in heart, we fully surrender to *God's Ins, Outs, Ups, and Downs of Resources*. As our time, talent, and treasure come *in*, we recognize *God is our Provider*. As our resources go *out*, we demonstrate *God is our Passion*. As our gifts build *up*, we discover *God is our Purpose*. When our resources go *down*, we trust that *God is our Protector*. The ultimate clarity of God appeared in Jesus Christ, and He is our model for a wise and generous heart. He empowers us to honor our heavenly Father with our resources.

Joy in Suffering: Joy Begins With Humility

Philippians 1:1–2

IDENTIFY the area in your life where you are experiencing despair, and ask three questions. First, are you inwardly focused? Second, are you going through it alone? Third, are you allowing God to use your despair for ministry to others? Your answers are most likely yes, yes, and no.

Paul wrote his letter to the church he had helped found in Philippi with the theme of joy amidst suffering. That's right; it is possible to experience joy even when we suffer. *Joy* is a deep internal acceptance that a loving, wise, and gracious heavenly Father is thoughtfully orchestrating every event of my life to shape me to be like Christ. The opposite of joy is despair (anxiety or sorrow), our typical response to difficult circumstances. In the first eleven verses of Philippians, Paul introduced a paradigm shift from despair to joy amidst suffering. Let's look at the first two verses.

First, Paul demonstrated that joy begins with humility: "Paul and Timothy, servants of Christ Jesus, To all God's holy people in Christ Jesus at Philippi, together with the overseers and deacons: Grace and peace to you from God our Father and the Lord Jesus Christ" (Philippians 1:1–2).

Notice that Paul referred to himself as a servant of Christ. Paul communicated the countercultural theme that he is a servant by choice. Consequently, any suffering will be seen through the eyes of a servant, eyes that refocus from inward to outward.

Today, continually recite, "I'm a servant of Christ." Or as one young lady wrote on her hand as a reminder, "I'M A SOC." Bend the knees of your heart to Him, and watch your despair begin to be transformed into joy.

Joy in Suffering: Joy Grows in Ministry

Philippians 1:3–8

ARE you suffering in a particular area of your life and attempting to go through it alone? Paul taught that joy grows in community: "I thank my God every time I remember you. In all my prayers for all of you, I always pray with joy because of your partnership in the gospel from the first day until now, being confident of this, that he who began a good work in you will carry it on to completion until the day of Christ Jesus. It is right for me to feel this way about all of you, since I have you in my heart and, whether I am in chains or defending and confirming the gospel, all of you share in God's grace with me. God can testify how I long for all of you with the affection of Christ Jesus" (Philippians 1:3–8).

Paul's reason for joy was the church's partnership for the gospel (Philippians 1:4–5). This meant they had surrendered all of their resources for the cause of Christ. Paul painted the picture of a business focused on communicating Christ's message of new life to a world full of despair. Joy was perpetuated by Paul's confidence that God, who began a good work (salvation) in the church, would complete it.

Today, rather than going it alone, share your burdens with another person and discover how they can be divided. At the same time, tell that person your joys and watch them be multiplied.

Joy in Suffering: Joy Prays for Ministry

Philippians 1:9–11

ARE you allowing God to use your suffering to minister to others?

Recognizing despair, anxiety, and sorrow comprised the natural response to suffering, Paul taught it was possible to experience joy, to take pleasure in Christ, even when we struggle. First, Paul demonstrated that joy begins with humility (Philippians 1:1–2). Second, Paul communicated that joy grows in community (Philippians 1:3–8). Third, Paul taught that joy prays for ministry.

"And this is my prayer: that your love may abound more and more in knowledge and depth of insight, so that you may be able to discern what is best and may be pure and blameless for the day of Christ, filled with the fruit of righteousness that comes through Jesus Christ—to the glory and praise of God" (Philippians 1:9–11).

Paul's prayer request was that love would abound more and more through experience and intimacy so the church would be sincere, literally judged by the light. *Sincere* conveyed a picture of pottery or marble that was the same all the way through. Potters and marble cutters would cover flaws with wax. The only way their pieces were proven to be either genuine or full of wax was to be held to the light.

When we pray for ministry, that God will use our suffering to draw others to Him, our despair is transformed into joy. Consequently, His light shines through our lives so that we reflect Christ's image.

Pray that God will use your suffering to draw others to Him. Exchange your despair for joy as you reflect Christ's image. He can use you to save a life from suicide, restore another for eternity, free a grudge-holder from the prison of withholding forgiveness, or further someone's journey to full surrender. He who began a good work will complete it!

Chains Of Suffering: Link Our Passion With Christ

Philippians 1:12–18a

W HAT chains are holding you back from joy?

Typically, the answer to this question is one that deals with our personal discomfort, rather than Paul's chains referenced in Philippians. Paul was imprisoned for advancing the kingdom of Christ. Our chains are often a result of advancing our own kingdoms. Paul's paradigm shift links our circumstances with Christ in order to find joy amidst suffering. We are to link our passion, perspective, and priorities with Him (Philippians 1:12–30). If any of these three links in our chain are broken, then we will not be able to experience chains of joy.

First, we link our passion with Christ. Paul taught:

"Now I want you to know, brothers and sisters, that what has happened to me has actually served to advance the gospel. As a result, it has become clear throughout the whole palace guard and to everyone else that I am in chains for Christ. And because of my chains, most of the brothers and sisters have become confident in the Lord and dare all the more to proclaim the gospel without fear. It is true that some

preach Christ out of envy and rivalry, but others out of goodwill. The latter do so out of love, knowing that I am put here for the defense of the gospel. The former preach Christ out of selfish ambition, not sincerely, supposing that they can stir up trouble for me while I am in chains. But what does it matter? The important thing is that in every way, whether from false motives or true, Christ is preached. And because of this I rejoice" (Philippians 1:12–18a).

Paul was chained to a Roman soldier for his passion for Christ. As a result of Paul's passion, the gospel advanced through the entire palace guard. Passion flows from the heart.

What gets you up in the morning? What energizes you? What makes you cry? The answers to these three questions reveal your passion. Link your heart with Christ to experience joy amidst suffering.

Chains Of Suffering: Link Our Perspective With Christ

Philippians 1:18b–26

WHAT do you see when you look at the chains that are holding you back from joy?

Usually, we focus on our personal discomfort that often stems from advancing our own agendas. Paul offered something different. He taught we could experience joy amidst suffering by first linking our passion with Christ (Philippians 1:12–18a). This connects our hearts with His. Second, in order to experience joy amidst suffering, we link our perspective with Christ.

Paul shared: "Yes, and I will continue to rejoice, for I know that through your prayers and God's provision of the Spirit of Jesus Christ what has happened to me will turn out for my deliverance. I eagerly expect and hope that I will in no way be ashamed, but will have sufficient courage so that now as always Christ will be exalted in my body, whether by life or by death. For to me, to live is Christ and to die is gain. If I am to go on living in the body, this will mean fruitful labor for me. Yet what shall I choose? I do not know! I am torn between the two: I desire to depart and be with Christ, which is better by far; but it is more necessary for you that I remain in the body. Convinced of this, I know that I will remain, and I will continue with all of you for your progress and joy in the faith, so that through my being with you again your boasting in Christ Jesus will abound on account of me" (Philippians 1:18b–26).

Whereas passion is a matter of the heart, perspective is a focus of the eyes. Paul saw every opportunity as one to advance Christ's kingdom. Regardless of the circumstances, Paul exalted Christ.

What is your perspective of your chains? Find a friend to pray with you to have Paul's perspective. Allow the Holy Spirit to refocus your eyes.

Joy in Serving Christ's Interests

Philippians 2:1–2

WOULD you rather serve or be served? There's something inside each of us that longs to be served. Often, it's why we buy, rent, sell, lease, or seek goods and services and even affects who singles choose to date. However, greater joy is actually discovered through serving, rather than being served.

Serving is the sweet spot of joy.

The apostle Paul said that this joy is discovered at the intersection of serving Christ's interests, our unselfish interests, and the interests of others. Arthur Ash, the great tennis player who gave his life to serving both on and off the court, advocated that joy could only be found in serving others. Just like the heart of the tennis racket is the sweet spot, so the sweet spot of joy resides in the heart of Christ the Servant.

First, we must be united with Christ in order to serve His interests.

Paul taught: "Therefore if you have any encouragement from being united with Christ, if any comfort from his love, if any common sharing in the Spirit, if any tenderness and compassion, then make my joy complete by being like-minded, having the same love, being one in spirit and of one mind" (Philippians 2:1–2).

Too often, we pretend to unite ourselves with Christ only to seek our own selfish desires. However, joy comes when we humbly unite our hearts with Christ in order to serve His interests. Jesus, who was humble in heart (Matthew 11:29), taught His followers that humility toward God would be rewarded in a reconciled relationship with Him (Luke 18:14).

Fully surrender your heart, desires, and life to serve Christ. Prayerfully, offer your calendar, your business card, and your checking account to be used for the advancement of His kingdom. Begin to experience joy in serving Him.

Joy in Serving Our Unselfish Interests

Philippians 2:3–4

HAVE you ever struggled with how to navigate through conflict when your personal interests are at stake?

The apostle Paul discovered joy at the intersection of serving Christ's interests, our unselfish interests, and the interests of others (Philippians 2:1–4). Let's look at what it means to serve our unselfish interests.

Paul taught: "Do nothing out of selfish ambition or empty pride, but in humility consider others more important than yourselves. Each of you should look not only to your own interests, but also to the interests of the others" (Philippians 2:3–4 BSB).

That's right, it is acceptable to serve our own interests when they flow from a humble heart surrendered to Christ. An example is wisdom (Proverbs 1:7; 9:10). Solomon confirmed: "He who gets wisdom loves his own soul" (Proverbs 19:8 NKJV).

This week, unselfishly seek a balanced budget, health, good relationships, and growth in wisdom. Solicit a friend to help you in an area of need. Meet once a week to discuss your progress. You will discover joy in serving.

Joy in Serving Others

Philippians 2:3–4

R ICK Warren said that you know whether you are a servant by how you feel when you are treated like one. Paul revealed that serving brings joy.

Paul instructed us as believers to serve the interests of others, considering them better than ourselves: "Do nothing out of selfish ambition or empty pride, but in humility consider others more important than yourselves. Each of you should look not only to your own interests, but also to the interests of the others" (Philippians 2:3–4 BSB).

People outside Christ often attempt to connect with others, but it can be superficial and self-serving. Paul taught us to serve others from a heart that seeks their interests in Christ. Peter said that we should use our gifts from God to serve others in a way that releases God's grace (1 Peter 4:10).

Today, focus on considering others better than yourself, looking for opportunities to serve them as if they were royalty. Make your muscles move with your prayers and allow God to use your challenges to serve someone going through a similar situation. Go find that person and serve them. You will experience joy.

Christ Our Example of Humility

Philippians 2:5–11

WOULD those closest to you describe you as humble or proud? Either is a heart condition.

When our hearts are hard, we exalt ourselves in pride. When our hearts are soft, we humbly exalt others. *Humility* and *humanity* come from the same Latin word, *humus*, meaning "from the ground." We often refer to a humble person as being "down to earth." Humility always has an object. Therefore, to be humble we must bend the knees of our hearts, first to God and then to others.

Paul penned a literary pendulum describing the humility of God: "In your relationships with one another, have the same mindset as Christ Jesus: Who, being in very nature God, did not consider equality with God something to be used to his own advantage; rather, he made himself nothing by taking the very nature of a servant, being made in human likeness. And being found in appearance as a man, he humbled himself by becoming obedient to death—even death on a cross! Therefore God exalted him to the highest place and gave him the name that is above every name, that at the name of Jesus every knee should bow, in heaven and on earth and under the earth, and every tongue acknowledge that Jesus Christ is Lord, to the glory of God the Father" (Philippians 2:5–11).

Paul gave the example of Christ, who being God, descended from heaven to die on a cross, only to be exalted to the highest place in the heavenly realm. The apostle painted a portrait of Christ's humility in serving the Father (Philippians 2:5) that was fleshed out in serving others (Philippians 2:6–8), so that they would serve the Lord (Philippians 2:9–11).

Contrast Christ's emptying with Adam, who being man, ascended to be like God (Genesis 3). Both accounts led to death, one willingly, one unwillingly. Unfortunately, our stories all resemble Adam's. The only way to be reconciled with God is to fully surrender our hearts to Christ, recognizing that in His kingdom, the pathway up is down.

This week, take the downward path. Start your day on your knees in prayer. Ask God to reveal His heart to you as you humble yourself to others. When you first see your family, ask how you can pray for them during the day. When you go to work, bend the knees of your heart to serve others. At the end of your workday, call your spouse and ask if you can pick up anything on the way home. God will lift you up by giving you His heart and drawing others to Himself.

Connect With the Light, Be a Rapid Holy Spirit Responder

Philippians 2:12–13

WHEN God prompts you through His Spirit, how quickly do you respond? Too often, we are slow to move when God calls. Consequently, we miss the blessing He has in store for us and those He desires us to engage.

Paul invited the church at Philippi to connect with the light of Christ, who provided the energy to obey through the indwelling of the Holy Spirit: "Therefore, my dear friends, as you have always obeyed—not only in my presence, but now much more in my absence—continue to work out your salvation with fear and trembling, for it is God who works in you to will and to act in order to fulfil his good purpose" (Philippians 2:12–13).

Paul charged his audience to "work out" their salvation with fear and trembling, or humility. "Work out," *katergazomai* in Greek, connoted digging in mines. In other words, these first century believers were to live out their salvation by the power of God, who was "at work" (*energeo*) in them. The same holds true for us today.

Today, connect with the light of Christ and become a Rapid Holy Spirit Responder. When He prompts you to act according to His good purpose, respond immediately with obedience. He might prompt you to help a coworker in need. He might prompt you to help your children with their homework. He could prompt you to meet with a hurting friend. In any circumstance, His vision will be followed by His provision.

Reflect the Light

Philippians 2:14–16a

HAVE you complained or argued, this week? Did you swear when someone cut you off on the highway? Did you slam a competitor over losing an account? Did you pop a gasket when the official missed a violation in your child's game? There's something fallen inside each of us that believes we will find satisfaction in complaining or arguing a bad call in our lives. When we complain or argue, we do so from darkness in our hearts.

Paul called the church at Philippi to reflect the light of Christ: "Do everything without grumbling or arguing, so that you may become blameless and pure, 'children of God without fault in a warped and crooked generation.' Then you will shine among them like stars in the sky as you hold firmly to the word of life" (Philippians 2:14–16a).

Paul offered practical advice to experience joy in serving. "Do everything without grumbling or arguing" (Philippians 2:14) to become blameless and pure, shining like stars (Philippians 2:15). *Blameless* meant "without fault." *Pure* carried a picture of refined metal that was not weakened by mixed impurities. In order to be blameless, we must confess our shortcomings to God, who then purifies us from our mixed motives. This empowers us to be free from complaining or arguing in order to shine like stars, as we hold out the word of life (Philippians 2:16a). Paul used imagery of harbor towers whose fires directed ships into the port during the night. When we hold out the word of life, we reflect the guiding light of Christ.

Memorize Philippians 2:14 and reflect the light of Christ by doing everything without complaining or arguing. Be blameless and pure when serving others. Confess to God your desire to serve your selfish interests and allow Him to purify you from mixed motives. Hold out the Word of life, so others can see the light of Christ.

Direct Others to the Light

Philippians 2:16b–30

Do you see every encounter with another human being as a divine appointment to point them to God?

Paul challenged the Philippians to direct others to the light of Christ: "And then I will be able to boast on the day of Christ that I did not run or labor in vain. But even if I am being poured out like a drink offering on the sacrifice and service coming from your faith, I am glad and rejoice with all of you. So you too should be glad and rejoice with me" (Philippians 2:16b–18).

Paul compared his life with a cup of wine being poured on a sacrifice near the end of a ceremony to seal the act of honoring the deity. Paul equated his hardship with the seal stamped on the sacrificial gifts and works of the church at Philippi. This sacrifice brought joy in serving. Paul concluded with examples of those who directed others to Christ's light, discovering service as the sweet spot of joy (Philippians 2:19–30).

Be intentional about directing others to the light of Christ. See every day as an opportunity to guide someone from darkness. Ask the Holy Spirit to examine your calendar and reclaim your appointments for the purpose of serving others, so they will serve God.

Joy in Believing

Philippians 3:1–21

WHEN my oldest daughter was in sixth grade, she played in her first organized school basketball game with her dad as the coach. All ten girls traveled around the court like an amoeba with a player occasionally emerging from the crowd with the ball. Then it happened, my daughter broke free from the mass of players and shot the rock with perfect form. It banked off the glass into the basket, scoring the first bucket of her career. Elated, she repeatedly jumped for joy, celebrating her accomplishment as if she had won the NCAA Final Four.

There was just one problem. She had scored at the other team's basket. After a teammate pointed out her dilemma, her joy turned into tears of embarrassment. I substituted her out of the game, pulled her close to me, and said, "Now you know what it's like to score, so go out and shoot at the right basket."

The apostle Paul taught that accomplishments become embarrassments when we shoot at the wrong goal: "Brothers and sisters, I do not consider myself yet to have taken hold of it. But one thing I do: Forgetting what is behind and straining toward what is ahead, I press on toward the goal to win the prize for which God has called me heavenward in Christ Jesus" (Philippians 3:13–14).

Joy comes from believing in Christ, fully surrendering our lives to Him and discovering forgiveness from the penalty of sin and freedom from the power of sin. However, if we think we can earn our way to this salvation by keeping the law, we will be embarrassed at judgment.

Are you shooting at the wrong goal? Forget, strain, and press on. Forget what is behind. Strain toward what is ahead. Press on toward the goal of the development of Christ in you. Make your definition of success to be shaped like Christ. Win, lose, or draw by the world's standards, your heart can grow closer to His.

Beware of Legalistic Accomplishments

Philippians 3:1–6

Do you ever find yourself following the letter of the law, but missing the spirit of the law, placing rules over relationships? Consistently placing man-made precepts over people is legalism, and Paul warned the Church at Philippi to beware of legalistic accomplishments.

"Further, my brothers and sisters, rejoice in the Lord! It is no trouble for me to write the same things to you again, and it is a safeguard for you. Watch out for those dogs, those evildoers, those mutilators of the flesh. For it is we who are the circumcision, we who serve God by his Spirit, who boast in Christ Jesus, and who put no confidence in the flesh—though I myself have reasons for such confidence. If someone else thinks they have reasons to put confidence in the flesh, I have more: circumcised on the eighth day, of the people of Israel, of the tribe of Benjamin, a Hebrew of Hebrews; in regard to the law, a Pharisee; as for zeal, persecuting the church; as for righteousness based on the law, faultless" (Philippians 3:1–6).

Legalism believes keeping the law will lead to salvation. It places confidence in our ability to save ourselves, which is religion. As a

Hebrew Pharisee from the tribe of Benjamin, named after Israel's first king, Paul communicated he had every right to boast about being faultless in his legalistic righteousness. When we operate in this fashion, we make rules greater than relationships. Jesus described this as straining out a gnat while swallowing a camel (Matthew 23:24). We follow the letter of the law only to miss the spirit of the law.

Do you ever strain out the gnat to swallow a camel? Keep a daily score card of the times you place rules over relationships. It might occur when you exit the parking lot of a concert or sporting event, preventing cars from exiting in front of you. It might happen in the express checkout line at the grocery, and you notice the person in front of you has more than twelve items in her cart. It might unfold when you win an argument with your spouse or when your child's playing time on his sports team doesn't meet your standard of fairness. Placing rules over relationships strains out gnats and swallows camels.

Legalistic Accomplishments Become Embarrassments

Philippians 3:7–11

HAVE you ever found yourself judgmentally approaching someone caught in their sin?

Typically, we carelessly approach a misguided family member we think should know better. We self-righteously share a verse from our favorite translation of the Bible, emphasizing what "true righteousness" should look like, giving little or no thought to our relative feeling condemned. This is the unfortunate scene when we attempt to correct sinners with a holier-than-thou approach, one that keeps track of our own legalistic accomplishments.

Paul taught that legalistic accomplishments become embarrassments because we shoot at the wrong goal.

"But whatever were gains to me I now consider loss for the sake of Christ. What is more, I consider everything a loss because of the surpassing worth of knowing Christ Jesus my Lord, for whose sake I have lost all things. I consider them garbage, that I may gain Christ and be found in him, not having a righteousness of my own that comes from the law, but that which is through faith in Christ—the righteousness

that comes from God on the basis of faith. I want to know Christ—yes, to know the power of his resurrection and participation in his sufferings, becoming like him in his death, and so, somehow, attaining to the resurrection from the dead" (Philippians 3:7–11).

Paul considered all his legalistic fervor as rubbish compared to experiencing Christ (Philippians 3:8). Only Christ provides the righteousness required by God. His holiness is applied to our eternal score card when we fully surrender our lives to Him (Philippians 3:9). The ground is level for all sinners at the foot of the cross.

Surrender your legalistic score card to Christ, reciting Philippians 3:9: "And be found in him, not having a righteousness of my own that comes from the law, but, that which is through faith in Christ—the righteousness that comes from God and is by faith." Experience freedom from the penalty and power of sin through faith in Him.

Humbly Turn Toward the Goal of Love

Philippians 3:12–16

WHAT words would those closest to you use to describe how you apply your faith to most relationships? Do you act with a perspective of religion or one of grace? Do you emphasize rules or relationship? Do you condemn or accept a fellow believer exercising a liberty you resist? Are you critical of someone committing a transgression against you or do you overlook the offense? Do you tell others about the sin in order to rally them in support of your position or do you take the matter to God? If you answered, yes, to the first option in one or more of these questions, you might be acting in legalism, rather than love.

Paul directed believers to humbly turn toward the goal of love and press on toward the high calling of God in Christ who loved them first.

"Not that I have already obtained all this, or have already arrived at my goal, but I press on to take hold of that for which Christ Jesus took hold of me. Brothers and sisters, I do not consider myself yet to have taken hold of it. But one thing I do: Forgetting what is behind and straining toward what is ahead, I press on toward the goal to win the prize for which God has called me heavenward in Christ Jesus. All of us, then, who are mature should take such a view of things. And if on some point you think differently, that too God will make

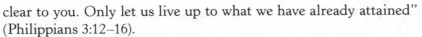

clear to you. Only let us live up to what we have already attained"
(Philippians 3:12–16).

Rome's pagan culture communicated that particular religions
completed citizens in such a way that made them flawless. Although
Christ lives in us as believers, we are not flawless (Philippians 3:12).
However, we are complete in Christ, who graciously matures us as
works in progress pursuing the goal of love (Philippians 3:14–15).
This progress on Restoration Road can be two steps forward and
one step back.

Forget the embarrassment of your past legalistic efforts and
humbly turn toward the goal of love by asking God to give you His
perspective of grace. Seek ways to demonstrate to others that your
relationship with them is more important to you than rules. Rather
than correcting or condemning a friend who exercises a liberty you
resist, accept him in Christ. Instead of criticizing someone for sinning
against you, overlook the offense. Rather than repeating that matter
to someone else, keep it confidential and surrender it to God who will
make you new again.

Serve Like Christ

Philippians 3:17–21

WHAT is your motive when you serve? Are you looking for something in return for your time or do your sacrificial efforts actually result in joy?

Paul invited the church at Philippi to join with others in community to humbly serve like Christ: "Join together in following my example, brothers and sisters, and just as you have us as a model, keep your eyes on those who live as we do" (Philippians 3:17). Paul noted that enemies of Christ have destruction as their destiny. Their god is their stomach; their glory is their shame; and their mind is on earthly things (Philippians 3:19). In contrast, as believers, our destiny is to be shaped like Christ. He is our God; our glory is in Him; and our minds are set on heavenly things (Philippians 3:20–21).

Join with other believers to humbly serve like Christ. Search for someone in need, even a past offender in your life, and recruit your small group or rally a few believing friends to meet that need. Avoid receiving benefit or credit.

Accomplishments become embarrassments when we shoot at the wrong goal. Joy comes from believing in Christ; however, if we think we can earn our way to salvation by keeping the law, we will be embarrassed at judgment. When we become aware of our legalistic efforts, we are in a position to surrender them to Christ, who turns us toward the goal of love, so we may serve in community.

Joy in Giving

Philippians 4:1

WHEN we worry, we misalign our hearts (mind, will, emotions, and spirit). It often looks like this: our minds are focused on the future, afraid we cannot control it; our wills reside in the present, frustrated our expectations are not met; our emotions are locked in the past from prior hurts; our spirits remain hindered in our vertical connection to God. When one piece of the heart is out of alignment, the whole thing hurts. Just like a misaligned spine needs adjustment, so our hearts need to be realigned in Christ.

Worry is the problem; prayer is the solution; and peace is the result.

The apostle Paul shared in Philippians 4:1–9 that prayer offers peace for worried hearts. Paul pleaded for peace in relationships and offered his prescription for peace with God, peace with others, and peace within ourselves.

Paul taught: "Therefore, my brothers and sisters, you whom I love and long for, my joy and crown, stand firm in the Lord in this way, dear friends" (Philippians 4:1).

As you encounter friends and family, find joy in giving grace to all of them. Stand firm in the GRACE God has given you in Christ and liberally issue God's Riches At Christ's Expense to everyone you encounter. You will experience God's three-dimensional peace as you practice joy in giving.

Peace With God

Philippians 4:4

WHEN we worry, we have a divided inner being, one foot in with God and one foot out, trusting in ourselves more than Him. Worry is the problem, prayer is the solution, and three-dimensional peace is the result.

Paul prescribed peace with God, and he communicated how: "Rejoice in the Lord always" (Philippians 4:4a). Notice he did not say, "sometimes." Too often, we allow anxiety to overcome us, and we go on autopilot, trusting in ourselves, rather than God. This robs us of the joy and peace found in Christ, who discovered joy in suffering for us (Hebrews 12:2).

Peace is a function of trust. When we trust God, we are filled with His peace. The prophet Isaiah proclaimed: "You will keep in perfect peace those whose minds are steadfast, because they trust in you" (Isaiah 26:3).

Next time you worry, thank God for the opportunity to find joy in Him, as you identify with the sufferings of Christ. He will fill you with peace as you trust in Him.

Peace With Others

Philippians 4:5

WHEN you worry, are you harsh with those around you? If we are honest, each of us will admit this is often the case. Worry robs us of joy and peace and leads us to being harsh with anyone in our vicinity, including God.

For worriers, Paul first prescribed peace with God. Second, he prescribed peace with others. The apostle instructed: "Let your gentleness be evident to all. The Lord is near" (Philippians 4:5). God's proximity to us is as close as the air that is in and around us. When we have peace with Him in our hearts, He frees us to have peace with others through gentleness, rather than harshness.

Gentleness is power under the Spirit's control. Solomon, an advocate of gentleness, taught that there is joy for those who promote peace (Proverbs 12:20), continuing that an anxious heart weighs a man down but a kind word cheers him up (Proverbs 12:25).

If you find yourself worrying, thank God for the opportunity to find joy in Him, and also surrender any harshness to the Holy Spirit and be soft with others, even when it's difficult. Use kind words to promote peace and joy. God will renew your relationships with His perfect peace.

Peace Within Ourselves

Philippians 4:6–7

DO you ever worry so much that your heart hurts?

For worriers, Paul first prescribed peace with God, peace with others, and, finally, peace within ourselves. The apostle wrote that we should not worry about anything. Rather, we should pray about everything so Christ would align our hearts with His, giving us perfect peace.

"Do not be anxious about anything, but in every situation, by prayer and petition, with thanksgiving, present your requests to God. And the peace of God, which transcends all understanding, will guard your hearts and your minds in Christ Jesus" (Philippians 4:6–7).

Anxiety's misaligned inner being divides trust between God and ourselves, which actually pains our hearts. Prayer is worry's antidote because it places our trust solely in Christ. Prayer is our inner being continually connected with God's, where He shapes our hearts to be like Christ's. In that connection, His desires become our desires.

If you begin to worry, pray—go online with God and upload your requests to Him. He will download His presence, and you will experience the peace of your heart aligned with His.

Christic-Like Qualities

Philippians 4:8–9

HAVE you noticed that we practice what we ponder? The focus of our minds affects our behavior. When we dwell on Christ, our lives are filled with peace. When we don't, we experience chaos.

Paul summarized a list of Christ-like qualities to ponder and put into practice.

"Finally, brothers and sisters, whatever is true, whatever is noble, whatever is right, whatever is pure, whatever is lovely, whatever is admirable—if anything is excellent or praiseworthy—think about such things" (Philippians 4:8).

Interestingly, the opposite characteristics are traits of Satan. That's why we should focus on what is *true* (John 14:6), rather than *false* (John 8:44); *noble* (James 2:7), not *useless* (2 Corinthians 2:11); *right* (Philippians 1:1; 3:9), as opposed to *wicked* (Acts 13:10); *pure* (1 John 3:3), instead of *mixed* (2 Corinthians 11:14); *lovely* (Ephesians 2:14; 1 Corinthians 13:6), rather than *selfish* (James 3:15–16); *admirable* (Luke 4:18), over *shameful* (1 Peter 5:8–10); *excellent* (Hebrews 5:9; 7:28), in lieu of *mediocre* (1 John 3:8); and *praiseworthy* (Philippians 2:10–11), over *accusatory* (Revelation 12:10).

Paul vividly anchored the scale for our thoughts. When we focus on the mind of Christ, we avoid what is false, useless, wicked, mixed, selfish, shameful, mediocre, and accusatory. With every thought, we stand at a crossroads, whether to pursue qualities of Christ or those of Satan. Pondering Christ gives us a heart reconciled with His that puts His characteristics into practice and gives us peace (Philippians 4:9). Focusing on the traits of the devil causes us strife.

Memorize Paul's list of Christ-like character traits, remembering that we practice what we ponder, and practice makes perfect peace.

Contentment

Philippians 4:10–13

W HAT is the secret to contentment?

Two thousand years ago, stoic philosophers referred to contentment as "self-sufficiency," or "to be independent of external circumstances." Contentment literally means "to be held together." Inside each of us is a desire to hold it all together. Paul closed his letter to the church at Philippi describing the secret to attaining this inner peace: trust in the Giver, not the gifts.

"I rejoiced greatly in the Lord that at last you renewed your concern for me. Indeed, you were concerned, but you had no opportunity to show it. I am not saying this because I am in need, for I have learned to be content whatever the circumstances. I know what it is to be in need, and I know what it is to have plenty. I have learned the secret of being content in any and every situation, whether well fed or hungry, whether living in plenty or in want. I can do all this through him who gives me strength" (Philippians 4:10–13).

First, Paul taught the secret to freedom from allowing circumstances to control our emotions is to trust in the Giver, Christ

(Philippians 4:10–13). Paul thanked the church for their gift to his ministry to advance the kingdom of Christ. He noted he had learned, whether in plenty or in want, the secret to contentment was that he could do all things through Christ who gave him strength (Philippians 4:13).

We must grasp the power of the word *through*. Every circumstance, whether we win, lose, or draw in the world's eyes, is an opportunity to grow in our intimacy with Christ, as we live through our Restorer who continually renews us. True inner peace comes only in Christ. In essence, Paul described contentment as Christ-sufficiency.

Do you trust in the Giver or the gifts? How many times have you stopped during your day and asked God for His guidance in making decisions? Try the Philippians 4:13 Experiment and do everything through Christ, who will restore your heart.

Don't Trust in the Gifts

Philippians 4:14–23

DO you believe in God's principle of replenishment or do you worry about having enough resources to be content? In our fallen perspective, we have a tendency to trust in only what we can see. Paul called the church at Philippi to trust in the Giver, not the gifts (Philippians 4:14–23).

Charlatan philosophers of Paul's day would stand on street corners of cities like Philippi, gathering followers with their good looks, expensive clothes, and articulate speech, in hopes of laying siege to the money of the unsuspecting citizens. Paul painted the church's gift to him as radically different from money given to the selfish philosophers because he did not benefit financially. Instead, the money was used to advance the kingdom of Christ. We see the same paradigm today.

Paul called followers of Christ to be content enough to give their time, talent, and treasure to the kingdom, describing this generosity as a fragrant offering pleasing to the Giver of life and its resources (Philippians 4:18). He concluded with a powerful promise from the teachings of Jesus: "My God will meet all your needs according to the riches of his glory in Christ Jesus" (Philippians 4:19). Paul believed in God's restoration of hearts and resources.

When you find yourself behaving as if you are trusting in the gifts and not the Giver, ask God to transform your heart. Trust in Christ the Giver not the gifts by being content enough to give your time, talent, and treasure to someone in need, advancing His kingdom. You might give to a church, a Christian school, a youth organization, or even spend time with a young person needing guidance.

Worry is the problem, prayer is the solution, and peace is the result. When we take up Paul's challenge, we can experience peace with God, peace with others, and peace within ourselves, discovering true contentment in Christ-sufficiency. Fully surrendering our lives to Christ brings us joy that empowers us to trust in the Giver, not the gifts, generously sharing with others in need because we believe in God's restoration of our hearts and our resources.

Wisdom in Conflict Management Styles

Proverbs 3:5–6

HOW do you manage conflict?

Solomon realized we were guaranteed conflict on this side where two objects would repeatedly attempt to occupy the same space at the same time. Consequently, he left us nearly 1,000 wise sayings for conflict management.

Psychologists describe a grid of five conflict management styles, each determined by our perspective of another person's interest versus that of our own: (1) *compromise* (moderate toward another's interest/ moderate toward our interest); (2) *compete* (low toward another's interest/high toward our interest); (3) *accommodate* (high toward another's interest/low toward our interest); (4) *avoid* (low toward another's interest/low toward our interest); and (5) *collaborate* (high toward another's interest/high toward our interest).

The challenge is discerning when to apply each conflict management style. Fortunately, Proverbs offers insight to this question: "Trust in the Lord with all your heart and lean not on your own understanding; in all your ways submit to him, and he will make your paths straight" (Proverbs 3:5–6).

Wisdom in conflict management styles begins with trusting in the Holy Spirit to guide us toward God's interest. When we seek His guidance, He makes our paths straight, or smooth.

Today, practice the *Five-Second Rule*. When two objects attempt to occupy the same space at the same time, take five seconds to ask God, "What do You want me to do?" He will smooth your paths with wisdom to manage your conflict.

Wisdom in Conflict Management Styles: Compromise

Proverbs 25:8

DURING interpersonal conflict, when do you compromise? Compromise is moderate toward another's interest and moderate toward our interest. Each party in the conflict gives in a little. Consequently, we should compromise when both choices at hand are acceptable to us. The key word is *acceptable*. In conflict, if we can accept both choices (our initial position or the proposed compromise) because they have similar outcomes, then we should consider compromise.

Often, we see compromise as similar to competing for the best deal. However, Proverbs says that we need to exercise caution in competing because we are not always as right as we think we are: "What you have seen with your eyes do not bring hastily to court, for what will you do in the end if your neighbor puts you to shame?" (Proverbs 25:7c–8).

Proverbs tells us that partiality toward ourselves is not good, and it often takes very little incentive for us to demonstrate it: "To show partiality is not good—yet a person will do wrong for a piece of bread" (Proverbs 28:21). Thus, compromise can be wise.

Are you in a conflict where you have hardened your heart to a workable compromise? Give in a little to the other person's proposal or initiate a compromise.

Wisdom in Conflict Management Styles: Compete

Proverbs 2:12, 16; 19:8

DURING interpersonal conflict, when do you compete? Compete means we will pursue our own interest at the expense of another's, making the perceived task of greater importance than the relationship. It usually implies a zero-sum game. We will win while the other person equally loses. Proverbs says that wisdom will save us from wicked competitors whose words are perverted: "Wisdom will save you from the ways of wicked men, from men whose words are perverse" (Proverbs 2:12).

When engaging in conflict, we run a high risk of losing, especially when the other person is willing to say one thing and do another. However, when there is a moral issue at stake, we must compete. Proverbs describes a man who is vulnerable to a woman who is not his wife, imploring that wisdom will save him from her seductive words: "Wisdom will save you also from the adulterous woman, from the wayward woman with her seductive words" (Proverbs 2:16).

When we are about to sin, we need to compete wisely for our own interest. Solomon said that it is wise to love your own soul: "The one who gets wisdom loves life; the one who cherishes understanding will soon prosper" (Proverbs 19:8).

Are you in a conflict of right versus wrong by biblical standards—an affair, an illegal business proposition, a lie, or a threat to someone's life? Compete for what is right in God's sight. Read the above verses, and go to a trusted friend for wisdom on how to compete for what is right with all your might.

Wisdom in Conflict Management Styles: Accommodate When Wrong

Proverbs 6:1–5

ARE you caught in a conflict that would dissolve if you would merely accommodate another person's interest? Solomon offered four scenarios when it is wise to accommodate.

First, we must accommodate another's interest when we are wrong. Solomon instructed that if we have been trapped by a foolish decision, then we should go, humble ourselves, accommodate the other person involved, and be free (Proverbs 6:1–5).

It is foolish to conceal our sin; it is wise to confess it: "He who conceals his sins does not prosper, but whoever confesses and renounces them finds mercy" (Proverbs 28:13).

A wise person finds goodwill in accommodating another, but only a fool mocks at accommodation: "Fools mock at making amends for sin, but goodwill is found among the upright" (Proverbs 14:9). If we have played the fool and exalted ourselves over another person, or if we have planned evil, we need to accommodate (Proverbs 30:32–33).

Examine your heart and behavior. Are you wrong about how you are managing your conflict and attempting to defend that wrong? If so, simply ask the person with whom you are in conflict, "What can I do to accommodate you?" God will use your humble heart to begin reconciling the relationship.

Wisdom in Conflict Management Styles: When to Accommodate

Proverbs 17:9

ARE you experiencing a conflict where you are winning the argument but potentially losing a valued relationship? Perhaps it's time to consider how to accommodate the other person. Proverbs provides four circumstances when we should accommodate our counterpart in conflict.

First, remember we accommodate when we are in the wrong (Proverbs 6:1–5). If pride has fueled our choices, then we should confess our foolish behavior to the person we have offended (Proverbs 28:13) and accommodate their interest (Proverbs 30:32–33).

Second, we accommodate when the issue is of greater importance to the other person involved. Sometimes, it will cost us little or nothing and greatly profit our counterpart in conflict to accommodate them. Solomon taught that it is to our glory to accommodate an offender (Proverbs 19:11). Even when we accommodate an enemy by meeting their needs, they may feel ashamed by their sinful actions (Proverbs 25:21–22).

Third, we accommodate when confronting might bring irreparable damage. Occasionally, our risk to confront is greater than the

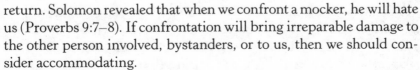

return. Solomon revealed that when we confront a mocker, he will hate us (Proverbs 9:7–8). If confrontation will bring irreparable damage to the other person involved, bystanders, or to us, then we should consider accommodating.

Fourth, we accommodate when the relationship is of greater value than our personal stakes. The maintenance of a friendship is frequently much more important than what we lose by accommodating another person. At that point, we should simply accommodate. Solomon revealed: "Whoever would foster love covers over an offense, but whoever repeats the matter separates close friends" (Proverbs 17:9).

Ask the Holy Spirit to examine your contribution to the conflict. Would you rather win the relationship or win the argument? Assuming the friendship is more significant to you than the dispute, go to that person and say, "I am so sorry for my contribution to our conflict. Our relationship means more to me than our differences. How can I help us reconcile?"

Wisdom in Conflict Management Styles:
Avoid

Proverbs 26:4–5; 20:3; 26:17

ARE you risking combat with a fool? Are you thinking of getting involved in a quarrel that is not your own without being asked? Perhaps, it's time to consider how to avoid the person with whom you are experiencing tension. Proverbs provides two scenarios when we should avoid our counterpart in conflict.

First, we should always avoid combat with a fool because we cannot win. "Do not answer a fool according to his folly, or you yourself will be just like him. Answer a fool according to his folly, or he will be wise in his own eyes" (Proverbs 26:4–5).

If we answer according to his tangled web of folly, then we will become like him. If we engage with a fool and let his words go idly by, then he will be wise in his own eyes. Solomon taught: "It is to one's honor to avoid strife, but every fool is quick to quarrel" (Proverbs 20:3).

Second, we should avoid a quarrel that is not our own when we are not asked to help: "Like one who grabs a stray dog by the ears is someone who rushes into a quarrel not their own" (Proverbs 26:17). When we engage in such a conflict, we will feel the pain of the teeth of those involved lacerating our flesh.

Are you nearing combat with a fool? Are you thinking of getting involved in a quarrel that is not your own without being asked? If the answer to either question is yes, then avoid the conflict. God's wisdom in conflict management will protect you from the consequences of foolish choices.

Wisdom in Conflict Management Styles: Collaborate

Proverbs 11:27; 13:15; Philippians 2:3–4

HOW often do you collaborate when you experience interpersonal conflict? God's design for wise conflict management is that we work together to seek win-win solutions. Solomon said that we find what we seek: "Whoever seeks good finds favor, but evil comes to the one who searches for it" (Proverbs 11:27).

In order to discover goodwill, we must literally co-labor with the other person involved in our conflict. This includes a journey inside each party to move from the positions to the underlying interests of the conflict. Often, the interests of both parties are the same.

Paul taught: "Do nothing out of selfish ambition or empty pride, but in humility consider others more important than yourselves. Each of you should look not only to your own interests, but also to the interests of the others" (Philippians 2:3–4 BSB).

We need the Holy Spirit's insight to discover another person's interests in order to collaborate. Solomon observed: "Good understanding wins favor, but the way of the faithless is difficult" (Proverbs 13:15 BSB). *Understanding* is insight. When we ask the Spirit of God to shine light into another person's heart, we are able to see his or her underlying interests. Then we can understand those interests and collaborate for a win-win solution to conflict management. God's wisdom will move us through conflict to community.

Commit today to collaborating through the conflict in your life. Co-labor with others for wise, win-win solutions by looking not only to your own, unselfish interests, but also the interests of others, including those of Christ (Philippians 2:1–5).

Leading Difficult People Through Listening

James 1:19

H AVE you ever encountered a difficult person? At least four exist. They include the aggressive, the complainer, the people pleaser, and the passive resistive. The first two are direct in their challenges. The latter two are indirect. Beware, the difficult person might be you!

Each of us has a bent toward one of these behaviors; left to ourselves, outside surrender to Christ, we borrow the difficult behavior from each of the four types. A difficult person is *disconnected* from the hearts of others, *undeflected* through his difficult behavior, *non-reflected* in his heart condition by those whom he encounters, and *misdirected* toward foolishness over wisdom.

When dealing with a difficult person, our first inclination often stems from our sinful nature, which will be foolish, rather than wise. We will be slow to listen, quick to speak, and quick to become angry, damaging our relationships. When we are surrendered to being led by the Spirit of Christ, we will be wise. Jesus's half-brother James taught: "My dear brothers and sisters, take note of this: Everyone should be quick to listen, slow to speak and slow to become angry" (James 1:19).

Solomon instructed: "To answer before listening—that is folly and shame" (Proverbs 18:13).

When you encounter a difficult person, be quick to listen, slow to speak, and slow to become angry. It won't be you restoring your relationships; rather, it will be Christ in you.

Connect With Their Heart Like a LEGO

Proverbs 20:5

IN order to listen and lead the difficult person, we must make at least four wise movements: (1) *connect* with their heart like a *LEGO* (Proverbs 20:5); (2) *deflect* their difficult behavior like a *shield* (Proverbs 17:9); (3) *reflect* their heart like a *mirror* (Proverbs 27:19); and (4) *direct* them toward wisdom like a *highway sign* (Proverbs 24:11–12). Each practice is performed uniquely with each respective difficult type (1 Thessalonians 5:14).

A difficult person is disconnected from the hearts of those around him. Their coworkers, family members, and friends often become stuck on his external behavior and never make a connection with their heart. In order to do so, we must ask questions about their choices, thoughts, feelings, and even prayers. Then we must listen. Solomon said: "The purposes of a person's heart are deep waters, but one who has insight draws them out" (Proverbs 20:5).

Are you drawing out the deep waters of the difficult person's heart? When you encounter any individual, recognize that they have the capacity to be difficult in at least one of the following ways: as an aggressive, a complainer, a people pleaser, or a passive resistive. Before any difficult behavior begins, connect with that person's heart. Ask questions and learn about their choices, thoughts, feelings, and prayers. This will establish a heart connection through listening and serve as preventive maintenance for the relationship. When that person becomes difficult, ask yourself why. Now that you have a heart connection, you can examine their desires and continue to do so through asking and listening.

Deflect Difficult Behavior Like a Shield

Proverbs 17:9

HOW well do you deflect difficult behavior?

Difficult behavior includes coarse words, a rude tone of voice, demeaning facial gestures, evil eye contact, improper use of the hands and body, and even ignoring a person altogether. Most people never get past these flaming arrows because they cannot control their own prideful responses to the negative behavior.

We need to deflect difficult behavior to Christ who gives us the power to do so because He has conquered sin at the cross, fully paying its penalty once and for all. Deflecting moves past the unpleasant behavior without disengaging from the relationship. Proverbs records: "Whoever would foster love covers over an offense, but whoever repeats the matter separates close friends" (Proverbs 17:9). Deflecting covers over an offense.

When you encounter difficult behavior, remain engaged with the person's heart and deflect his sin like a shield. Humble your heart to Christ and the person who is being difficult. This will allow you to be wise in deflecting their flaming arrows. Consequently, it will not be you, but Christ in you who will do the deflecting.

Reflect the Heart Like a Mirror

Proverbs 27:19

WHEN dealing with a difficult person, do you struggle to reflect that person's heart in a way that communicates you understand their desires? Unfortunately, most of us rarely stay engaged long enough to get that far and see that deeply.

Because so few people connect with a difficult person's heart, and even fewer deflect the difficult behavior, rarely does anyone reflect the difficult person's will, intellect, spirit, and emotions. Reflecting is paramount to the difficult person's behavior being revealed to him in a nonthreatening way through questions and images.

Solomon taught: "As water reflects the face, so one's life reflects the heart" (Proverbs 27:19).

When you are engaging with a difficult behavior, connect with the person's heart, deflect their flaming arrows, and reflect your journey to understanding their desires that you gain from listening. Do this in the form of a sincere question so you are not presuming you know their desires completely and accurately. Possibly use relevant images that will engage the person's heart in an unthreatening fashion. Continue to learn and lead through listening.

When you humbly and wisely reflect the difficult person's heart through listening, it won't be you leading; rather, it will be Christ in you.

Direct Difficult People Toward Wisdom
Like a Highway Sign

Proverbs 24:11–12

A FTER connecting, deflecting, and reflecting, comes the directing. When the difficult person understands we are engaged with their heart, they become more open to our suggestions. This is when we want to direct them toward wisdom. Often, this is most effective when we offer multiple wise choices.

In one of the Thirty Sayings of the Wise, Solomon wrote: "Rescue those being led away to death; hold back those staggering toward slaughter. If you say, 'But we knew nothing about this,' does not he who weighs the heart perceive it? Does not he who guards your life know it? Will he not repay everyone according to what they have done?" (Proverbs 24:11–12). God calls us to direct others towards wisdom.

Next time you encounter a difficult person, connect with their heart like a LEGO, deflect their difficult behavior like a shield, reflect your understanding of their heart to them like a mirror, and direct them toward wisdom like a highway sign by offering wise alternatives for them to consider. When you lead wisely through listening, God will provide a path for you to navigate through conflict to community.

Leading the Aggressive

James 1:19

DO you have an aggressive person in your life?

The aggressive raises the volume of their voice in order to take control of the task at hand. The volume increases as the conflict escalates. They often see victory defined by the axiom, "The loudest voice wins."

In order to take control of their counterpart in the conflict, the aggressive often uses insults, which are designed to garner a reaction from the recipient. When the recipient reacts with the intended response, they yield emotional control to the aggressive.

To accomplish their end goal, the aggressive steam rolls over any competition, including innocent bystanders. This works for them because most people allow it to occur.

The aggressive will not be robbed of control or their will. They will leverage their difficult behavior to maintain control of not only accomplishing their desired task, but also the people in their way. James offered profound wisdom to deal with difficult people, including the aggressive: "My dear brothers and sisters, take note of this: Everyone should be quick to listen, slow to speak and slow to become angry" (James 1:19).

In order to lead the aggressive, we must listen to their heart—their will, mind, emotions, and spirit. The chambers of the heart can be discovered by learning their choices, thoughts, feelings, and even their prayers. Connect with their heart like a LEGO (Proverbs 20:5). Deflect their difficult behavior like a shield (Proverbs 17:9). Reflect their heart like a mirror (Proverbs 27:19). Direct them toward wisdom like a highway sign (Proverbs 24:11–12).

In an example from the Bible, Jonathan used wisdom's tools to lead his aggressive father King Saul through listening (1 Samuel 20:24–34). Saul had exploded with his son Jonathan who modeled most of what we see in Proverbs for wisely leading an aggressive through listening: (1) *answer gently* (Proverbs 15:1), (2) *ignore insults* (Proverbs 12:16), (3) *confront lovingly* (Proverbs 25:12; 15:31), and (4) *offer choices*, all of which are wise alternatives acceptable to you (Proverbs 8:10; 16:16).

Leading the Aggressive Through Listening:
Answer Gently

Proverbs 15:1

DOES the aggressive person in your life ratchet up their tone to get what they want?

The aggressive will be loud, so rather than be intimidated by the volume, answer gently. Solomon offered: "A gentle answer turns away wrath, but a harsh word stirs up anger" (Proverbs 15:1). This is one of the most powerful and useful verses in the Bible. A harsh word just adds fuel to anger's fire, but a gentle one smolders it. Rather than going with our fallen inclination to raise the volume as well, we must answer gently. Each word in this verse is vital.

First, we must answer, or the aggressive will run over us. They will respect the fact that we clearly communicate a response.

Second, the style of the answer should be gentle, powerful and under the Spirit's control. This will help bring the volume down. A gentle answer gets us connected with the aggressive person's heart like a LEGO. They stop their rage and begin to think about our response. Jonathan appeared to gently answer his irate father King Saul (1 Samuel 20:24–29).

Next time you encounter an aggressive person, listen for any good hidden in the heart of the person and affirm it. "That's really a good idea!" or "You are really on to something!" are examples. Sometimes, the gentle affirmation will take place in a question, "Could you please explain that?"

All the while, remember that it's difficult to argue in a whisper.

Leading the Aggressive Through Listening:
Ignore Insults

Proverbs 12:16

WHAT is your first reaction to an insult? Do you reciprocate or even debate its validity?

The aggressive person designs and deploys an insult to generate a reaction—one that gives them control. When we do not react, the insult is defused. We must ignore insults, rather than immediately showing our annoyance. Solomon taught: "Fools show their annoyance at once, but the prudent overlook an insult" (Proverbs 12:16).

Someone in my life used insults as a way to gain the upper hand in business negotiations. At the outset of experiencing his behavior, I would debate the insult, which would escalate our discussion into a heated discourse, giving him the upper hand. Then I read Proverbs 12:16, so I tried applying it. The first time I ignored his insult, it appeared he didn't know what to do because I didn't give him the reaction he wanted. I must say, everything changed after that.

Ignoring an insult includes maintaining listening body posture and attentive facial expressions as we deflect flaming arrows soaring our way. Jonathan ignored his father King Saul's insult.

Next time an aggressive person insults you, ignore it, deflecting their demeaning words like a shield. Paul said that we should take up the shield of faith that allows us to extinguish all the flaming arrows of the evil one (Ephesians 6:16). This deflects the heart-piercing words of an insult, placing us in a position of wisdom and strength that only God can provide.

Leading the Aggressive Through Listening: Confront Lovingly

Proverbs 25:12; 15:31; 28:23

HOW do you confront the aggressive in your life? By text? Through email? Possibly, not at all?

God calls us to lovingly confront the aggressive: "Like an earring of gold or an ornament of fine gold is the rebuke of a wise judge to a listening ear" (Proverbs 25:12). *Confront* literally means "face-to-face." Confronting by text, telephone, through another person, or via letters or emails is not actually confronting because it is not face-to-face. To confront lovingly means we have the difficult person's best interests in mind.

When we confront the aggressive in love, we increase the chances that they will listen to us: "Whoever heeds life-giving correction will be at home among the wise" (Proverbs 15:31). Confronting lets the aggressive know we have peered beyond their behavior into their heart, getting to their ultimate desire for control. At the same time, confronting actually increases the aggressive person's level of respect for the confronter: "Whoever rebukes a person will in the end gain favor rather than one who has a flattering tongue" (Proverbs 28:23).

Jonathan confronted his aggressive father King Saul face-to-face with relevant questions (1 Samuel 20:32).

In one of Scripture's most insightful statements regarding our wise conflict management with difficult people, Paul taught to confront the aggressive (1 Thessalonians 5:14). This needs to be done in total humility, recognizing we are capable of the same sin (Galatians 6:1). Oftentimes, we can seek to better reflect a person's heart by learning more when we ask the simple question, "May I have the opportunity to better understand what you are saying?"

Next time you engage with an aggressive person, lovingly confront them face-to-face with the fact that you have connected with their heart. Because you have deflected their difficult behavior you can reflect your understanding of their desires.

Leading the Aggressive Through Listening: Give Wise Choices

Proverbs 8:10; 16:16

DO you ever feel hopeless in your attempts to deal with the strong will of an aggressive person? Solomon offered a secret to leading the aggressive through listening.

In order to direct the aggressive toward wisdom, we must offer choices to the aggressive so that they are not robbed of their God-given will: "Choose my instruction instead of silver, knowledge rather than choice gold" (Proverbs 8:10). The strong will of an aggressive always needs to make a choice. In order to effectively be used by God, we can offer wise alternatives. Solomon taught: "How much better to get wisdom than gold, to get insight rather than silver!" (Proverbs 16:16).

It is imperative these choices are wise alternatives that are acceptable to us. This allows the aggressive to always choose, while we remain in agreement with their choice. When we don't listen to the aggressive, we rob them of choosing wisdom. "Would you like to call Bill or go see him to reconcile?" is an example of giving a choice from acceptable alternatives.

Whereas Jonathan's questions were open-ended, he allowed his father King Saul the opportunity to choose wisdom. In Jonathan's scenario, his father was still aggressive when Jonathan left him to choose (1 Samuel 20:32–34). Sometimes, that will be the case. When the aggressive remains heated and out of control, it might be necessary for us to leave the scene after engaging wisely.

The next time you are faced with an aggressive person, after answering gently, ignoring their insults, and confronting them lovingly, offer wise choices, all of which are acceptable to you. This will help you direct the aggressive toward wisdom.

Leading the Complainer Through Listening

Philippians 2:14

DO you frequently encounter a complainer in your life? How does each interaction make you feel?

The second difficult person is the direct hitter known as the complainer. A complainer whines for at least four reasons: they fear being misunderstood; they focus on the negative; they fight to be right, seeing issues in life as black and white (right or wrong); and they frustrate their perfectionist self from their unmet, unrealistically high expectations.

The complainer lives in fear of being misunderstood. Consequently, they often over-describe issues in such detail that they leave the listeners more confused than before they began to speak. The complainer focuses on and remembers the negative. Although ninety percent of a person, task, or object might be positive, the complainer focuses on and analyzes the ten percent that is negative, frequently defining the whole as such. This often discourages those they encounter.

The complainer's desire for security comes with an embedded passion to be right. Consequently, they fight to be mistake-free, creating neat, tidy compartments of right and wrong. This compartmentalizing creates boundaries that did not previously exist, oftentimes leaving others feeling compartmentalized as well.

The complainer is a perfectionist who routinely imposes unrealistic expectations on themselves and others. As a result, they are often frustrated and so are those around them. Consequently, we must be careful not to complain ourselves. The apostle Paul taught: "Do everything without grumbling or arguing" (Philippians 2:14).

In order to lead the complainer, we must listen to their heart—their will, intellect, emotions, and spirit. These four chambers of the heart can be discovered by learning about their choices, thoughts, feelings, and even their prayers.

Read Luke 5:30–39 to discover how Jesus listened to and led a group of religious complainers who whined about Jesus and His disciples dining with tax collectors and "sinners" at Matthew's party. Jesus connected, deflected, reflected, and directed, implementing four wise practices. He: *comforted, encouraged, rephrased absolute statements with a question,* and *taught excellence rather than perfection.*

The next time you encounter a complainer, apply Jesus's four practices. It won't be you leading the complainer through listening; rather, it will be the Spirit of Christ in you.

Leading the Complainer Through Listening: Comfort

Proverbs 16:24; 25:11

OUR first step in leading a complainer through listening is to comfort them, connecting with their heart. *Comfort* literally means "to call alongside." It comes from the Latin, *com* meaning "together" and *fortis*, which is translated "strong." Comfort strengthens together.

Comforting a complainer means that we come alongside them and communicate the words, "I understand." This short sentence builds an emotional bridge between the complainer's heart and ours. They are comforted by the connection of understanding, which opens the door to encouragement. Solomon counseled: "Gracious words are a honeycomb, sweet to the soul and healing to the bones" (Proverbs 16:24). He also said: "A word fitly spoken is like apples of gold in settings of silver" (Proverbs 25:11 BSB). The right word at the right time is comforting and priceless.

The complaining Pharisees asked why Jesus and His disciples dined with tax collectors and "sinners" (Luke 5:30). Jesus's response to the Pharisees: "It is not the healthy who need a doctor, but the sick" (Luke 5:31) communicated He had understood their perspective. Paul said that our comfort comes from God and is designed to overflow into others (2 Corinthians 1:3–5).

The next time you encounter a complainer, connect with their heart—their desire for security and their fear of being misunderstood. Comfort them with the phrase, "I understand." Follow these words with describing an experience in your own life that is similar to the complainer's scenario.

Jesus called the Holy Spirit the *Comforter*. When you comfort the complainer, it won't be you; rather, it will be the Spirit of Christ in you, who comes alongside the difficult person and strengthens together.

Leading the Complainer Through Listening: Encourage

1 Thessalonians 5:14; Proverbs 12:25; 15:23

*E*NCOURAGEMENT includes the Latin, *cor*, which means "heart." An encourager breathes life into the hearts of others. A discourager sucks the life right out of them. Encouragement is imperative when leading a complainer through listening.

Encouraging the complainer means that we reveal the positive in the situation, breathing life into their heart. In essence, we offer hope. Shifting their focus from the negative to the positive provides an environment for the complainer's anxiety to change to courage. Paul encouraged believers in Thessalonica to encourage the timid, those who focused on the negative (1 Thessalonians 5:14).

Solomon advised: "Anxiety weighs down the heart, but a kind word cheers it up" (Proverbs 12:25). Listening to and leading the complainer by deflecting their behavior with encouragement—in spite of their negativity—will actually bring us joy (Proverbs 15:23). The Pharisees were so focused on the negative they had created 1,500 additional laws to protect followers from breaking the Torah. Jesus encouraged the Pharisees to see the positive with His underlying mission: "I have not come to call the righteous, but sinners to repentance" (Luke 5:32).

After comforting the complainer, deflect their negative behavior and encourage them to see the positive in the situation. The focal point of their new, positive perspective can center on a person or task. It might capture a unique quality in the complainer or another person involved in the conflict, or even focus on a benefit from the task of processing the conflict. It won't be you encouraging the complainer; rather, it will be Christ in you.

Leading the Complainer Through Listening: Rephrase Absolute Statements With a Question

Colossians 4:5–6; Proverbs 27:9

QUESTIONS generate answers, but statements produce resistance. Questions help us lead a complainer through listening.

Because they see issues as black and white (right or wrong), the complainer fights to be right and is notorious for making absolute statements that leverage the words *always* and *never*. For example, "You never call me!" When we listen wisely, we *rephrase an absolute statement in the form of a question*: "Do you really mean *never*?" This gently implies the exaggeration just made by the complainer, causing them to wrestle with their perspective and readjust their statement. Often, they will discover their desire to be objective has led them to be quite subjective.

Paul likened this wise kind of response to salt, saying that we should be wise in the way we act towards outsiders so that we may know how to answer everyone (Colossians 4:5–6). Solomon equated this earnest counsel with joy to the heart: "Perfume and incense bring joy to the heart, and the pleasantness of a friend springs from their heartfelt advice" (Proverbs 27:9).

In Luke 5:33 Jesus rephrased a Pharisee's absolute statement ("John's disciples often fast and pray, and so do the disciples of the Pharisees, but yours go on eating and drinking") in the form of a question: "Can you make the friends of the bridegroom fast while he is with them?" (Luke 5:34). Jesus was saying that it was the right time to celebrate because God was among them.

Follow comfort and encouragement with reflection, reflecting the complainer's heart to be right by rephrasing an absolute statement in the form of a question. Be alert for words like *always* and *never*. Ask, "Do you really mean always? Do you really mean never?" It won't be you leading the complainer through listening; rather, it will be Christ in you.

Leading the Complainer Through Listening: Teaching Excellence Rather Than Perfection

Proverbs 20:9; 28:13; 13:14; 24:13–14

I S the complainer in your life a perfectionist? If so, they—most likely—possess a propensity to learn. Therefore, we can teach them how excellence, not perfection, is God's design. Teaching excellence rather than perfection to the complainer means we communicate how God intends us to manage our expectations. *Proverbs*, which means generally true most of the time, teaches us how to do so.

Excellence features two components: *authenticity* and *wisdom*. The complainer is a frustrated perfectionist, but is willing to learn. While their high expectations can be beneficial at times, the complainer has a blind spot to the fact that everyone and everything except God will fall short. Whereas perfectionism implies flawlessness, *excellence* recognizes *authenticity*, the truth about one's strengths and shortcomings, and *wisdom*, the intersection of God's righteousness with street smarts—shrewdly doing the best with what we have.

Authenticity implies that someone is genuine, or true. We often refer to an authentic person as "the real thing." The truth is that no one can say they are perfect, or without sin (Proverbs 20:9). Authenticity demands we confess our sin to God and others and discover His restorative mercy (Proverbs 28:13).

Teaching wisdom is a fountain of life, which turns a complainer from the snares of death (Proverbs 13:14). Solomon painted the picture of wisdom energizing the soul, providing eternal hope: "Eat honey, my son, for it is good; honey from the comb is sweet to your taste. Know also that wisdom is like honey for you: If you find it, there is a future hope for you, and your hope will not be cut off" (Proverbs 24:13–14).

In response to the complaining Pharisees, Jesus taught excellence (authenticity and wisdom) versus perfection through a parable about the old being unable to contain the new. The old, perfectionist, religious system could not hold captive the new, authentic expression of Christ's kingdom in one's heart (Luke 5:35–39).

Someone might say, "Hey, in the Sermon on the Mount, Jesus called his disciples to be perfect" (Matthew 5:48). Perfect means complete. We are to be complete in our love for all, including difficult people (Matthew 5:43–48). This occurs only when we surrender our hearts to the authenticity and wisdom of Christ.

Comfort, encourage, rephrase any absolute statement in the form of a question, and then direct the complainer to excellence—authenticity and wisdom—over perfection. Help the complainer recognize the truth about the situation and wisely readjust their expectations, which are thwarted on their audience. Give them a safe place to accurately express their personal strengths and shortcomings and offer wisdom for them to do the best with what they have. Do this by modeling excellence over perfection yourself. Humbly communicate authenticity and wisdom, rather than an embellished image of flawlessness. Follow Jesus's example of listening and leading the complainer. He implemented the wisdom we glean from Proverbs. It's no wonder Paul referred to Christ as the wisdom of God (1 Corinthians 1:24).

Leading the People Pleaser Through Listening

Proverbs 18:2; 26:22–25, 27–28; 29:5

THE third difficult person is the people pleaser who is noticeably people-oriented as opposed to the task-oriented aggressive and complainer. They agree with everyone. Consequently, the people pleaser is indirect in their difficult behavior. They create negative conflict when they promise everyone what they want to hear. The result is unmet expectations because the people pleaser is unable to do what they promised when the interests of two parties collide. Their desire to please flows from an underlying motive to bring significance to themselves as they seek attention, acceptance, affection, and approval. They utilize at least four persuasive tools that stem from their gift to gab: gossip, exaggeration, flattery, and a chameleon complex that desires to say yes.

The people pleaser gossips, although they never see themselves as doing so. In their nonstop conversational banter, the people pleaser shares unverified and even classified information about other people. Their desire for significance creates a seemingly insatiable desire to be the bearer of news as they delight in airing their own opinions (Proverbs 18:2). This idle conversation can be contagious: "The words of a gossip are like choice morsels; they go down to the inmost parts" (Proverbs 26:22).

The people pleaser is gifted in leveraging emotions for their persuasive pleas. In order to do so, they exaggerate facts with their words and nonverbal cues. Their loud tone of voice, animated hand gestures,

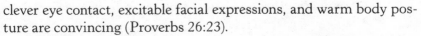

clever eye contact, excitable facial expressions, and warm body posture are convincing (Proverbs 26:23).

The people pleaser uses charming words to get what they want, including praise from others. This is flattery. In essence, the people pleaser tells others what they want to hear (Proverbs 26:24–25, 28). This creates a net that can snag their audience: "Those who flatter their neighbors are spreading nets for their feet" (Proverbs 29:5).

The people pleaser is passionate about pleasing people. Their low expectations of self and others, combined with their love to have fun, provide an agreeable atmosphere where they genuinely want to say yes to everyone they encounter. In essence, they become difficult by default. When they say yes to two different persons who have opposing interests, they create negative conflict when those interests collide (Proverbs 26:27).

In order to lead the people pleaser, we must listen to their heart—their will, intellect, emotions, and spirit. These four chambers of the heart can be discovered by learning about their choices, thoughts, feelings, and prayers.

Wisdom works when we *connect*, *deflect*, *reflect*, and *direct* the people pleaser through four wise practices: *don't gossip, don't be gullible, don't give in*, and *graciously support them in the wisest direction*.

Leading the People Pleaser Through Listening: Don't Gossip

Proverbs 20:19; 26:20, 22

DO you want to hear a secret? Why is gossip so enticing? The more we speak, the more likely we are to gossip. This is a looming risk when we interact with the people pleaser.

The people pleaser often speaks now and thinks later. We need to be careful not to do the same. Gossip is unnecessary talk about others. It often includes untrue statements (slander) as well as true statements that are confidential. Solomon said: "A gossip betrays a confidence; so avoid anyone who talks too much" (Proverbs 20:19). He likened gossip to throwing wood on a fire: "Without wood a fire goes out; without a gossip a quarrel dies down" (Proverbs 26:20).

Gossip offers deceptive pleasure because it attempts to satisfy our desire for significance—apart from Christ. Solomon recorded: "The words of a gossip are like choice morsels; they go down to the inmost parts" (Proverbs 26:22). We either lift ourselves up or bring others down through gossip. We must be careful not to do so when we engage with a people pleaser. Even if we nod in agreement, the people pleaser will quote us to their next audience as the perpetuator of the rumor at hand.

The next time you encounter a people pleaser, connect with their heart by avoiding gossip. In their heart, the people pleaser desires significance apart from Christ and leads with their emotions. Do not assume their gossip is true, and do not perpetuate a conversation that breaches confidence. Be careful not to nod your head in agreement to gossip nor utter, "Uh huh." Remember without wood a fire goes out, without gossip a quarrel dies down (Proverbs 26:20).

Leading the People Pleaser Through Listening:
Don't Be Gullible

Proverbs 26:23; 14:15

EXAGGERATION is a powerful tool leveraged by the people pleaser. Distorted facts, recollections that stretch the imagination, and embellished stories all cleverly mishandle the truth. Solomon noted: "Like a coating of silver dross on earthenware are fervent lips with an evil heart" (Proverbs 26:23). Just like that coating of glaze over earthenware makes the outside look better than it truly is on the inside, so exaggerated words allow the people pleaser to appear more significant on the surface than they feel in their heart.

The Bible warns us not to be gullible to exaggeration: "The simple believe anything, but the prudent give thought to their steps" (Proverbs 14:15). Simple, or gullible, is the first of five progressive words for fool in the Hebrew language. We must deflect the indirect difficult behavior of the people pleaser and remain connected with their heart by not becoming gullible to exaggeration.

After connecting with the heart of the people pleaser by not gossiping, next deflect their difficult behavior by not becoming gullible to exaggeration. In unthreatening fashion, ask for verification of facts or other eyewitnesses when wisdom tells you the people pleaser is exaggerating. "Were you really there?" "Who else saw that?" "What would they say?" "Where could I download a list of those facts?" These are all examples of wise questions that deflect exaggeration.

Leading the People Pleaser Through Listening: Don't Give In

Proverbs 26:24–25, 28

THE people pleaser uses flattery to gain an advantage. When a compliment comes our way, we are often tempted to give in because we like what we hear. *Flattery* comes from the Hebrew word for *smooth*. Designed to snag its target, flattery is a smooth way to capture the heart and life of another person (Proverbs 29:5). Flattery is differentiated from a compliment, not merely by whether it is true, but by whose interest is at heart. Paul taught: "For such people are not serving our Lord Christ, but their own appetites. By smooth talk and flattery they deceive the minds of naive people" (Romans 16:18). The people pleaser uses flattery for their advantage (Jude 1:16). We give in to flattery by believing what we hear, foolishly surrendering our heart to the people pleaser, and acting on the deceitful compliment.

Solomon commanded, "Don't give in to flattery." This is a shrewd practice to reflect the heart of the people pleaser: "Enemies disguise themselves with their lips, but in their hearts they harbor deceit. Though their speech is charming, do not believe them, for seven abominations fill their hearts" (Proverbs 26:24–25). When we don't give in to the people pleaser's net, we won't be tripped up and snagged. The people pleaser will realize we have not fallen prey to their deceptive tactics, and they will begin to wrestle with their own heart that desires significance apart from Christ. Solomon described the flatterer's disingenuous intent and the painful result: "A lying tongue hates those it hurts, and a flattering mouth works ruin" (Proverbs 26:28).

Connect with the heart of the people pleaser by recognizing their desire for significance apart from Christ and don't gossip. Deflect their difficult behavior and don't be gullible to their exaggerations. Reflect their heart and don't give in to flattery. Simply smile and say, "You sound really convincing, but I need some time to pray about it."

Leading the People Pleaser Through Listening: Graciously Support Them in the Wisest Direction

Proverbs 4:11; 24:11; 1 Thessalonians 5:14

H AVE you ever noticed how the people pleaser in your life has a tendency to agree with almost everyone? The people pleaser is weak in willpower, and their desire for significance apart from Christ leads them to be a chameleon as they continually adjust their values to accommodate whomever they are with at the moment.

In their effort to be popular, the people pleaser foolishly says yes to everyone they encounter. The people pleaser says yes to the Sunday school budget increase and the new elder retreat committing the same finite dollars twice. The people pleaser says yes, promising the same car on the same Friday night to two different teenage siblings. The people pleaser says yes to two appointments at two different locations at the same exact time. The people pleaser says yes to the differing values and opinions of two people with opposing views. Only after two persons or groups with opposite interests experience each other's carte blanch from the people pleaser does negative conflict occur. The result is an over-commitment of life's resources: time, talent, and treasure.

The people pleaser needs a new benchmark for success—wisdom. Their desire to please will motivate them to try wisdom when it is *graciously* presented as an alternative, and they feel *supported* to get there. *Grace* means "undeserved love"—where one finds ultimate significance in Christ (2 Corinthians 8:9). *Support* means that they will not go there alone.

Solomon believed in graciously supporting one toward wisdom: "I instruct you in the way of wisdom and lead you along straight paths" (Proverbs 4:11). Solomon compelled young leaders to shrewdly save those who are directed toward foolishness: "Rescue those being led away to death; hold back those staggering toward slaughter" (Proverbs 24:11). The weak-in-willpower people pleaser will become warm toward a wise alternative when they are emotionally supported in that direction. Paul said that we should support the weak (1 Thessalonians 5:14).

Connect with the heart of the people pleaser by recognizing their desire for significance apart from Christ, and don't gossip. Deflect their difficult behavior, and don't be gullible to their exaggerations. Reflect their heart, and don't give in to flattery. Finally, direct them toward wisdom and graciously support them in the wisest direction.

After being prompted with wisdom from the Holy Spirit and the Bible say, "Based on my understanding of the Bible, this direction would be a wise solution for you. Your gifts would greatly honor God. I would love to help you get there." The people pleaser will want to please you with wise behavior. If they are an unbeliever, use discretion in your use of the Bible and God in your conversation (Matthew 7:6). God will use you to wisely lead the people pleaser in your life through listening.

Leading the Passive Resistive Through Listening

Proverbs 26:12–15

DO you have a passive resistive person in your life?

The fourth difficult person is the people-oriented passive resistive who is inactive and immovable. The fact the passive resistive is people-oriented, means they can be averse to task and be nice about it. Consequently, their passive resistance makes them indirect in their difficult behavior—on the surface we might not immediately recognize this negative conflict.

The passive resistive primarily focuses on their desire for *contentment*. This is directly correlated to their spirit, the window to the mystical world that allows them to keep it together amid immediate conflict in the physical realm. Unfortunately, this is divorced from and at the expense of those around them. In their difficult behavior, they can attempt to satisfy their desire for contentment apart from Christ. The relaxed, passive resistive stubbornly attempts to hold themselves together in order to be content.

The passive resistive portrays at least four difficult characteristics: avoiding conflict at all costs; lack of initiative—searching for the easy routine; slowness to change, to process, and to commit; and stubborn pride—internally demanding respect and honor (Proverbs 26:12–15).

If you are in a conflict with a passive resistive, ask God for His insight to connect with their heart. See past their negative behavior into their desires. God will use you to bring His restoration to your relationship.

Characteristics of the Passive Resistive

Proverbs 26:12–16

THE passive resistive avoids conflict at all costs. The only thing the passive resistive will do quickly is run from conflict. However, this perpetuates negative conflict due to their unwillingness to address any perceived tension. King Solomon referred to the passive resistive as a sluggard: "A sluggard says, 'There's a lion in the road, a fierce lion roaming the streets!'" (Proverbs 26:13). The passive resistive sees potential conflict as a lion roaming loose on the streets, ready to devour.

The passive resistive lacks initiative. They want life to be easy, or free from conflict; therefore, they are reluctant to begin new tasks. Sometimes, they even resist beginning a new day. Solomon gave us clear imagery: "As a door turns on its hinges, so a sluggard turns on his bed" (Proverbs 26:14). The door turning on its hinges represents the oftentimes negative routine of the passive resistive who might see themselves as being in a groove when they are actually in a rut.

The passive resistive is slow to change, slow to process, and slow to commit. That's why some Bible translations substitute *slothful* for *sluggard*. A sloth is a lazy, furry animal about the size of a common housecat found in South America and the West Indies. His name stems from his slow motion, often hanging upside-down in the tree

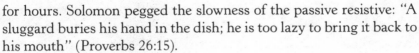

for hours. Solomon pegged the slowness of the passive resistive: "A sluggard buries his hand in the dish; he is too lazy to bring it back to his mouth" (Proverbs 26:15).

Internally, the passive resistive demands respect and honor because they proudly see themselves as wise. Solomon taught: "A sluggard is wiser in his own eyes than seven people who answer discreetly" (Proverbs 26:16). The king also declared: "Do you see a person wise in their own eyes? There is more hope for a fool than for them" (Proverbs 26:12). The Hebrew word for *fool* in this verse is *kesil*, meaning stupid—one who repeats the same gullible behavior.

Ask the Holy Spirit if you are exhibiting any passive resistive behavior in your relationships. If so, surrender your negative conflict to Him and take a first step toward restoration by confessing your resistance to those experiencing the consequences of your stubborn inaction. If someone else in your life is passive resistive, begin to pray for that person every day. God will use you to bring initiative to the relationship.

Leading the Passive Resistive Through Listening: Be Peaceful

Proverbs 12:20; 16:7; Romans 12:18

WHEN leading the passive resistive through listening, first, we need to be peaceful. Stirring up anger and anxiety increases the amount of conflict perceived by the passive resistive and shuts down the joy of any forward movement. Solomon observed: "Deceit is in the hearts of those who plot evil, but those who promote peace have joy" (Proverbs 12:20). We need to be gentle in our communication, modeling harmony, or the passive resistive will not even hear us. Solomon taught: "When the LORD takes pleasure in anyone's way, he causes their enemies to make peace with them" (Proverbs 16:7).

Peaceful communication features a passion for reconciliation. This allows us to connect with the heart of the passive resistive who desires contentment. That desire for contentment is actually satisfied in peace. Paul instructed: "If it is possible, as far as it depends on you, live at peace with everyone" (Romans 12:18). He reiterated Scripture's consistent theme that Jesus Christ is the peace of God (Ephesians 2:14). Only He can satisfy the desire for contentment through reconciliation of our relationship with God as well as our relationships with others.

When you encounter a passive resistive, first, connect with their heart's desire for contentment and be peaceful. Communicate gently by softening your tone of voice and choice of words. Speak in a tone of reconciliation. Resist the temptation to make loud, combative statements like, "Why won't you support this project?" Instead, with a soft peaceful tone, offer, "Do you have any questions or insights about our small steps toward improvement?" Christ, the peace of God, will equip you to lead the passive resistive through listening.

Leading the Passive Resistive Through Listening: Be Patient

Proverbs 25:15

ARE you impatient with the passive resistive person in your life?

When leading the passive resistive through listening, first, we need to be peaceful. Second, we must be patient. Wise King Solomon witnessed the power of patience: "Through patience a ruler can be persuaded, and a gentle tongue can break a bone" (Proverbs 25:15).

Leading the passive resistive person requires patience, which allows us to deflect their resistance to taking initiative. To be patient is to be understanding (Proverbs 14:19), calm (Proverbs 15:18), and one who overlooks an offense (Proverbs 19:11). If we aren't patient, enduring the passive resistive person's slothful responses, we will never effectively communicate wisdom. This means time. Paul said that we should be patient with everyone. This includes the passive resistive (1 Thessalonians 5:14).

After connecting with the passive resistive person's heart by being peaceful, next deflect their passive resistance through patience. Be understanding, be calm, and overlook their offenses. Give them time. As you surrender to the guidance of the Holy Spirit, He will give you peace and patience to lead the passive resistive through listening (Galatians 5:22).

Leading the Passive Resistive Through Listening: Reveal a Painless First Step

Proverbs 1:32–33; 14:15; 6:6–8

IS the passive resistive in your life reluctant to change?

When leading the passive resistive through listening, first, we need to not only be *peaceful* and *patient*, but also, we need to *reveal a painless first step*. This first step must be easy with little perceived conflict: "For the waywardness of the simple will kill them, and the complacency of fools will destroy them; but whoever listens to me will live in safety and be at ease, without fear of harm" (Proverbs 1:32–33). Listening to wisdom guides us to offering the complacent passive resistive a safe, easy, and confident first step.

Remember, a passive resistive person dislikes change. They often consider it evil, so change must be presented in simple, bite-sized portions. In an unthreatening fashion, this reflects our understanding of the desire for contentment resident in their heart. Step-by-step, we work through their indecision stemming from their slowness to process and reluctance to commit. Solomon said that a prudent man gives thought to his *steps* (Proverbs 14:15), and that a sluggard can learn from an ant who stores its food in summer and gathers it at harvest—*one step at a time* (Proverbs 6:6–8).

Connect with the heart of the passive resistive and be peaceful. Deflect their difficult behavior and be patient. Reflect their heart and reveal a painless first step. Make it practical by breaking the end goal into small steps. Reveal only one painless step at a time, or the passive resistive will perceive too much conflict and not act at all. All the while, surrender to the Holy Spirit who will guide you to lead the passive resistive through listening.

Leading the Passive Resistive Through Listening: Humbly Provoke Them Toward Wisdom

Proverbs 11:2; Hebrews 10:24

WHEN leading the passive resistive through listening, first, we need to be *peaceful*. Second, we must be *patient*. Third, we need to *reveal a painless first step*. Fourth, we need to *humbly and positively provoke the passive resistive toward wisdom*.

We must express the positive benefits of change revealed in that painless first step. The passive resistive harbors a stubborn pride, a hidden will of iron, that demands respect and honor. Humility is the only concept that can soften pride because it does not rob the passive resistive of their will. Solomon revealed: "When pride comes, then comes disgrace, but with humility comes wisdom" (Proverbs 11:2).

Whereas pride is a hard heart, humility is a soft heart—one that will lead the passive resistive toward wisdom. Humbly demonstrating the positive outcomes of the painless first step lessens the passive resistive person's barrier to change. The writer of Hebrews penned: "And let us consider how we may spur one another on toward love and good deeds" (Hebrews 10:24).

Connect with the heart of the passive resistive and be peaceful. Deflect their difficult behavior and be patient. Reflect their heart and reveal a painless first step. Finally, direct them toward wisdom by humbly and positively provoking them toward the intersection of God's heart and street smarts. Model a soft heart while communicating the positive outcomes of the painless first step.

Wisdom will allow you to navigate through conflict toward community. When you listen to the passive resistive and when you follow God's priceless pearls of instruction, it won't be you leading; rather, it will be Christ in you.

God Devises Ways for Life

2 Samuel 14:14

DO you devise ways for those outside Christ to find life with God or to remain separated from Him? Be careful, there is no neutral. We all devise ways to either pull people toward God or to push them away from Him. The determining factor is how we respond to the life-giving inspiration of the Holy Spirit.

The Bible says that when it comes to the banished, God devises ways for life: "Like water spilled on the ground, which cannot be recovered, so we must die. But that is not what God desires; rather, he devises ways so that a banished person does not remain banished from him" (2 Samuel 14:14).

Nephesh is the Hebrew word for *life*, also translated *soul*, or *breath*. God pulls toward those who are separated from Him by breathing life into their souls so they may turn to Him and experience reconciled relationships. In contrast, left to our flawed nature, we push people away from God. In fact, the Hebrew word for *estranged* literally means "to push away."

Now here's the question that each of us must ask: "If the Spirit of God dwells in me, do I devise ways so that a banished person may not remain estranged from God?" In order to do so, we must: inhale the breath of life from God and exhale His breath of life to others.

God Devises Ways for Life:
Pushing When God Is Pulling

2 Samuel 13:1–39

THE Bible teaches God devises ways for life for those who are estranged from Him. Despite our sinful nature, which often pushes others away, God still pulls the banished toward His abundant and eternal life. Let's examine a story from the Bible where people were pushing when God was pulling.

Amnon Devises a Way to Push

King David's son, Amnon, fell in love with his half-sister, Tamar. Literally lovesick because it seemed impossible for him to be with her, Amnon was approached by his friend and cousin, Jonadab, who inquired about his gloomy appearance. The two devised a way for Amnon to be alone with Tamar. Amnon pretended to be ill, garnering the presence of his father the king from whom he requested none other than Tamar to come to his house and prepare food for him. An unsuspecting David obliged. What followed cut deeply into David's family legacy, scarring it for generations.

A scheming Amnon gazed at Tamar with shameless intent while she kneaded the dough, formed it into bread, and then placed it in the brick oven. As the aroma of freshly baked bread filled Amnon's house, lust filled his heart. When Tamar served him the warm bread, he refused to eat, ordering their servants to leave. Still devising a way to violate his sister without any witnesses, Amnon requested Tamar to feed him as he lay in his bed. When a vulnerable Tamar approached her deceitful brother, he grabbed her, whispered his dishonorable intentions, defied her warning, and stole her innocence.

Absalom Devises a Way to Push

When news hit the king, he was furious, but he ignored the law requiring Amnon's banishment. Consequently, Tamar's full brother

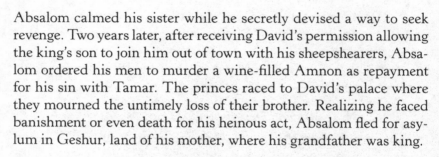

Absalom calmed his sister while he secretly devised a way to seek revenge. Two years later, after receiving David's permission allowing the king's son to join him out of town with his sheepshearers, Absalom ordered his men to murder a wine-filled Amnon as repayment for his sin with Tamar. The princes raced to David's palace where they mourned the untimely loss of their brother. Realizing he faced banishment or even death for his heinous act, Absalom fled for asylum in Geshur, land of his mother, where his grandfather was king.

David Devises a Way to Push

All the while, David's heart longed for his son Absalom. However, the king allowed his son to remain banished without contact for three years until David's military leader Joab (meaning *Jehovah-fathered*), devised a way to persuade the king to reconcile with Absalom (2 Samuel 14:1).

Are you pushing or pulling? Maybe your story is not as dramatic as the one you just read, but regardless of your circumstances, you are either pushing people away from God or being used by Him to pull them close. There is no neutral.

God Devises Ways for Life: A Way to Pull

2 Samuel 14:1–22

MOTIVATED by a desire to pull David toward reconciled relationships, to see the king's heart mended by renewing his relationship with his son (2 Samuel 14:1), to honor God (2 Samuel 14:13, 16–17), to maintain Israel's military strength (2 Samuel 14:16), and to improve his own relationship with David (2 Samuel 14:22), Joab sent his messenger about ten miles south of Jerusalem to Tekoa where he solicited the help of a wise woman. Disguised as a grieving widow, the undercover agent traveled to Jerusalem and fell before the king as she presented him with her parable masterminded by Joab.

While in the fields, her sons argued. With no one to separate them, one son stole the breath of life from his brother. Now the entire clan was coming to kill her sole remaining heir who also represented her only means of survival. She begged for David's protection from the avenger of blood. Empathizing with the woman's plight, the king promptly ordered her son's safety.

With the confirmation of the king's ruling, the wise woman of Tekoa unveiled her true motive. David listened intently only to learn he had been the antagonist in yet another parable. "The woman said, 'Why then have you devised a thing like this against the people of God? When the king says this, does he not convict himself, for the king has not brought back his banished son?'" (2 Samuel 14:13).

With David's blood boiling, the woman seized the moment to craft one of the most insightful word pictures ever expressed to the shepherd turned king: "Like water spilled on the ground, which cannot be recovered, so we must die. But that is not what God desires; rather, he devises ways so that a banished person does not remain banished from him" (2 Samuel 14:14). The wise woman of Tekoa had just painted a portrait of God on the inner canvas of the king. If God devises ways for life, would the man after God's own heart do the same?

In order to be used by God to advance His kingdom, David would have to inhale the breath of life from God and exhale His breath of life to others. The same holds true for us today.

Are you inhaling and exhaling God's breath of life and being used by His Spirit to pull the estranged to Christ? Is He laying anyone on your heart who is outside a saving relationship with the Savior? If so, daily pray for that person to discover eternal life in Him.

God Devises Ways for Life: Inhale the Breath of Life From God

2 Samuel 14:14

AFTER being confronted by the wise woman of Tekoa about reconciling with his exiled son Absalom, David was faced with whether he would inhale the breath of life from God who devises ways so that the banished may not remain estranged from Him. First, David would have to remember his own sin and God's justice, mercy, and grace.

Justice

"Like water spilled on the ground, which cannot be recovered, so we must die" (2 Samuel 14:14a). Amnon was dead and could not be brought back to life. According to the law, Amnon should not have had sex, let alone forced, with his sister (Leviticus 18:9). The penalty was to be banished, or cut off, from the people (Leviticus 18:20; 20:17). David exchanged justice for license with Amnon, fostering an opportunity for Absalom to execute revenge.

We have one opportunity at life on this side where we fall short of God's perfection, and then we die to face judgment (Hebrews 9:27). Christ is the justice of God. He paid the price for our sin (Hebrews 10:10).

Mercy

"But that is not what God desires" (2 Samuel 14:14b). The Latin Vulgate states: "Nor does God will the destruction of the soul" (2 Samuel 14:14b). God exhaled mercy. God provided Amnon, David, and Absalom mercy so they would return to Him. In the Garden of Eden, God breathed life into the clay (Genesis 2:7). In the original

Hebrew, that breath of life suggested a continual inhaling and exhaling. Consequently, God did not merely breathe into man one time and walk away. Rather, He continued to inhale and exhale through His creation.

In Christ, we find that breath of life only by His mercy (Romans 9:15–16). God does not give us what we deserve, eternal banishment from Him. Instead, He offers us mercy: less than we deserve.

Grace

"Rather, he devises ways so that a banished person does not remain banished from him" (2 Samuel 14:14c). *Chashab* is the Hebrew word for *devise*, which is contrasted with David devising Absalom's banishment referenced in the previous verse (2 Samuel 14:13). If God devises ways to forgive and reconcile, will David? Will we? Contrast this with the fact God hates a heart that devises wicked schemes (Proverbs 6:18). Both Amnon and Absalom had devised wicked schemes. According to the law, two or more witnesses to a premeditated murder allowed for the death penalty (Number 35:30). This stipulation would have weighed heavily in Absalom's decision to flee Jerusalem.

Each of us must remember we were once banished, and God devised a way we could turn and not remain estranged from Him. In order to restore our fellowship with Him, the Father did not condone our sin, nor condemn us beyond His reach; rather, He paid the price for our transgressions and devised a pathway home. Justice, mercy, and grace flow from the heart of the Father who devises ways for life.

Banishment and Grace

2 Samuel 14:14

H AVE you ever felt banished from God? There is a way back home.

"Like water spilled on the ground, which cannot be recovered, so we must die. But that is not what God desires; rather, he devises ways so that a banished person does not remain banished from him" (2 Samuel 14:14).

"Banished," spoken by the wise woman of Tekoa, is a repeated Old Testament reference to God's people, the benefactors of the Divine, who devised ways so that they would not remain estranged from Him. This was true from the beginning. After the first sin in the Garden, justice was issued and death occurred. An animal was killed for its skin to cover Adam and Eve (Genesis 3:21). Then mercy was unveiled as God instituted physical death for man so that he would not live in the dilapidated state of sin forever (Genesis 3:22). Consequently, God banished Adam and Eve from the Garden of Eden (Genesis 3:23). However, God did not banish them from His presence. He offered grace through the prophesied Christ (Genesis 3:15).

The story of God's grace to reconcile banished people continued throughout the Old Testament. Just prior to the Israelites entering the Promised Land, God spoke to His people through Moses: "Even if you have been banished to the most distant land under the heavens, from there the LORD your God will gather you and bring you back" (Deuteronomy 30:4).

Hundreds of years later, though King David's successors had sinned, God still issued grace: "But the LORD was gracious to them and had compassion and showed concern for them because of his covenant with Abraham, Isaac and Jacob. To this day he has been unwilling to destroy them or banish them from his presence" (2 Kings 13:23).

God devised ways for life. Our sin against God requires death. Through His justice, mercy, and grace, God devised a way that we would not remain estranged from Him. Christ is the way (John 14:6).

Justice is getting what we deserve. Mercy is not getting what we deserve. Grace is getting what we do not deserve. Do you understand that you deserve justice from God? Are you ready to ask for mercy? If so, God will give you grace, His undeserved love, His unmerited favor, discovered only in Christ. Take a deep breath. Hold it for five seconds. Exhale. Let that be a reminder of God inhaling and exhaling His breath of life through you.

David Inhaled the Breath of Life:
Worship, Word, Workout

Psalm 103; 23:3

IN an attempt to reconcile David with his banished son Absalom, the wise woman of Tekoa seized the moment at the conclusion of her parable to craft one of the most insightful word pictures ever expressed to the shepherd turned king (2 Samuel 14:14). We have to ask, "How did David respond to these words about God?" We know David allowed Absalom to return to Jerusalem, though their relationship was strained for the balance of Absalom's life (2 Samuel 14:23–24, 32–33). However, a snapshot inside David's heart appears in his words of Psalm 103 where David painted a picture of inhaling God daily.

First, David inhaled God's breath of life in his soul (*nephesh*) in *worship* of Him (Psalm 103:1–17). David penned: "Praise the LORD, my soul; all my innermost being, praise his holy name" (Psalm 103:1). He remembered he was once banished from God, and he had received forgiveness, God's justice and mercy offered by grace, in order to not be estranged from Him (Psalm 103:3–17). Second, David inhaled the *Word* of God (Psalm 103:18–20). David wrote: "Praise the LORD, you his angels, you mighty ones who do his bidding, who obey his word" (Psalm 103:20). Third, David inhaled the *works* of God: "Praise the LORD, all his heavenly hosts, you his servants who do his will. Praise the LORD, all his works everywhere in his dominion. Praise the LORD, my soul" (Psalm 103:21–22). In his familiar psalm, David expressed only God can renew the breath of life in us when he composed: "He refreshes my soul" (Psalm 23:3).

Inhale the breath of life from God. Read Psalm 103. Remember you were once banished, and God devised a way for you not to remain estranged from Him. Christ is the way, and His Spirit devised a unique way for you to find life in Him. Therefore, commit to three spiritual pursuits in order to inhale God each morning: worship, Word, and workout.

First, worship God by listening to a style of worship music that speaks to your heart. Music affects the central nervous system, but worship music breathes life into the soul. As you listen, pray to God, praising Him for Who He is and thanking him for forgiving you. Second, read the Word. Begin your morning by reading the Bible. Start with at least one verse. Breathe in and live the day through the oxygen the Word provides. Third, start your day with a workout. Whether walking one hundred steps in God's creation or training for a marathon, release the norepinephrine and endorphins in your body that offer a relaxed energy throughout the day (1 Timothy 4:8). You might even do all three at the same time by listening to worship music while reading your Bible and climbing on the elliptical machine.

When you begin your day by inhaling God's breath of life through worship, the Word, and working out, God will use you to exhale His breath of life to everyone you encounter.

Exhale the Breath of Life to Others

1 Peter 3:15

DO you secretly maintain a list of transgressions that disqualify sinners from the reach of God? Our beliefs affect our behavior, especially when encountering those who have blatantly sinned against God. Consequently, we must examine God's passion for the lost to find life in Him and His desire to use us in the process.

David not only inhaled God's breath of life, he also exhaled His breath of life to others by yielding to God's ways.

We must yield to God devising ways in us to help the banished not remain estranged from Him. When we were banished, God reconciled us in Christ in order to use us to reconcile others to Him (2 Corinthians 5:16–21). Not only must we inhale the breath of life from God, but also, we must exhale the breath of life to others by yielding to the Spirit of Christ in us.

When we yield to God devising ways in us to help restore the banished, we exhale the breath of life to others through the same methods in which we inhaled the breath of life: worship, Word, and workout. Jesus's disciple Peter said: "But in your hearts revere Christ as Lord. Always be prepared to give an answer to everyone who asks you to give the reason for the hope that you have. But do this with gentleness and respect" (1 Peter 3:15). Worship sets apart Christ as Lord in our hearts. The Word prepares us to give an answer to everyone who asks us to give the reason for our hope. Workout is how we exhale life to the banished with gentleness and respect.

Exhale the breath of life to others through worship, the Word, and working out your faith with gentleness and respect. Yield to the Holy Spirit who devises ways in you to help the banished not remain estranged from Him.

Exhale the Breath of Life: Worship, Word, Workout

1 Corinthians 14:24; Hebrews 4:12

LET'S examine three specific ways to exhale God's breath of life to others in order to be used by Him to pull them toward their Creator.

First, we *worship* God by communicating His character to others. The Hebrew word *yadah* is often translated as *confess*, meaning "to exhale" to God. Our first step to reconciling the banished is not toward them, but toward God. Exhaling is how we remove waste both physically and spiritually. As a result, we must be willing to confess our sins to God and appropriately to others, demonstrating our yielding to God's justice, mercy, and grace. When we worship God, we exhale the breath of life to others who will be drawn to Him (1 Corinthians 14:24).

Second, we communicate the *Word* of God to others. The more we get into God's Word, the more His Word gets into us. Consequently, His Word appears in our words. When we humbly and wisely share His Word with others, they draw nearer to Him (1 Corinthians 2:1–5; Colossians 4:5–6; 2 Timothy 3:16). The writer of Hebrews taught: "For the word of God is alive and active. Sharper than any double-edged sword, it penetrates even to dividing soul and spirit, joints and marrow; it judges the thoughts and attitudes of the heart" (Hebrews 4:12).

Third, we *workout* God's redemptive and restorative breath of life in us by living out our salvation. Paul wrote: "Continue to work

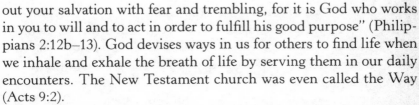

out your salvation with fear and trembling, for it is God who works in you to will and to act in order to fulfill his good purpose" (Philippians 2:12b–13). God devises ways in us for others to find life when we inhale and exhale the breath of life by serving them in our daily encounters. The New Testament church was even called the Way (Acts 9:2).

David yielded to God's devising ways in him to help the banished not remain estranged from the Lord. In his crown jewel psalm, David exhaled the breath of life to others. First, David worshiped God in the presence of others (Psalm 145:1–3). Second, David exhaled God's Word to others by writing the inspired Word. Third, David exhaled to others God's just, merciful, and gracious work in him by working out, or living out, his redemption and restoration (Psalm 145:4–21).

God's breath of life in David catapulted him from shepherding sheep to shepherding His people as their king: "He chose David his servant and took him from the sheep pens; from tending the sheep he brought him to be the shepherd of his people Jacob, of Israel his inheritance. And David shepherded them with integrity of heart; with skillful hands he led them" (Psalm 78:70–72).

When we exhale the breath of life to others that we inhale from God, we are used by Him to pull them toward Him. Today, exhale worship, the Word, and the working out of your restoration in Christ. God will use you to make others new again.

Never Give Up

2 Chronicles 15:7

DO you ever feel like giving up?

Amidst life's challenges or even lack of them, we often say, "I give up." These words weighed with finality flow from the heart. Whether we are overextended or just plain bored, how do we never give up?

Before the words "I give up" leave our lips, a crack is formed in one of the hardened chambers of our spiritual hearts (will, intellect, spirit, or emotions). The crack is *discouragement*, and it leads to *disconnectedness*.

Courage stems from the Latin word for *heart*, which is *cor*. Consequently, to be *discouraged* is literally "to lose heart." On the inside, the *will* says, "I will not;" the *mind* says, "I think not;" the *spirit* says, "I pray not;" or the *emotions* say, "I want not." Unfortunately, when one chamber cracks, the other three follow suit. The result is a three-dimensional disconnectedness: (1) from who we were designed to be, (2) from God, and (3) from others. Much like the case with concrete, a crack separates what once was connected. In order to never give up, each of us must first reconnect in our hearts and say, "I choose, I think, I pray, and I want to surrender to God's design for my life."

When faced with an obstacle, we either give up or live up to God's design for our lives—the unique expression of Christ in us. If we ever give up, we will never live up to who God designed us to be. The Bible calls us to never give up in three contexts that provide us the secret to enduring life's challenges. Never give up on yourself, God, or each other.

King Asa was instructed: "But as for you, be strong and do not give up, for your work will be rewarded" (2 Chronicles 15:7).

Memorize 2 Chronicles 15:7. When discouraged, don't disconnect. Run to God who will give you the courage to endure.

Never Give up on Yourself

Hebrews 12:1–3

W HEN faced with seemingly insurmountable challenges, are you tempted to give up on yourself?

After describing a season in which God's leaders gave up, Azariah son of Oded challenged King Asa of Judah to be strong and not give up (2 Chronicles 15:7). King Asa's response to the call to not give up on himself was clearly stated in the following verse: "He took courage" (2 Chronicles 15:8). The writer went on to describe Asa's heart as "fully committed to the LORD" (2 Chronicles 15:17).

"*Give up*" is *raphah* in Hebrew, meaning "to sink or to relax, to lose courage." Interestingly, we tend to *sink* when we *lose* or *relax* when we *win*. Our perspective of a challenge can appear either too big when we are defeated or too small when we are victorious. In either event, we lose courage. Victorious King David's sin with Bathsheba stemmed from him not going to war in the spring as was customary to kings.

Jesus never gave up on Himself. In His high priestly prayer, Jesus said to His heavenly Father: "I have brought you glory on earth by finishing the work you gave me to do" (John 17:4). On the cross, Jesus confirmed He had indeed finished what He had started (John 19:30).

The writer of Hebrews called believers to model His endurance: "Therefore, since we are surrounded by such a great cloud of witnesses, let us throw off everything that hinders and the sin that so easily entangles. And let us run with perseverance the race marked out for us, fixing our eyes on Jesus, the pioneer and perfecter of faith. For the joy set before him he endured the cross, scorning its shame, and sat down at the right hand of the throne of God. Consider him who endured such opposition from sinners, so that you will not grow weary and lose heart" (Hebrews 12:1–3). These verses paint a picture

of a runner who, prior to a race, would throw off the training weights that were hooked in his uniform so that he would be free to endure the upcoming challenge.

Sin trusts in our own design, rather than God's. Consequently, it is a heavy burden that hinders us from persevering toward the unique expression of Christ in us. Because it begins in the heart, sin entangles itself into the fabric of our lives, discouraging and disconnecting us from who we were designed to be. Therefore, never giving up on ourselves means never giving up on humbling our hearts to God's design for our lives, as was the pattern of Jesus. Paul challenged Timothy: "Join with me in suffering, like a good soldier of Christ Jesus" (2 Timothy 2:3).

In order to endure, or never give up on ourselves, we forever live up to God's design. When discouraged enough to quit, we have the courage to commit all four chambers of the heart in order to finish what we start—the advancement of God's kingdom in us.

In what area of your life have you noticed a crack of discouragement in your heart? Is it one where your challenge seems too big because you have been defeated or one where your challenge appears too small, leaving you restless from multiple victories? Is discouragement surfacing in your marriage, parenting, ministry, education, friendships, or career? Identify that specific area of life. Next, confess to the Father your shortfall from the heart of Christ. Ask Him to restore your heart to be like His.

Never Give Up on God

Luke 18:1

WHEN it seems as though chaos abounds all around you, are you tempted to give up on God? Luke recorded the purpose of Jesus's Parable of the Persistent Widow: His disciples should "always pray and not give up" (Luke 18:1). The expression "not give up" is *egkakeo* in Greek, meaning "to lose heart" (NASB), or "to grow weary." When we begin to give up on God, we lose courage, or endurance, in our hearts, and we cease praying and obeying. Our discouragement leads to disconnectedness from our pursuit of Him. Yet, in this flailing condition, we still have hope.

Paul taught us to pray continually (1 Thessalonians 5:17). *Prayer* is being online with God 24/7. It is the intimate connection of our hearts with our heavenly Father where He shapes our desires in accordance with Christ's. Within this context, we make our petitions and requests (Philippians 4:6). God calls us to live out this connection in *obedience*, which literally means, "to listen under." Therefore, obedience makes our muscles move with our prayers.

Jesus never gave up on the Father. He prayed alone with Him daily; He lived a life of obedience; and He endured until the end, praying His Spirit into the Father's hands (Luke 23:46). In order to never give up on God, we must pray continually, remaining online with the Almighty 24/7. At the same time, we must make our muscles move with our prayers in obedience to Him. We never give up so that we will forever live up to God's design to pray and obey.

Have you given up on God, disconnecting from Him by not praying and obeying? Confess this to your gracious heavenly Father and ask Him to restore the heart of Christ in you. Write "Pray and obey" on your daily calendar as a reminder to connect with God in every task and relationship.

Never Give up on Each Other

Galatians 6:9–10; Hebrews 10:25

ARE you tempted to give up on someone? Has the advancement of the kingdom of God in that person skidded to what appears to be a screeching halt?

Paul explained the what and why of not giving up on each other: "Let us not become weary in doing good, for at the proper time we will reap a harvest if we do not give up" (Galatians 6:9). The what of not giving up is "doing good": the why is the "harvest."

Next, Paul unmistakably described the who of not giving up, or the audience who receives our good deeds: "Therefore, as we have opportunity, let us do good to all people, especially to those who belong to the family of believers" (Galatians 6:10). The who of not giving up is "all people, especially the family of believers." The writer of Hebrews elaborated on the family of believers never giving up on one another, telling his readers to continue "not giving up meeting together, as some are in the habit of doing, but encouraging one another—and all the more as you see the Day approaching" (Hebrews 10:25).

"*Give up*" is *egkataleipo* in Greek, meaning, "to desert." Rather than discouraging others toward disconnectedness, believers are called to never desert each other and to encourage their spiritual family members toward connectedness both in community with others and communion with God. That is exactly what Azariah son of Oded did with King Asa of Judah (2 Chronicles 15:7).

Jesus never gave up on His disciples (John 17:12). Jesus never gave up on us; He prayed that we would be encouraged toward connectedness—to live in community with each other and in communion with the Father and Son, so the world may be encouraged toward the same connectedness (John 17:20–23). When we are tempted

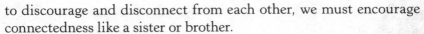

to discourage and disconnect from each other, we must encourage connectedness like a sister or brother.

Ask the Spirit of God to reveal to you the cracks in the heart of the person on whom you are tempted to give up, namely the desires they are attempting to satisfy apart from God. Next, ask for wisdom to encourage that person toward connectedness with God and others. Finally, go to that person and listen to their story, serve them in the way God has prompted you, and encourage communion with the Father and community with others.

When you never give up on yourself, never give up on God, and never give up on each other, you will realize it is not merely you enduring life's challenges; rather, it is Christ in you. In the words of the apostle Paul: "May the God who gives endurance and encouragement give you the same attitude of mind toward each other that Christ Jesus had, so that with one mind and one voice you may glorify the God and Father of our Lord Jesus Christ" (Romans 15:5–6).

When you have the courage to commit with all your heart,
    Then you will finish all that you start.
When you never give up on God and continue to pray,
    Your muscles will move with your prayers as you obey.
When you never give up on each other—from your friends
      you'll never flee—
    You will encourage them toward communion and community.
When you never give up, it's not merely you others will see,
    Rather, it is Christ in you . . . the way you were
        designed to be.

The Prison of Withholding Forgiveness

Colossians 3:13

ARE you holding on to an offense and withholding forgiveness from anyone?

A few years ago, at the beginning of a school year, I received a call early in the morning from my daughter's teacher who was coordinating chapels for the school. She confided she had lost her chapel speaker for the first four weeks of the school year and asked if I could teach one of the sessions. When I inquired what she wanted me to talk about, she replied, "Anything about Jesus." I said, "Praise the Lord! I'm in."

I went on with my workout, continuing to think about the worksheet I was preparing for my upcoming radio broadcast. The topic was "The Parable of the Unforgiving Debtor." I am bald, and I am slow. Consequently, it took me awhile to realize I could teach this parable at the school's chapel.

A couple of days later, I was standing in front of a group of elementary school students challenging them to forgiveness, which means "to let go." I asked them to examine their hearts for any white-knuckling, or holding on, of unforgiveness, which creates a prison around us. With the music playing, heads bowed, eyes closed, and palms up, an electric impulse of conviction ran up my spine.

I am sensitive, and my wife grew up the youngest of four with two teasing elder brothers. Consequently, her occasional tone of voice she used to battle them hurts my feelings. Right there in the chapel, I realized I had been teaching about not withholding forgiveness, while at that very same time, I had been withholding forgiveness from my spouse. I rushed home that morning, stood in front of the elliptical machine while she was exercising, and fell on my knees pleading for forgiveness. She accepted.

This incident describes a typical husband and wife thing. However, it serves as a model of how we condemn others who have unrestored hearts. We are called to look into the eyes of even the unrestored and authentically say with our hearts and our mouths, "Please forgive me," and "I forgive."

The apostle Paul taught: "Bear with each other and forgive one another if any of you has a grievance against someone. Forgive as the Lord forgave you" (Colossians 3:13).

When we let go, we let God use us to restore others.

The Parable of the Unforgiving Debtor

Matthew 18:21–35

JESUS likened withholding forgiveness to a prison. The irony is the person who will not forgive is the one locked inside the four walls. *Forgive* means "to let go." In order to forgive someone who has wounded us, we must let go of four prison walls that incarcerate us in the prison of unforgiveness. In Jesus's parable of the unforgiving debtor, He described three scenes illuminating the three applications of the story (Matthew 18:21–35).

Scene one portrays the largest debt ever incurred (150,000 years' wages) being forgiven, or let go, vertically from the king to his servant (Matthew 18:21–27). In Christ, God our King has let go of the largest debt ever incurred—our sin against Him. Write down the date, time, and place where God's forgiveness was appropriated to your own life.

Scene two paints a similar scenario; however, the debt incurred horizontally between the forgiven servant and his fellow servant is comparatively quite small (100 days' wages) (Matthew 18:28–31). The servant who had been forgiven the largest debt ever incurred would not let go of the small horizontal debt with his fellow servant. He wanted to hold on.

Are you holding on to a horizontal debt? If so, write it down on that same sheet of paper where you recorded the date, time, and place where you surrendered your vertical debt to Christ. Something about the reality of ink on paper will allow you to connect with the point of scene two in Jesus's parable. The vertical debt you were let go in

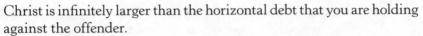

Christ is infinitely larger than the horizontal debt that you are holding against the offender.

Scene three casts a dark reality: withholding forgiveness horizontally results in imprisonment (Matthew 18:32–35). Word of the forgiven servant's behavior reached the king who responded by throwing the unforgiving servant into prison. Jesus concluded the parable with quite possibly the most sobering words in Scripture: "This is how my heavenly Father will treat each of you unless you forgive your brother or sister from your heart" (Matthew 18:35).

As we see in Jesus's concluding statement, forgiveness flows from the heart. A proud heart is hard, unforgiving, and holds on to offenses. A humble heart is soft, forgiving, and lets go. When we hold on, we remove the vertical from the horizontal, taking matters into our own hands. Consequently, we break up the cross into four pieces—each piece representing a prison wall. Ironically, the one incarcerated is not the offender, but the withholder.

Do you want to be free? Remember Christ paid a debt He did not owe because we owed a debt we could not pay. Let go of any horizontal debt you are white-knuckling and release the Forgiver in you. Choose to. Think to. Pray to. Want to. The King will set you free.

Forgiveness Flows from the Heart

Matthew 6:14–15

ARE you characterized and known as a forgiver?
Forgiveness does not occur horizontally in relationships without first occurring vertically with God in Christ. So, we are not the one forgiving, or letting go. Christ in us lets go. In order to forgive others, we must first be forgiven by God. Freedom in Christ from the penalty, power, and, one day, the presence of sin leads to freedom in relationships with others: "For if you forgive other people when they sin against you, your heavenly Father will also forgive you. But if you do not forgive others their sins, your Father will not forgive your sins" (Matthew 6:14–15). Forgiveness frees us for reconciliation.

Forgiveness always precedes reconciliation, but reconciliation does not always follow forgiveness because reconciliation takes two.

Forgiveness welds together two ideas: justice and mercy. Both are found in Christ and are displayed in their ultimate clarity at the cross. Consequently, the key that unlocks the prison of withholding forgiveness is cross-shaped (humility toward God and others).

This week, try the instant forgiveness experiment. Every time you are wronged, instantly let go of the offense and the offender. Do this by remembering the biggest debt ever incurred was let go in Christ. While the offense against you horizontally might hurt, it pales in comparison to the weight of your sin against God. You will not be the one letting go; rather, it will be Christ in you. He will set you free.

The Prison Wall of Revenge Comes in Three Levels

Romans 12:17–21

OFTENTIMES, our first reaction to someone who wrongs us is revenge, the first of four prison walls of withholding forgiveness. Revenge means retaliation, or repayment, and comes in three levels: greater, same, or lesser. Which do you favor? When our talent, treasure, or time is damaged, we are tempted to repay the offender with either greater, the same, or lesser damage to their corresponding resource. Revenge takes the matter into our own hands and removes it from God's—the horizontal removed from the vertical.

The apostle Paul taught: "Do not repay anyone evil for evil. Be careful to do what is right in the eyes of everyone. If it is possible, as far as it depends on you, live at peace with everyone. Do not take revenge, my dear friends, but leave room for God's wrath, for it is written: 'It is mine to avenge; I will repay,' says the Lord. On the contrary: 'If your enemy is hungry, feed him; if he is thirsty, give him something to drink. In doing this, you will heap burning coals on his head.' Do not be overcome by evil, but overcome evil with good" (Romans 12:17–21).

Revenge is the enemy of loving our neighbor—the greatest horizontal commandment (Leviticus 19:18)—and the enemy of loving God—the greatest vertical commandment (Deuteronomy 6:5). Love, not revenge, fulfills the law (Romans 12:10; Galatians 5:14).

Forgiveness does not occur horizontally in relationships without first occurring vertically with God in Christ. So, we are not the one forgiving, or letting go. Christ in us lets go. Freedom in Christ from the penalty, power, and, one day, the presence of sin leads to freedom in relationships with others (Matthew 6:12, 14–15).

There is a direct correlation between the amount that we perceive we've been forgiven vertically and how liberally or conservatively we forgive horizontally (Luke 7:41–43). Remember Jesus was not standing idly by watching us be harmed; rather, He was being harmed with us (Hebrews 4:14–16; 10:10, 18).

Think of a setting where you have done, currently are doing, or would do someone harm in a similar fashion done to you. Connect the offender's sin with the sin in you.

Start the instant forgiveness experiment. For the next two weeks, instantly let go of every wrong committed against you (your talent, treasure, and time). You will begin to experience freedom in Christ in an entirely new way.

The Prison Wall of Resentment

Jeremiah 2:19b

H AS withholding forgiveness of your offender swelled the anger and bitterness inside you? The second prison wall is resentment, which means literally "to feel again." It is bitterness, or a poison of the heart. Whereas revenge emphasizes our will, resentment emphasizes our emotions.

Resentment hardens our heart to God's. Job's friend said that the godless in heart harbor resentment (Job 36:13). When we hold on to resentment, we shut out the Spirit of God in our lives. Some of us even resent God's rebuke, or correction (Proverbs 3:11).

When we harden our hearts to God, we drink in bitterness—the poison of the heart—that turns us away from God (Deuteronomy 29:18; cf. Deuteronomy 32:32; Hebrews 12:15). God said: "Consider then and realize how evil and bitter it is for you when you forsake the LORD your God and have no awe of me" (Jeremiah 2:19b). We tend to do this in one of two ways: condemnation or license.

Condemnation is justice without mercy. The prophet Amos wrote that justice turns into bitterness when rejecting God (Amos 5:7). He went on to say that bitterness is poison (Amos 6:12). License is mercy without justice. Often times when we harbor resentment, we focus on God's mercy at the expense of His justice. We are so hurt from the offender's sin against us, only to discover we merely issue license to be hurt again and again.

Forgiveness welds together justice and mercy. This is displayed in its ultimate clarity at the cross of Christ where God's justice and

His mercy intersect in the sweet spot of His grace. Forgiveness is the vehicle that transports His grace.

Resentment hardens our heart to our offender and even to others because we protect our pride. The Bible describes this hardening as foolish. Solomon said that a mocker resents correction; he will not even consult the wise (Proverbs 15:12). This horizontal hardening of the heart occurs in the same two ways as the vertical: condemnation or license. When we condemn the offender horizontally, we curse them (Judges 5:23). The apostle Paul said that the lips of those with hearts hardened to God drip with poison (Romans 4:13; cf. Psalm 10:7).

When we issue license to the offender, we tend to weep from feeling the pain over and over again (Judges 21:12) because we issue mercy without any form of justice, or boundaries. Whether, we curse with a heart of condemnation or weep with a heart of license, we continue to feel the offense over and over again. The result is a heart full of resentment and its poison of bitterness. Hubert Humphrey said: "Bitterness, or resentment, is like drinking poison and expecting your enemy to die."

Pray, asking God to identify any bitterness in your heart. Pour it out to Him.

How to Let Go of Resentment Vertically With God

Ephesians 4:31–32; Psalm 62:8b; Lamentations 2:19

IN order to let go of resentment vertically with God, we must pour out our bitter resentment and drink in God's sweet antidote: restoration of forgiveness, kindness, and compassion in Christ. Paul wrote: "Get rid of all bitterness, rage and anger, brawling and slander, along with every form of malice. Be kind and compassionate to one another, forgiving each other, just as in Christ God forgave you" (Ephesians 4:31–32).

First, we must pour out our bitter souls to God (Mark 11:25). In her bitterness of soul, Hannah wept and prayed (1 Samuel 1:10–11). She poured out her soul to God (1 Samuel 1:15). David penned: "Pour out your hearts to him, for God is our refuge" (Psalm 62:8b). Jeremiah taught: "Pour out your heart like water in the presence of the Lord" (Lamentations 2:19). In order to let go of resentment, we must pray, or pour out our bitterness, confessing our resentment, whether condemnation or license, to God.

Second, we must drink in God's sweet antidote of restoration in Christ (Psalm 116:12–13). God restored sweetness to Hannah's bitter soul (1 Samuel 1:20). The psalmist said that God restores sweetness to bitter souls (Psalm 71:20; cf. Isaiah 5:20). God pours out His Spirit of love into our hearts (Romans 5:5; 1 Timothy 1:14). Similarly, Christ poured out His blood for the forgiveness of sins (Matthew 26:28; Leviticus 4:7; 17:11).

Peter told Simon the Sorcerer that the word of God delivers us from bitterness (Acts 8:25). In order to let go of resentment, we must

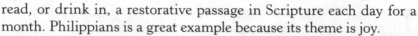

read, or drink in, a restorative passage in Scripture each day for a month. Philippians is a great example because its theme is joy.

Pour out the bitter by praying the following prayer in confession, repentance, and freedom each day during the next month until you feel the poison of bitterness removed from your heart:

"God, I am harboring resentment against _____ for _____. I want to let go of the offender's horizontal debt that pales in comparison to the largest debt ever recorded, my sin against You, which You let go of me in Christ. Free me from this imprisonment of holding on to resentment."

Drink in the sweetness by supporting your prayer, reading through each of the four chapters of Philippians every day for thirty days. Read two chapters in the morning and two in the evening. Drink in God's sweet restoration of joy described by David (Psalm 51:10–12).

How to Let Go of Resentment Horizontally in Relationships

Ephesians 4:31–32

To let go of resentment horizontally in relationships, we must follow Paul's teaching: "Get rid of all bitterness, rage and anger, brawling and slander, along with every form of malice. Be kind and compassionate to one another, forgiving each other, just as in Christ God forgave you" (Ephesians 4:31–32).

First, we must pour out the bitter poison of resentment and let go of all condemnation or license toward the offender (Ephesians 4:31; Proverbs 24:17–18).

Second, we must drink in the sweet antidote of God's restoration in Christ, by recalling how the offender might have once honored us in his heart (Gideon and the Ephraimites in Judges 8:3). This frees us from seeing the offender as malicious 100 percent of the time. Then, we exhibit mercy, sharing God's sweetness, His kindness and compassion flowing from our hearts, to the offender, implementing wise boundaries, including justice (Ephesians 4:32; cf. 2 Timothy 2:23–24).

Pray daily for the next month that God's Spirit will empower you to pour out all condemnation or license toward the offender: *"God, through the power of your Holy Spirit, please help me to let go of all condemnation or license toward _____ for _____. I can't do it on my own, but through Christ in me, You can. Give me wisdom to establish boundaries that might be necessary for freedom."*

Copy and paste the text of Ephesians 4:31–32 on your smartphone so you can carry it with you. Read those verses aloud each day,

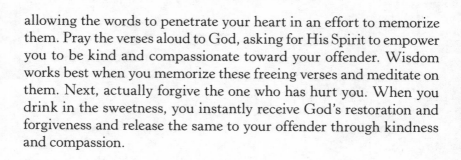

allowing the words to penetrate your heart in an effort to memorize them. Pray the verses aloud to God, asking for His Spirit to empower you to be kind and compassionate toward your offender. Wisdom works best when you memorize these freeing verses and meditate on them. Next, actually forgive the one who has hurt you. When you drink in the sweetness, you instantly receive God's restoration and forgiveness and release the same to your offender through kindness and compassion.

The Prison Wall of Regret

Psalm 10:4

REGRET, the third prison wall of withholding forgiveness, is the thought we could change the past. When we withhold forgiveness from holding on to regret, we think about how we could have changed the past in a way that would have eliminated or minimized the offense. In order to be free, we must let go of regret. Whereas revenge emphasizes the will, and resentment emphasizes the emotions, regret emphasizes the mind. Consequently, regret is intellectual sorrow. Words of regret are usually prefaced with, "I could've, would've, or should've."

Regret is pride's way of holding on to the thought that we could change the past—either the offense and its consequences, the offender, or our behavior. It flows from a hardened heart that crowds out our thoughts for God: "In his pride the wicked man does not seek him; in all his thoughts there is no room for God" (Psalm 10:4).

Regret commits at least two offenses: it fears and protects. Regret fears the loss of our pride, and it protects our pride. In essence, regret is anxiety about the past. Anxiety is a divided mind—one that only partly trusts in God and partly trusts in ourselves.

Fear and protection are the two defense mechanisms of our fallen mind of pride. Every inclination of our thoughts is bent toward evil, trusting in ourselves rather than God (Genesis 6:5; 8:21). Jesus said that these evil thoughts come from a divided mind (Matthew 12:25; 15:19; Mark 7:21). Holding on to regret is an evil thought rooted in pride that is diametrically opposed to God's design because it trusts in ourselves, not God.

FEAR can be defined in an acrostic: frustrated expectations assume regret. Fear stems from unrealistic expectations about the past offense, the offender, or our behavior. It minimizes or reduces expectations that people will sin against us, and that we might not respond wisely. Unmet expectations are the cause of frustration that feeds regret, which leaves us saying, "I could've, would've, or should've."

Protection seeks to defend our unrealistic expectations in order to keep our pride. In our mind, we think if we can protect our pride in changing the past, then we can be victorious over the offender.

Regret imprisons us in the past and robs us of the present and the future. When we are imprisoned by withholding forgiveness and holding on to regret, we do not trust God's forgiveness. When we don't trust God, we are not loving Him with all of our mind—the vertical portion of the greatest commandment (Matthew 22:37; cf. Deuteronomy 6:5). This robs us of fully experiencing His presence and the future He has designed for us.

How Does Regret Affect
Our Relationships?

Psalm 139:23–24

IS regret of someone's past sin against you stifling your relationships? In the heat of conflict, did you raise your voice to abnormal decibels or say something you wish you hadn't that led to the offense against you? Are you constantly rethinking your actions, surmising you could have changed something to have totally avoided the negative interaction? If so, you are holding on to the thought that you could have changed the past.

Regret works by fearing and protecting. We live out the thought that we could change the past, not only in our relationship with an offender, but also in our relationships with others. The danger is we define ourselves by the past offense and its subsequent regret—the thought that we could have changed it. This violates the horizontal portion of the greatest commandment to love our neighbor, including our offender (Matthew 22:39).

As an example from the Bible of someone who allowed thoughts about the past to imprison him, King Saul feared David, God's anointed successor to the throne. Saul's thoughts of "I could've, would've, or should've" were often followed by the words "killed David." Saul's divided mind led to his repeated protection of his own kingdom as well as an on-again, off-again relationship with David and others around him.

Is regret causing you to fear and protect? Are you constantly thinking, "I could've, I would've, I should've changed the past?" Ask the Holy Spirit to search your heart for the sin of regret. Pray David's refining prayer: "Search me, God, and know my heart; test me and know my anxious thoughts. See if there is any offensive way in me, and lead me in the way everlasting" (Psalm 139:23–24). Ask Him to lead you down a new path, one that finds freedom in the Forgiver.

How Do We Let Go of Regret Vertically With God?

Philippians 4:6–7

OFTENTIMES, we utter the words, "I'm struggling to forgive God for allowing this tragedy to happen to me," when in fact we cannot forgive God because He has not sinned against us. However, we can let go of regret, the thought that we could have changed the past, which tends to be the core issue.

In order to let go of regret vertically with God, we must repent, which means "to change our mind." This represents a 180-degree turn from thinking we could change the past to changing the past thinking. Rather than holding on to the thought that we could change the offense, the offender, or our past behavior, we learn to change our thoughts about the past. We trust in God for the freedom of forgiveness.

Repentance is a turning that includes two components, one representing what we turn from, the other what we turn to: we let go of the past and we hold on to the present. Whereas intellectual sorrow leads to imprisonment, repentance comes from godly sorrow that leads to salvation's freedom and leaves no regret (2 Corinthians 7:10). Paul said that he let go of the past in order to hold on to the present that led to his vertical future (Philippians 3:13–14).

In order to let go of the past, we must recognize that God does not change the past, and yet, His most frequent Old Testament command is "Fear not." We must humble our mind by letting go of fear and protection language ("I could've, I would've, or I should've").

God removes our fear and protection perspective when we pray, asking Him to search us and reveal any regret—any anxious thoughts that we could change the past, thoughts of fear and protection (Psalm 139:23–24). Then, we let go. When imprisoned by anxious thoughts, prayer aligns our mind with Christ's (Philippians 4:6–7).

Next, we hold on to the present (which leads to the future) by learning wisdom and receiving forgiveness discovered in the presence of God. Wisdom changes our language from words that hold on to regret to words that hold on to learning: "We can learn, we will learn, and we shall learn to repent and be free from the imprisonment of regret."

The best way to garner wisdom is to read the Bible, storing its wisdom in our mind (Hebrews 4:12) so that we might trust God (Proverbs 22:17–19). Only when we trust God can we love Him with all our mind (Matthew 22:37), focusing on things above (Colossians 3:2) and receiving the mind of Christ (1 Corinthians 2:16). Jesus taught: "Learn from me" (Matthew 11:29).

Read aloud these two verses: "Do not be anxious about anything, but in every situation, by prayer and petition, with thanksgiving, present your requests to God. And the peace of God, which transcends all understanding, will guard your hearts and your minds in Christ Jesus" (Philippians 4:6–7). Make this your prayer to God. He will free you from the imprisonment of regret.

How Do We Let Go of Regret Horizontally in Relationships?

Philippians 2:3

IN order to let go of regret horizontally in relationships, we must repent, trusting in God for the freedom of forgiveness. Rather than harboring the thought that we could change the offense, the offender, or our past behavior, we change our thoughts about the past. We let go of the past and hold on to the present.

In order to repent and let go of regret, first we must let go of our past fear and protection, releasing our unrealistic expectations that we are holding against the offender. We pray and ask God two revealing questions, which can uncover our hidden cause of regret: *"What do I fear?"* and *"What am I protecting?"* If we are honest, each answer will include the word, pride.

Second, we must hold on to the present and learn to love our offender with our mind because they are our neighbor (Matthew 22:39). In order to do this, we must first read the Bible to learn the prerequisite to loving him. Paul said that in humility we need to consider others better than ourselves (Philippians 2:3). This includes our offender. Thus, we turn from the thought that we could change the past to changing our thoughts about the past. This frees us to live and learn in the present.

Picture the offender against whom you are holding on to regret and subsequently withholding forgiveness. Pray to God, asking, "What do I fear? What am I protecting?" Then, confess the fear and protection of pride that you are white-knuckling. Read Philippians 2:3, speaking each word aloud: "Do nothing out of self-ambition or vain conceit. Rather, in humility value others above yourselves." Ask God to teach you how to wisely humble yourself toward the offender.

Freedom From Regret

2 Corinthians 10:5

ARE you still holding on to regret, imprisoned by the thought that you could have changed the past?

In order to be free from regret, we must continue to practice the instant forgiveness experiment. When someone sins against us, we can instantly let go of the prison wall of regret by *repenting*: letting go of the past and holding on to the present. Rather than operating with pride, we live in humility toward Christ and others. We give up pride's fear and protection language ("I could've, would've, or should've") for humility's words of learning ("I can, I will, and I shall"). We accomplish this by following the apostle Paul's teaching: "We demolish arguments and every pretension that sets itself up against the knowledge of God, and we take captive every thought to make it obedient to Christ" (2 Corinthians 10:5).

When someone sins against you, instantly let go of the thought that you could change the past and repent by changing your thoughts about the past. Let go of the past fear and protection and hold on to the present and learn. Renew your mind daily through prayer and the Scriptures by taking every thought captive and making it obedient to Christ. The Spirit of God and the Word of God will free you to live wisely among the people of God.

The Prison Wall of Resisting Blessing

Matthew 5:43–48

ARE you withholding something positive from a person who has sinned against you?

Resisting blessing is not wishing someone well before God and others. Whereas the other three prison walls of withholding forgiveness hold on to negatives, resisting blessing white-knuckles a positive. We withhold wishing the offender well before God and others—the ultimate goal of forgiveness. This withholding occurs in our heart—our will, emotions, mind, and spirit. Whereas *revenge* emphasizes the *will*, *resentment* emphasizes the *emotions*, and *regret* emphasizes the *mind*, *resisting blessing* emphasizes the *spirit*. We choose to withhold spiritual blessing of our offender. In a word, it is *hate*—not loving our neighbor, including our enemy. We yield to our prideful desire to treat others as they treat us.

Jesus addressed this in the Sermon on the Mount: "You have heard that it was said, 'Love your neighbor and hate your enemy.' But I tell you, love your enemies and pray for those who persecute you, that you may be children of your Father in heaven. He causes his

sun to rise on the evil and the good, and sends rain on the righteous and the unrighteous. If you love those who love you, what reward will you get? Are not even the tax collectors doing that? And if you greet only your own people, what are you doing more than others? Do not even pagans do that? Be perfect, therefore, as your heavenly Father is perfect" (Matthew 5:43–48). Jesus called us to love and pray for those who sin against us.

Have you wished your offender well before God and others? Ask Jesus to give you His heart to do so. Don't resist blessing the person who harmed you. Rather, seek the Holy Spirit's guidance to love and pray for the one who did you wrong.

How Does Resisting Blessing Affect Our Relationship With God?

1 John 4:20

A RE you involved in a conflict where you simply cannot bless the offender?

Resisting blessing does not wish our offender well before God. It treats others as they treat us. Jesus said that His followers had been taught a legalistic interpretation of the greatest horizontal commandment to love one's neighbor (Matthew 5:43). They had learned to treat others as they were treated by them. "Hate your enemy" did not come from Moses' Law, but from the Pharisees as an abuse of Leviticus 19:18. In fact, the Law stated that hate was not to flow from anyone's heart (Leviticus 19:17).

When we resist blessing our offender, we harden our heart toward God. This occurs in at least two ways.

First, resisting blessing impedes our love for God. When we resist blessing our offender, we are not loving our neighbor whom Jesus defined as everyone, including our enemy (Luke 10:36–37). Rather,

we hate them. When we hate our enemy who is made in God's image, we are not loving God: "Whoever claims to love God yet hates a brother or sister is a liar. For whoever does not love their brother and sister, whom they have seen, cannot love God, whom they have not seen" (1 John 4:20).

Second, resisting blessing our offender affects our vertical relationship with God by hindering our prayers because we will not pray for our offender, wishing him well before the Almighty. For example, Peter said that a husband's prayers are hindered when he is inconsiderate and disrespecting toward his wife (1 Peter 3:7). When we hold on to resisting blessing our offender, we are inconsiderate and disrespectful of someone else created in God's image.

Confess the white-knuckling of your offender to God, agreeing with His perspective of blessing. Ask Him to renew your heart to be like His.

Praying for an Offender

Matthew 5:43–48

HAVE you tried praying for the person who wronged you? If so, what did your prayer sound like? Too often we hold on to resisting blessing our offender.

Resisting blessing does not wish our offender well before God or others; it treats others as they have treated us, hardening our heart toward our enemies. Rather than love our offender, we actually hate them because we will not wish them well. As a result, we will not love them in a way that God wants us to love them, and we surely will not pray for them, even when praying with other people. We find ourselves withholding positive conversation or behavior from our offender and about our offender with others.

Jesus offered a different way. We let go of resisting blessing by wishing our offender well before God and others. This occurs in two ways, we: love our enemy and pray for them even when they persecute us (Matthew 5:43).

We begin by wishing our enemy well before God. We *love* our enemy by *praying* for them to be blessed in the exact same way we want to be blessed by God (Matthew 5:44). This releases the heart of Christ in our vertical relationship with God who loves both the righteous and the unrighteous (Matthew 5:45). Christ loved His enemies and prayed for those who persecuted Him (Luke 23:34). We love God by being His child, surrendering to Christ in us (Galatians 4:7).

Today, read Matthew 5:43–48, then pray. At the close of your prayer, review the dominant theme you have requested from God for your life. Now pray that same blessing for your offender.

How Do We Let Go of Resisting Blessing Horizontally in Relationships?

Matthew 7:12

CAN you honestly say that you love your offender? In order to truly let go of resisting blessing our enemy horizontally in relationships, we wish our enemy well before others.

First, we *love* our enemy by serving them in order to meet a legitimate need in their life. This love fulfills the Law: "So in everything, do to others what you would have them do to you, for this sums up the Law and the Prophets" (Matthew 7:12). Second, we *pray* for them when we are with a close confidant with whom we share most of our walk with Christ. If prompted by the Holy Spirit, we then pray with our offender that God would bless them in the same way that we have asked God to bless us. All of this is prerequisite to, not a result of, reconciliation. This treats our offender differently than we were treated, which exhibits the humble, forgiving, and wise heart of Christ rather than the proud, unforgiving, and foolish heart that is opposed to Him (Matthew 5:46–47).

During the next week, love your enemy by discovering a need you can meet. It might be a house that needs cleaning, leaves that need raking, children that need watching, clothes that need replacement, a car that needs repair, a vendor that needs recommendation, or a potential customer that needs referral. Ask your mutual walk partner in Christ to pray with you in order to bless your offender. After serving your offender, if prompted by the Holy Spirit, humbly pray with them, requesting God's blessing in their life.

Continue to practice the instant forgiveness experiment. When someone sins against you, instantly let go of the four prison walls of *revenge, resentment, regret,* and *resisting blessing.* Do this by humbling your heart to Christ in you. He is complete in His love for all, including your enemies (Matthew 5:48; cf. Luke 6:36; Deuteronomy 18:13).

Guard Your Heart From Satan's Schemes

Proverbs 4:23–27

A**RE** you being tempted to commit an act apart from God's design for your life?

When we read David's instructions to his son, Solomon, in Proverbs 4:1–9, we recognize the King of Israel was warning his eventual successor that he would be tempted toward foolish behavior. Wisdom would be his weapon to apply his relationship with God to his circumstances. The Hebrew word for *wisdom* is *chokmah*, which is the intersection of the vertical (God's heart) with the horizontal (street smarts). Wisdom delivers us from temptation. The key that unlocks this gateway to God's protection is humility. When we humble our hearts to the Spirit of God, His wisdom flows through us (Proverbs 1:7; 9:10).

Our enemy, Satan, is a schemer. However, the Bible exposes his strategy (2 Corinthians 2:11). Just remember the fishing analogy: bait, hook, line, and sinker. First, Satan *baits* us with *temptation* (Matthew 4:3). Second, he *hooks* us in the *deceit* of dissatisfied desires

(2 Corinthians 11:14). Third, he lifts the *line* from the water with the *accusation* of evil before God and others (Revelation 12:10). Fourth, he *sinks* us in *destruction* (1 Peter 5:8; John 10:10).

Solomon taught that Satan's prey is our hearts, mouths, eyes, and feet: "Above all else, guard your heart, for everything you do flows from it. Keep your mouth free of perversity; keep corrupt talk far from your lips. Let your eyes look straight ahead; fix your gaze directly before you. Give careful thought to the paths for your feet and be steadfast in all your ways. Do not turn to the right or the left; keep your foot from evil" (Proverbs 4:23–27).

Are you facing a decision where you know what is right, but you are being tempted to do the opposite? Turn to the wisdom of God in Jesus Christ. Run to Him. He will renew your heart and direct your paths toward freedom in a wise choice only He can provide.

Satan Is a Tempter

Matthew 4:3–11

SATAN is a tempter. Too often, we see temptation as a sin; however, temptation is not from God, and being tempted is not a sin (James 1:13–14). Jesus was tempted in every way that we are, and yet He did not sin (Hebrews 4:15).

Wisdom delivers us from temptation. Jesus Christ is the wisdom of God (1 Corinthians 1:24), and His Spirit leads us away from falling prey to any temptation, whether it be lust of the flesh, pride of life, or lust of the eyes (1 John 2:16).

Jesus was tempted with the lust of the flesh: "The tempter came to him and said, 'If you are the Son of God, tell these stones to become bread.' Jesus answered, 'It is written: "Man shall not live on bread alone, but on every word that comes from the mouth of God"'" (Matthew 4:3–4).

Jesus was tempted with the pride of life: "Then the devil took him to the holy city and had him stand on the highest point of the temple. 'If you are the Son of God,' he said, 'throw yourself down. For it is written: "He will command his angels concerning you, and they will lift you up in their hands, so that you will not strike your foot against

a stone."' Jesus answered him, 'It is also written: "Do not put the Lord your God to the test"'" (Matthew 4:5–7).

Jesus was tempted with the lust of the eyes: "Again, the devil took him to a very high mountain and showed him all the kingdoms of the world and their splendor. 'All this I will give you,' he said, 'if you will bow down and worship me.' Jesus said to him, 'Away from me, Satan! For it is written: "Worship the Lord your God, and serve him only."' Then the devil left him, and angels came and attended him" (Matthew 4:8–11).

When Jesus was tempted, He used the Word of God to defeat temptation and not sin. You can do the same. Next time you are tempted toward foolish behavior, recognize Satan's bait for what it is, an enticement into a trap. Recite the appropriate Scripture above used by Jesus. He will deliver you from the temptation and direct you toward wisdom.

Satan Is a Deceiver

2 Corinthians 11:14

HAVE you ever been deceived by Satan? Did you take his bait, only to discover you had been duped? Perhaps it was a lustful act, an angry tirade, a substance abuse, or a foolish risk that left you feeling dissatisfied.

Satan is a deceiver: "And no wonder, for Satan himself masquerades as an angel of light" (2 Corinthians 11:14). This means he will make the temptation, or bait, look good. However, it is all part of Satan's masquerade, which hides the danger inside the temptation. Within the bait, he disguises a hook—sin's hook of dissatisfied desires. Whereas Satan's bait falsely promises to satisfy our desires, the hook holds us captive when we fall prey to the temptation and sin. The deceitful hook of dissatisfied desires sets us up to be even more vulnerable to the original temptation.

Only Christ can truly satisfy our desires.

If you have been deceived by Satan, confess your sin of pursuing the temptation, remembering: "If we claim to be without sin, we deceive ourselves and the truth is not in us" (1 John 1:8). Turn to Christ, the truth of God, who will set you free from Satan's hook and make you new again. "If we confess our sins, he is faithful and just and will forgive us our sins and purify us from all unrighteousness" (1 John 1:9).

Find a confidant to whom you can confess your sin and restoration. Ask them to become a mutual walk partner, someone with whom you can share any temptation before falling prey to the enemy's hidden hook of sin and dissatisfied desires. Do the same for your friend. Christ will use both of you to bring His restoration to others.

Satan Is an Accuser

Revelation 12:10

HAVE you ever noticed how someone who makes an accusation typically practices the act that he accuses another of doing? Satan is the origin of the evil that he accuses humanity of committing.

Satan is an accuser: "Then I heard a loud voice in heaven say: 'Now have come the salvation and the power and the kingdom of our God, and the authority of his Messiah. For the accuser of our brothers and sisters, who accuses them before our God day and night, has been hurled down'" (Revelation 12:10).

Just like a fisherman pulls the line from the water to show everyone what he caught, so Satan lifts up his line to show God and others who he has snagged. He uses the line of accusation to convict us of sin against the Holy One.

Has Satan snagged you with his line of accusation? Perhaps you are even accusing someone else of a similar sinful behavior. Repent. Literally, see it differently. Pursue Christ's authentic design for your life. He will set you free.

Satan Is a Destroyer

1 Peter 5:8; John 10:10

ARE you experiencing destruction from falling prey to Satan's temptation? Did you succumb to his enticement, only to discover his bait concealed the hook of dissatisfied desires that trapped you in sin, and now you stand accused before God and others?

Satan is a destroyer: "Be alert and of sober mind. Your enemy the devil prowls around like a roaring lion looking for someone to devour" (1 Peter 5:8). Satan wants to wreck each one of us, so he tempts us to desire life apart from God. The result is death and destruction.

Jesus offered a solution to this pattern: "The thief comes only to steal and kill and destroy; I have come that they may have life, and have it to the full" (John 10:10). Christ has liberated believers from death and destruction to experience eternal and abundant life in Him.

The sinker that took the bait, hook, and line down is designed to take us down with it. Although the bait of temptation appears to be attractive, the hook of dissatisfied desires is disguised to keep us returning to the bait. The line of accusation presents us before God and others as fallen prey to Satan whose intent is to destroy us.

Don't be destroyed by desiring life apart from God. Regardless of your circumstances, Christ can and will set you free. Simply pray to Him, "I can't. You can. I can't free myself from the penalty of sin. God in Christ You can. I can't free myself from the power of sin, God in Christ You can." "I can't" is repentance. "You can" is faith. One day, Christ our Forgiver and Restorer will free us from the presence of sin in eternity with Him.

The Work of a Defeated Being

Hebrews 2:14–15; 1 John 3:8

WE have often watched football games where one team was way ahead of the other as the final seconds ticked down on the clock. With no hope of victory, the squad being trounced on the scoreboard resorted to cheap shots, baiting the winning players into a brawl, in an attempt to take them down. These are the characteristics of a defeated team.

The Bible makes it clear that Satan's bait, hook, line, and sinker are all the work of a defeated being, one who has already lost and desires to take down anyone he can. Jesus was not only victorious over the temptation of Satan, He also defeated him through His life, death, and resurrection: "Since the children have flesh and blood, he too shared in their humanity so that by his death he might break the power of him who holds the power of death—that is, the devil—and free those who all their lives were held in slavery by their fear of death" (Hebrews 2:14–15).

When tempted, we have a choice to either succumb to the bait and experience destruction or to turn to the One who conquered sin and death: "The one who does what is sinful is of the devil, because the devil has been sinning from the beginning. The reason the Son of God appeared was to destroy the devil's work" (1 John 3:8).

The next time you are tempted, don't take the bait of a defeated being. Instead, surrender the temptation to Christ who will deliver you from the deception of sin and destruction. You will be victorious in the arena where it counts for eternity.

Satan Preys on the Heart

Proverbs 4:23

PRIORITY number one is that we should guard our heart with wisdom because all of life flows from it: "Above all else, guard your heart, for everything you do flows from it" (Proverbs 4:23).

God gave us at least four primary desires: *significance* from being created in God's image (Genesis 1:27a); *contentment* from being blessed by God (Genesis 1:28a); *control* from being empowered by God to rule the earth (Genesis 1:28b); and *security* from being provided all that we need (Genesis 1:29). Ever since the first sin of pride—desiring the satisfaction of these desires apart from God—the bent of the human heart has been toward evil (Genesis 8:21). Satan preys upon these desires with his bait of temptation (1 John 2:16).

Desiring the tempting bait is sin (James 1:14–15). When we mull over the pursuit of the temptation, we desire satisfaction of our desires apart from God, which is the definition of sin. We wrongly think the bait will satisfy; however, outside Christ, our desires remain dissatisfied. The deceitful hook of dissatisfied desires holds us captive to the sin: "The righteousness of the upright delivers them, but the unfaithful are trapped by evil desires" (Proverbs 11:6).

Jesus instructed that the desire for life, either with or apart from God, flowed from the heart (Matthew 12:35). Consequently, Satan

accuses the person whose heart is hooked in sin with dissatisfied desires by lifting up his line to show God and others what he has caught—a heart that desired life apart from the Creator.

The sinker is that God hates a heart that devises wicked schemes (Proverbs 6:18). The sinner is destroyed from the pursuit of his own evil desires.

Inventory your heart: your will, mind, emotions, and spirit. This includes your choices, your thoughts, your feelings, and prayers—or lack of them. What or who are you desiring in your heart? Is it wise or foolish? The answer lies in whether you are hooked in the pursuit of dissatisfied desires apart from the heart of God. During the next two weeks, keep a journal of your challenging choices, your predominant thoughts, your prevailing feelings, and your prayers. Examine the results to determine whether your heart has been hard or soft toward God.

Satan Preys on the Mouth

Proverbs 4:24

HAVE you ever uttered something and then wished you hadn't? Solomon recognized the potential danger in our speech: "Keep your mouth free of perversity; keep corrupt talk far from your lips" (Proverbs 4:24).

John said that one of the three pathways temptation flows is from our hearts to our mouths. Each of us can fall prey to the bait of boasting, which is an overstatement of the truth. The temptation is to make ourselves sound better than we really are.

Deceitfully hidden in the bait of boasting is the hook of dissatisfied desires: "The words of a gossip are like choice morsels; they go down to the inmost parts" (Proverbs 26:22). Although boasting words that lift us up or bring others down originate in our hearts and travel to the ears and hearts of others, they never satisfy. Unfortunately, we often keep trying to discover satisfaction in our loose lips.

The misuse of our tongues gets us in trouble with God: "To fear the LORD is to hate evil; I hate pride and arrogance, evil behavior and perverse speech" (Proverbs 8:13). A humble heart fears, or reveres,

God who hates a proud heart that leads to evil behavior, including the sin of perverse speech. Satan accuses us before God and others by lifting up his line to show his trophy—those who have misused God's gift of language.

The sinker is those who fall prey to the bait, hooked in their dissatisfied desires, standing accused, are destroyed because God hates the misuse of the mouth (Proverbs 6:17, 19).

Ask a close friend to help you take an inventory of your words for two weeks. Are they wise or foolish? Ask the person to let you know when you are misusing your mouth including boasting or bringing others down. Agree to share the times of misuse that occur when your friend is absent. Be sure to identify any recurring persons who are frequent targets of your boasting. God will use this exercise to transform your speech, refocusing your intentions to His design for your words.

Satan Preys on Our Eyes

Proverbs 4:25

WHAT has been the focal point of your eyes this week? Think about the images that captured your gaze most frequently. Now here's the big question: What do those images reveal about your heart?

The second target of temptation is the lust of our eyes (1 John 2:16). In our peripheral vision, we see money, jewelry, cars, electronics, houses, clothes, and images of other objects we are tempted to desire at the expense of Christ. Oftentimes the objects, including other persons, are not evil; rather, our desire for them apart from God is. We move them from the peripheral to the focal point of our eyes.

Recognizing our vulnerability to let our eyes wander, Solomon taught: "Let your eyes look straight ahead; fix your gaze directly before you" (Proverbs 4:25). Often, we see things we desire apart from Christ, and they look good to us. However, Satan's strategy is to take us down, bait, hook, line, and sinker.

Solomon clearly communicated the danger of following our eyes without wisdom: "Death and Destruction are never satisfied, and neither are human eyes" (Proverbs 27:20). Outside Christ, we always see and want more. Most likely being aware of this verse and having received the personal instruction of Christ, John taught: "The world

and its desires pass away, but whoever does the will of God lives forever" (1 John 2:17). Juxtaposed in this verse are the desires of the world against the will of God. The former provides insufficient and temporary gratification, the latter abundant and eternal satisfaction. The deceitful hook hidden inside the bait is our eyes are never satisfied apart from Christ. We sin when we desire any satisfaction apart from Him.

Knowing evil entered through our eyes (Proverbs 6:25), Satan lifts his line from the waters of temptation and sin to accuse us before God and others. Jesus revealed that the eyes are inextricably linked with the heart (Matthew 5:28). When a man fixes his gaze on a woman who is not his wife, he desires her in his heart, which is an adulterous act.

The sinker is our personal destruction because God hates eyes that sin (Proverbs 6:17).

What is the focal point of your eyes? When you close them at night, replay the day's images with God. Ask Him to guide you in determining which images were wise and which ones were foolish. Then pray that God will empower you by His Spirit to focus your eyes on wise images. He will deliver you from temptation and draw you to His design.

Our Children's Eyes

Proverbs 2:10–11

WHAT is the focal point of your child's eyes? We are reminded that God hates eyes that sin (Proverbs 6:17). Still, when the day's images replay in our children's minds, they often include what they have seen on the internet, whether wise or foolish.

Our culture, especially the millennial generation, is bombarded by social media images on a daily basis. Each month the number of active users skyrocket, nearing two billion on Facebook, 700 million on Instagram, and 328 million on Twitter. When we place smartphones in our children's hands, we make them accessible 24/7. Approximately twenty percent of all teenagers have texted or posted nude or semi-nude photos or videos of themselves, and thirty-nine percent of all teens have posted or texted sexually suggestive messages (The National Campaign).

To win the battle for our children's eyes, here are four helpful tools to wisely navigate social media:

Pre-approve all persons who can contact your teenager.

Provide absolutely no connection with the real world such as an address or telephone number via social media.

Plan how to shut down your student's site before you start it. Realize the risk of posted information that can always be retrieved.

Prepare a prospective employer-approved webpage. Employers use social media sites to investigate and verify the credibility of resumes.

Solomon promised the benefits of seeking God's street smarts: "For wisdom will enter your heart, and knowledge will be pleasant to your soul. Discretion will protect you, and understanding will guard you" (Proverbs 2:10–11). This promise covers our eyes.

Satan Preys on Our Feet

Proverbs 4:26–27

WHEREVER our feet carry us, we can sin. Even our hands are subject to where our feet travel: "Give careful thought to the paths for your feet be steadfast in all your ways. Do not turn to the right or the left; keep your foot from evil" (Proverbs 4:26–27).

The third of the three pathways temptation flows is roundtrip from our hearts to our flesh (1 John 2:16). This bait includes the misuse or abuse of food, drugs, alcohol, sexual acts outside marriage, or other abuses of the body.

Deceitfully disguised in the bait is sin's hook. Solomon warned about the feet of the adulteress: "Her feet go down to death; her steps lead straight to the grave" (Proverbs 5:5). He continued saying parenthetically: "She is unruly and defiant, her feet never stay at home" (Proverbs 7:11). The irony of an adulterous relationship with either an inanimate object or a person is that it never truly satisfies our desire because it lies outside God's design for our lives.

When we sin, Satan accuses us before God and others. He claims our feet were quick to rush into sin (Proverbs 1:16). Referring to adultery, Solomon included in his diatribe: "Can a man walk on hot coals without his feet being scorched? So is he who sleeps with another man's wife; no one who touches her will go unpunished" (Proverbs 6:28–29).

Destruction is embedded in the sinker that God hates feet that are quick to rush into evil (Proverbs 6:18).

Sin begins with our feet when we walk toward a temptation with the desire to take it. During the next two weeks, think about whether you are walking toward temptation. It might be a cubicle that you

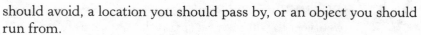

should avoid, a location you should pass by, or an object you should run from.

If you are a parent of a teenager, be proactive in his or her dating relationships. Indiana University Medical Center research shows that forty-one percent of girls ages fourteen to seventeen who have sex say they do so in order to keep their boyfriend from becoming angry. The temptation for a teenage girl and boy to walk where they should not go is strong. Consequently, we must guide them in straight paths by investing wisdom—God's heart combined with street smarts—into their lives.

Hope in Christ

1 Corinthians 10:13

D O Satan's schemes leveraging his bait, hook, line, and sinker leave you feeling hopeless?

There is hope, and that hope is Christ. He will guard our hearts. When temped with the bait, God always provides a way out in Christ: "No temptation has seized you except what is common to man. And God is faithful; he will not let you be tempted beyond what you can bear. But when you are tempted, he will also provide a way out so that you can stand up under it" (1 Corinthians 10:13). When deceived with the hook, Christ is the wisdom and power of God for us to become unhooked (1 Corinthians 1:24). When accused with the line, Christ intercedes on our behalf (Romans 8:34). When destroyed with the sinker, Christ defeated evil (Hebrews 2:14–15; 1 John 3:8).

We experience the hope of Christ through the *Word* of God, the *people* of God, and the *Spirit* of God. We connect with the Word of God when we read the Bible. Jesus quoted Scripture when He was tempted by Satan. Memorizing verses from the Bible is one of the most powerful tools to learn wisdom. We connect with the people of God when we enter into mutual walk with another Christ follower. We connect with the Spirit of God when we pray. We must model Christ's prayer of confidence in the Father who will lead us away from temptation and deliver us from evil (Matthew 6:13).

When we humble our hearts to the Spirit of God, His wisdom will flow through us: "Through love and faithfulness sin is atoned for; through the fear of the LORD evil is avoided" (Proverbs 16:6).

Why Does God Ask You to Walk Through a Door He Decides to Close?

Psalm 78:70–72

A FRIEND asked me this question, after sensing God's clear prompting to become a candidate in his company's search process for their new CEO, only to make it to the final four and not be selected. The search committee even communicated that he was a leading candidate for the next time the CEO position became available. Here's my answer to his insightful question.

Preparation of your heart and hands. If this has happened to you, God and your organization have both communicated you would lead. Now it's a matter of accepting your new journey of preparation. This is similar to David being anointed by Samuel, and then waiting and being prepared during Saul's reign. Here's insight into King David's journey: "He chose David his servant and took him from the sheep pens; from tending the sheep he brought him to be the shepherd of his people Jacob, of Israel his inheritance. And David shepherded them with integrity of heart; with skillful hands he led them" (Psalm 78:70–72).

Integrity means "complete." God is completing your heart and bringing the skills to your hands. In fact, we could insert your name and your current and future roles in place of David's above. You might try it and read it out loud.

Almost every subsequent King of Judah experienced the same preparation through a co-regency with an elder monarch. Each knew his eventual role, but the preparation was paramount, similar to our position as believers on this earth today. Even Jesus waited until the appropriate time to announce His kingdom.

Now you are free to grow with a clear perspective of the leadership role, void of any unhealthy ownership, as God prepares your heart and hands. It's an enjoyable place to be.

How to Be Thankful: The Magnifying Glass

1 Thessalonians 5:18

Do you ever focus on the negative at the expense of being thankful? The problem lies in the eyes of our hearts. Anxiety focuses on the negative, making it the antithesis of thanksgiving, which is a joyful attitude that occurs through prayer when our hearts are fully focused on God in Christ (Philippians 4:6).

Anxiety is a divided inner being, one where our hearts attempt to focus on the circumstances at the expense focusing on Christ. This halfhearted attempt at getting through conflict deters us from giving thanks to God. Yet Paul encouraged God's people to: "Give thanks in all circumstances; for this is God's will for you in Christ Jesus" (1 Thessalonians 5:18; cf. Ephesians 5:20; Colossians 3:17).

Paul's challenge can be pictured in the image of a magnifying glass that enlarges its focal point, while the images around it become fuzzy. When presented with conflict, we either focus on Christ or our circumstances. When we focus on Christ, our circumstances become fuzzy. However, when we focus on our circumstances, Christ becomes fuzzy. This foolishness of the heart darkens our divine focus (Romans 1:21) and leads to foolish, negative talk that flows from an ungrateful heart (Ephesians 5:4).

Today, focus on Christ, rather than your circumstances. Pray and ask Him to reveal any anxiety and make you new again.

How to Be Thankful: Peter and the Wind

Matthew 14:23–33

AN example of anxiety stemming from the focus of the eyes of the heart occurred with Jesus's disciple Peter. During the late night as His disciples sailed on the Sea of Galilee to Gennesaret, Jesus had finished praying in solitude on a mountainside near Bethsaida where He had fed 5,000 men (Matthew 14:23). When a storm hit, His disciples' boat nearly capsized as it tossed a considerable distance from shore (Matthew 14:24). Amid this conflict is precisely when Jesus walked on water to their boat (Matthew 14:25). When the disciples saw their Master, they experienced tremendous anxiety, thinking they had just encountered a ghost (Matthew 14:26). Jesus identified Himself and told His pupils to take courage and not be afraid (Matthew 14:27).

After confirming Jesus's identity, and with not only the eyes of his head, but also the eyes of his heart, focused on Christ, Peter jumped out of the boat and walked on the water, too (Matthew 14:28–29). Then Peter did something foolish. He shifted his focus away from Christ to the stormy circumstances, and he saw the wind, once again experiencing such anxiety that he cried out in fear (Matthew 14:30). Immediately, Jesus reached out His hand, catching not only Peter's

body, but also his heart with these words: "You of little faith . . . why did you doubt?" (Matthew 14:31). When they climbed into the boat, the wind died down, and the disciples worshiped Christ in thanksgiving for who He was, God in the flesh (Matthew 14:32–33).

We can learn a valuable lesson from Peter's story. Life is indeed like a magnifying glass. We magnify the focal point and what is around it becomes fuzzy. When we focus the eyes of our hearts on Christ, our circumstances become fuzzy, and we can be thankful in worship of who He is. When we focus the eyes of our hearts on our stormy circumstances, Christ becomes fuzzy and we experience anxiety, a halfhearted attempt at getting through conflict. Whether we are thankful or anxious depends on the focus of the eyes of our hearts.

Years later, Peter wrote: "Cast all your anxiety on him because He cares for you" (1 Peter 5:7).

Today, shift your eyes from the negative in your circumstances to the positive restoration in Christ.

How to Be Thankful: Look at the Downside

Psalm 28:7; 1 Timothy 1:12

WHEN we are tempted to be ungrateful, we must ask God to realign our focus 360 degrees: the downside, upside, inside, and outside. First, we must look at the downside.

Regardless of our circumstances, it could be worse. This is hindsight that is mindful. In a cry for help, David thanked God for His strength and protection: "The LORD is my strength and my shield; my heart trusts in him, and he helps me. My heart leaps for joy, and with my song I praise him" (Psalm 28:7).

David recognized apart from God his circumstances could have been worse. Confirming he could not have ministered without God, Paul informed Timothy: "I thank Christ Jesus our Lord, who has given me strength, that he considered me trustworthy, appointing me to his service" (1 Timothy 1:12). In other words, left to himself, Paul would not have been strong enough or faithful enough to be appointed to God's service. He was thankful for God in all circumstances.

What are your stormy circumstances? They might include a marital trial, debt, disappointment from a loss, an estranged relationship, a tragic accident, a lawsuit, or perhaps tremendous success that has translated into busyness. Where is your focus? Do you fix the gaze of your heart on Christ or the circumstances? Look at the downside. It could be worse. Consider journaling your choices, thoughts, prayers, and feelings as you recognize God's provision and protection. Write down how matters could be more severe. Then thank God for being your strength and shield.

How to Be Thankful: Consider the Upside

Hebrews 12:28–29

IN any trial, there's always an upside.

In stormy circumstances, it can and will get better. This is foresight that is hopeful. While in prison, Paul called those in Christ to devote themselves to prayer, being watchful and thankful because God would advance His kingdom through them (Colossians 4:2). Circumstances would get better.

The writer of Hebrews looked at the upside of God's kingdom with thankfulness: "Therefore, since we are receiving a kingdom that cannot be shaken, let us be thankful, and so worship God acceptably with reverence and awe, for our 'God is a consuming fire'" (Hebrews 12:28–29).

David wrote his Psalm of Thanks when the Ark of the Covenant was returned to Jerusalem, recognizing that God's blessings would follow (1 Chronicles 16:7–36). He thanked God for His righteousness that would prevail over the wicked (Psalm 7:17). The psalmists penned songs expressing their thanks to God for His continued deliverance (Psalm 100; 118; 136).

In spite of rebellious circumstances, Isaiah gave thanks because salvation would come through the Messiah (Isaiah 12:4). Daniel gave thanks as he looked at the upside of Babylonian captivity when interpreting King Nebuchadnezzar's dream (Daniel 2:23). He continued to give thanks on his knees in prayer three times a day under yet another foreign regime, even though it would lead him to the lion's den (Daniel 6:10). Nehemiah's two large choirs gave thanks for the upside God would provide after rebuilding the Jerusalem wall (Nehemiah 12:31, 40). The prophetess Anna thanked God for the redemption

He would provide through the infant Jesus when He was dedicated in the temple (Luke 2:38).

The upside in our circumstances is God will advance His kingdom through us when we focus on Christ, rather than the circumstances.

Look at the upside. Your circumstances can and will get better. Read Psalm 118 and Psalm 136. Then make a list of how your storm can improve by God advancing His kingdom through you. Thank God for what He will do. Memorize Psalm 100. Storing these fives small verses in your heart will equip you with a powerful resource to recall as you look at the upside and become thankful in all circumstances.

How to Be Thankful: Peer on the Inside

Psalm 139:23–24

WHEN we are imprisoned by perfectionism and tempted to be ungrateful, we must ask God to realign our focus and peer on the inside.

We can ask the Holy Spirit to examine our hearts. This is insight that is worshipful.

Our circumstances are not always the cause for our anxiety; rather, it is often our beliefs about our circumstances that create our emotional consequences. When we experience anxiety, we should pray a thank offering of our hearts to God (Philippians 4:6). The Old Testament writers saw a thank offering as worship, or a surrendering of the heart (Leviticus 7:12; 22:29; Psalm 116:17; Jeremiah 17:26; 33:11; Amos 4:5). Giving thanks is an act of worship where we focus on Christ, not the circumstances.

David said a thank offering fulfilled his heartfelt vow to God (Psalm 56:12; cf. Psalm 50:14). We can worship God because He is deserving of our praise. Hezekiah's thank offering came after repairing the temple (2 Chronicles 29:11). We can worship God when He makes things new. Manasseh prepared a thank offering after restoring Jerusalem's outer wall, removing foreign gods and images from the temple, dismantling all the pagan altars he had built on the temple hill and in Jerusalem, and restoring the temple altar (2 Chronicles 33:16). We can worship God when He triumphs in our hearts.

A thank offering honors God by not forgetting Him and prepares the way for us to find salvation (Psalm 50:22–23). The psalmist thanked God for that salvation (Psalm 116:12–13, 17). Paul called us to be thankful for the peace of Christ in our hearts (Colossians

3:15). Jesus thanked the Father for salvation evidenced in communion (Matthew 26:26–27; Mark 14:22–23; Luke 22:17, 19). Thankfulness comes from joy because God's unfailing love endures forever in our hearts (Psalm 107:1, 22).

Peer on the inside and ask the Holy Spirit to examine your heart. How do you need to grow internally? David was thankful in all circumstances by asking God to search and help him to surrender any anxiety inside his heart: "Search me, God, and know my heart; test me and know my anxious thoughts. See if there is any offensive way in me, and lead me in the way everlasting" (Psalm 139:23–24). Pray David's refining prayer of search and surrender. As God reveals areas of needed growth, write them down as an act of surrender. Then write a prayer of thanks to God for saving and growing your heart.

How to Be Thankful: Focus on the Outside

Acts 27:35–36

REGARDLESS of our circumstances, we can encourage others. This is outsight that is helpful. Jesus thanked the Father for listening in order to encourage others to do the same (John 11:41). The Levites thanked and praised the Lord every morning as an encouragement to God's people (1 Chronicles 23:30).

Paul was notorious for thanking God in order to encourage others. Among his fellow stranded travelers, Paul thanked God for His protection and provision during their shipwreck, recognizing both the downside and the upside from the inside (Acts 27:35). His gratitude encouraged those around him on the outside (Acts 27:36). Paul lived a life of 360-degree focus on Christ.

Jesus encouraged others with His generosity and thanksgiving. When He saw 5,000 hungry men, Jesus thanked the Father for His provision before He multiplied the five loaves and two tidbits of fish that left all of them encouraged (Matthew 14:19; 15:36; cf. Mark 6:41; Luke 9:16; John 6:11, 23). He did the same when feeding the 4,000 (Mark 8:6–7). Jesus thanked the Father for His provision before opening the eyes of the two on the Road to Emmaus (Luke 24:30–31). They left encouraged (Luke 24:31).

God created everything in order to encourage us. Paul told Timothy that everything God created is good, and nothing is to be rejected if received with thanksgiving because it is consecrated by the word of God and prayer (1 Timothy 4:3–5).

Focus on the outside. Amidst your stormy circumstances, encourage others by thanking God for them. Write in your journal the names of people for whom you are thankful and why. Pray for God

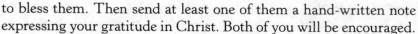

to bless them. Then send at least one of them a hand-written note expressing your gratitude in Christ. Both of you will be encouraged.

When faced with stormy circumstances, we are called to focus on Christ. Magnifying Him in our lives makes our circumstances fuzzy. When we are anxious and tempted to be ungrateful, we must ask God to realign our focus 360 degrees by surrendering the downside, upside, inside, and outside to Him. Giving thanks in all circumstances is God's desire for our lives in Christ. His hindsight, foresight, insight, and outsight provide us with the supercharged joy of thanksgiving that is mindful, hopeful, worshipful, and helpful.

Online With God 24/7

Psalm 37:4; 145

WHEN, where, and how do you pray? Is it only in times of crisis or need, possibly once a week at church?

Prayer is being online with God when our hearts are connected with His: "Take delight in the LORD, and He will give you the desires of your heart" (Psalm 37:4). Being online includes our uploads and God's download of His presence, along with links with others. Typically, we avoid prayer for two reasons: *cost* and *competence*. We do not want to risk the cost of our time, talent, or treasure; and we do not deem ourselves competent to pray. Consequently, we work offline from God, limiting our encounters with Him to a church building with a particular group of people functioning in a certain style for one hour on one given day of the week.

Addressing these barriers, David, who was the leader of the strongest superpower of his day, wrote what Spurgeon called his crown jewel psalm, a prayer song to God. Psalm 145, titled *a psalm of praise*, is an acrostic poem. Each verse (including 13b) begins with the successive letter of the Hebrew alphabet as a method to assist followers in memorizing the psalm.

Praise appears forty-eight times in Psalms 145–150 (the Hallel Hymns sung in the synagogues each morning), but David's idea of praise superseded the boundaries of a building, a particular group of people, a style, or the limits of one hour of a given day each week. Rather, he described praising God anywhere and everywhere as he painted a picture of being online with God 24/7, being a person who PRAYS (Praise, Renew, Ask, Yield, and Surrender to be Spirit-led). Interestingly, David's pattern of praise correlates with the flow of the Lord's Prayer evidenced in the life of Christ.

This week, take five minutes every waking hour to praise God for who He is. You will sense His presence in a new way.

Praise

Psalm 145:1–7; Matthew 6:9

HOW frequently do you take time to praise God?

Praise means "to bend down and to lift up." David bent the knees of his heart and lifted up the name of God daily: "I will exalt you, my God the King; I will praise your name for ever and ever. Every day I will praise you and extol your name for ever and ever" (Psalm 145:1–2). David's worship of the Lord was in full view for all to see as he communicated the heart of God to others who would transfer Yahweh's goodness to future generations (Psalm 145:3–7). When we praise God, we bend the knees of our hearts to lift Him up 24/7. This means we worship Him the most where others expect it the least, including in our work, play, homes, and churches.

In the Lord's Prayer, Jesus said: "Our Father in heaven, hallowed be your name" (Matthew 6:9). Heaven had three meanings: where we go when we die, the stars in the sky, or the air in and around us. Perhaps Jesus was emphasizing the close proximity of God, as close as the air in and around us.

When David praised his Creator, he experienced God's Person and power (Psalm 145:3–7). When we upload praise to God, He downloads His Person and power into our lives. This becomes evident in our communication of God to others. We transfer God's Person and power to them, both through our walk and our talk.

Praise God the most where people expect it the least. Praise Him 24/7, including in your work, play, home, and church. Identify any setting where you believe you are limiting your praise of God. Commit to lifting up God in that setting with your heart, desires, and life so that you worship Him 24/7. When you pray, praise your heavenly Father for Who He is (holy) and for being as close as the air in and around you. God will download His Person and power into your life, empowering you to link the same with others.

Renew

Psalm 145:8–13a; Romans 12:1–2; Matthew 6:10

HOW often do you renew your mind from the toxic thoughts that enter it?

David renewed his mind to be focused on God's kingdom rather than his own. A kingdom is the effective reach of one's will. In a monarchy, a king's will reached to the ends of his kingdom. However, atypical of an eastern ruler, David believed in an authority higher than himself. Similarly, we have the same opportunities to refocus our minds on God's kingdom within our personal kingdoms on earth. God desires that we experience His kingdom: His divine rule, reign, and order in the hearts and lives of people on this earth now and in the future. This occurs only with the supernatural renewing of our minds.

Paul taught: "Therefore, I urge you, brothers and sisters, in view of God's mercy, to offer your bodies as a living sacrifice, holy and pleasing to God—this is your true and proper worship. Do not conform to the pattern of this world, but be transformed by the renewing of your mind. Then you will be able to test and approve what God's will is—his good, pleasing and perfect will" (Romans 12:1–2).

In the Lord's Prayer, Jesus said: "Your kingdom come, your will be done on earth as it is in heaven" (Matthew 6:10). It was understood that after God's kingdom came, His will would be done on earth as in heaven. Jesus ushered in God's kingdom. As a result, this part of Jesus's prayer calls for the renewing of our minds in order to experience God's kingdom and will in our lives. This is a 180-degree turn from our world's standards. Jesus modeled this when He prayed for His Father's will (Matthew 26:39).

David advocated the depth and breadth of God's compassion, emphasizing that He was rich in love (Psalm 145:8–9). When we renew our minds to refocus on God's kingdom, we experience His passion, including His will for our lives. God desires we transfer His passion to the hearts and lives of others as we renew our minds (Psalm 145:10-13a).

Renew your mind 24/7 to refocus your efforts toward the advancement of God's kingdom, rather than your own. Memorize Romans 12:1–2. Recite it to God, praying to Him as you seek the renewal of your mind. God will download His passion, namely His will for your life, and you will link that passion with others.

Ask

Psalm 145:13b–16; Matthew 6:11

WHAT do you ask of God when you pray?

Because David depended on God, he asked Him to supply his needs. He recognized God as faithful, loving, restoring, giving, and satisfying (Psalm 145:13b–16). Today, we are offered the same opportunity to ask God to supply all our needs in Christ (Philippians 4:19).

In the Lord's Prayer, Jesus asked: "Give us today our daily bread" (Matthew 6:11). This referenced God's provision of Manna in the desert for the Israelites. It was an illustration of the people's total dependence on God to supply their needs to advance His kingdom.

When David asked God to supply all his needs, he received God's provision (Psalm 145:15–16). Consequently, David advanced the kingdom of God in others. When we ask God to supply our needs, we recognize our total dependence on Him to advance His kingdom through us and into others. Subsequently, He downloads His provision.

Ask God 24/7 to supply your needs to advance His kingdom through you and into others. When you pray, ask His Spirit to help you identify and provide any missing resource for you to communicate Christ to those in your life. God will download His provision and equip you to link His provision with others.

Yield

Psalm 145:17; Matthew 6:12

ARE you holding on to a past hurt by someone who has wronged you? If so, how is it affecting your relationship with God?

David recognized God's unlimited righteousness and love: "The LORD is righteous in all His ways and faithful in all he does" (Psalm 145:17). Righteousness and love are two components of forgiveness, God's vehicle that transports grace to others. *Forgive* means "to let go." When we let go, we yield. Just like a driver's response to a yield sign, when wronged, we slow down and let the other person go.

In the Lord's Prayer, Jesus said: "And forgive us our debts, as we also have forgiven our debtors" (Matthew 6:12). C.S. Lewis observed that, "as" was the most sobering two-letter word in all Scripture because the prayer is for God to forgive us in the same exact manner in which we have forgiven others. We have to yield all unsettled accounts to God, radically issuing to others the forgiveness we have received from Him. If we are not characterized and known as forgivers, then we have not truly received God's forgiveness (Matthew 6:14–15).

David yielded all unsettled accounts to God and experienced the Lord's peace through His righteousness and love. When we yield all unsettled relational accounts to God, He downloads His peace into our hearts, and we transfer that peace to our relationships with others. God's peace flows from His righteousness and love offered only in Christ.

Yield 24/7 all unsettled accounts to God. Let go and let God bring peace to your relationship with Him and your relationships with others. When you pray, seek the Spirit's guidance to reveal to you all unsettled relational accounts as you yield to Him. God will download His peace and help you link His peace with others.

Surrender to Be Spirit-Led

Psalm 145:18–21; Matthew 6:13

WHERE do you place your trust when you are tempted? We have an innate tendency to trust in our own strength, often falling prey to the temptation, rather than surrendering to the power of God who is present with us, ready, willing, and able to deliver us.

David was so in tune with the closeness of God that he called on Him in his times of need: "The LORD is near to all who call on Him, to all who call on Him in truth. He fulfills the desires of those who fear Him; He hears their cry and saves them. The LORD watches over all who love Him, but all the wicked He will destroy. My mouth will speak in praise of the LORD. Let every creature praise His holy name for ever and ever" (Psalm 145:18–21).

This included times of temptation. Though he did not get it right every time, David surrendered to be Spirit-led during the overall course of his life. We are guaranteed temptation on this side, but we are always provided a way out in Christ when we surrender to be Spirit-led (1 Corinthians 10:13).

In the Lord's Prayer, Jesus said: "And lead us not into temptation, but deliver us from the evil one" (Matthew 6:13). The Aramaic sentence structure might indicate, "Let us not sin when tempted," rather than, "Let us not be tempted." This is supported by the fact Scripture tells us God does not tempt anyone (James 1:13).

When David surrendered to be Spirit-led, he experienced God's protection (Psalm 145:19–20). When we surrender to be Spirit-led, God downloads his protection and uses us to transfer His protection to others.

Surrender your heart to be Spirit-led 24/7. When you are tempted, surrender to the Holy Spirit the bait and your desires that are luring you. When you wake up every morning, pray to God, surrendering your heart to Him. He will download His protection and guide you to link the same with others.

The House of Leadership:
The Footer of Humility

Proverbs 11:2; 9:10a; 22:4

Do you have a blueprint for success? Within your team, business, family, or nonprofit institution, do you have building plans to positively influence your target audience? Tucked away in the Bible's *Thirty Sayings of the Wise* is God's secret blueprint for any organization or movement to successfully lead its culture. It is His *House of Leadership*.

We must first dig down before God lays our foundation. Solomon taught: "When pride comes, then comes disgrace, but with humility comes wisdom" (Proverbs 11:2). Whereas pride is a hard heart that makes itself higher than others, humility is a soft heart that makes itself lower than others. Therefore, humility is bending the knees of our hearts first toward God and then toward people. Solomon's theme of Proverbs states: "The fear of the LORD is the beginning of wisdom" (Proverbs 9:10a). *The fear of the* LORD *is humility* toward God, our first step in the House of Leadership. This is the starting point for building a satisfied life: "Humility is the fear of the LORD; its wages are riches and honor and life" (Proverbs 22:4).

In order to lead any movement, we must be the first and most frequent to bend the knees of our hearts to God, like in the case of

Moses (Numbers 12:3). This prayerful clay heart translates in humility toward our peers. We listen more than we talk, we learn more than we teach, and we serve more than we are served, as God becomes the architect of our lives. Solomon declared God's role in the construction of any successful movement as nonnegotiable: "Unless the LORD builds the house, the builders labor in vain" (Psalm 127:1a). When our hearts are softened from pride to humility toward God and others, we are in the position for God to pour the footer and lay the foundation of wisdom in our lives.

Are you characterized and known by humility? Dig down for a heart transformation and bend the knees of your heart to God and others. Listen more than you talk. Learn more than you teach. Serve more than you are served.

The House of Leadership:
The Foundation of Wisdom

Proverbs 24:3a

IS the foundation of your life the rubble of foolishness or the firm foundation of wisdom?

After we humble our hearts to God, He lays our foundation. Left to ourselves, our foundation is foolishness, a progressive hardening of our hearts from wet cement to cured concrete in direct opposition to God. We deceive ourselves into believing that our foolishness represents a solid foundation when in reality it is quite brittle.

We begin as simple fools, progressing to stupid, then stubborn, followed by scorning, and finally secular—a journey from gullible to godless. However, Solomon communicated: "By wisdom a house is built" (Proverbs 24:3a). *House, bayith* in Hebrew, refers to any organization or movement. The foundation is where the vertical intersects with the horizontal—the definition of wisdom: God's heart (vertical) intersecting with street smarts (horizontal). Wisdom helps us apply our vertical relationship with God to our horizontal relationships and circumstances.

The Jews' ultimate name for God was *Wisdom*. The apostle Paul defined the wisdom of God not as a principle, but as a person—Christ (1 Corinthians 1:24). He went on to define Christ as the only foundation (1 Corinthians 3:11). This was not a new idea. Proverbs, the book of wisdom, described the preincarnate Christ as the wisdom of God (Proverbs 8:22–31). When we exchange foolishness for wisdom as the foundation of our lives, God begins to transform the rubble of our foolish failures into triumph in Christ.

Read a chapter in Proverbs each day, corresponding to the date of the month. Before you read, ask God to reveal the wisdom of Christ to you. Apply one verse from your daily reading to your calendar, seeing your entire day through its lens.

The House of Leadership:
The Framework of Understanding

Proverbs 24:3b

ARE you experiencing a conflict where your relationship is falling apart due to a misunderstanding?

After digging our footer and laying our foundation, God builds our framework. Solomon continued: "And through understanding it is established" (Proverbs 24:3b). *Understanding* is *insight* that occurs through the Holy Spirit (Proverbs 9:10). *Established* means "to build up." In order to build upon our foundation of wisdom, we must be equipped with the framework to see inside others.

Too often, we bring confusion to our relationships during interpersonal conflict when we take control, and are closed, heated, and blind. However, with understanding, we become Spirit-led (Proverbs 9:10; 3:5–6), teachable (Proverbs 15:32; 19:25; 17:10), cool (Proverbs 17:27), and insightful (Proverbs 20:5; 14:33; 28:11). Consequently, understanding sees inside a person's heart where we would like to build a bridge, moving us through interpersonal conflict laden with misunderstandings to divine insight into others.

Be plugged into the Holy Spirit. Live by the *Five-Second Rule.* Before every telephone call, text, email, encounter, or meeting, ask the Spirit of God to lead you. Prior to words or actions flowing from your body, ask Him, "What do You want me to do?"

Be teachable. Follow the *Times-Two Rule* by asking someone to coach you in an arena of your life where you can grow in understanding. Find someone who is wiser than you in that selected discipline. Meet at least once each month to pursue specific areas of improvement.

Be cool. Practice the *Ten-Second Rule.* Take your anger to God. As you begin to heat up, ask Him to *cool* you down keeping you *silent*

(Proverbs 11:12), *patient* (Proverbs 24:29), and *on a straight path* (Proverbs 15:21).

Be insightful. Apply the *Twenty-Second Rule* and look inside others. Take twenty seconds after each conversation to look past every person's words in order to peer inside their heart. Don't merely focus on their vocabulary, but reflect on what they were attempting to describe.

The House of Leadership:
The Furnishings of Knowledge

Proverbs 24:4

H OW well do you know the opposing person in your most current conflict?

Once our house is built, it is time to furnish it. Solomon concluded: "Through knowledge its rooms are filled with rare and beautiful treasures" (Proverbs 24:4). *Knowledge* is the connection of the innermost part of two or more persons through the Spirit of God. Consequently, knowledge is not merely information; rather, it is *intimacy*, an experiential connection with others. In essence, knowledge is a bridge we can cross to connect with the heart of another. Therefore, the House of Leadership is primarily about developing wise relationships.

Solomon's use of *rooms* refers to the inside of a house, imagery for any collection of relationships assembled to achieve a common goal—whether the association be in marriage, family, ministry, or the marketplace. Those relationships comprise *rare and beautiful treasures* in our hearts, the only riches on earth that will last for eternity. As a result, we must pursue relationship over remuneration in every association. If we don't, we build walls rather than bridges.

What walls need to come down in order for you to build a bridge? Ask the Holy Spirit to remove any sin of pride in you and help you connect with the heart and motives of your counterpart in your conflict. Make it your goal to restore the relationship. Pray that God will give you another rare and beautiful treasure for eternity.

The House of Leadership:
Building Walls or Bridges?

Proverbs 24:5b

ARE you building walls or bridges in your interpersonal conflict?

Left unchecked in conflict, we build four walls that disconnect us from others. First, we hold on to conflict, mulling over our selfish perspective of the two objects attempting to occupy the same space at the same time. Second, we foolishly seek the satisfaction of our selfish motives, neglecting to discover the motives of others involved in the conflict. Third, we fail to effectively communicate our motives. If we attempt to do so, we usually describe only our selfish desires, speaking with pride and foolishness. Finally, we leave the conflict unresolved. Today, marriages, families, ministries, teams, and marketplace relationships fail from a lack of intimacy, or knowledge.

Proverbs tells us that knowledge deepens our relationships and increases our strength to resolve conflict. Solomon taught: "Those who have knowledge muster their strength" (Proverbs 24:5b). Therefore, knowledge intimately navigates us through conflict to community in our relationships. Solomon gave us four steps to wisely connect with the innermost part of the person with whom we are having conflict: surrender our conflict to God (Proverbs 1:7), seek the motives of the persons involved (Proverbs 18:15), spell out our motives humbly and wisely (Proverbs 15:7), and solve the conflict by discovering common ground (Proverbs 11:9).

Surrender your conflict to God through prayer. Surrender your *motives, the person involved,* the *problem,* and *the outcome.* Ask God to shape your heart and desires to reflect His, giving you the knowledge for wise conflict management. Stop white-knuckling any selfish desires.

Seek the motives of the person involved in your conflict by *asking* and *listening.* Move from focusing on the outside to exploring the inside of your counterpart. First, *ask* questions that reveal motives of the heart: "What do you desire? Why?" Second, *listen* to what motives the person is attempting to describe.

Spell out your motives humbly and wisely. Use restraint by avoiding proud and foolish words.

Solve your conflict by discovering common ground in your motives with those of the other person involved. Use words that build bridges rather than put up walls. Don't be in a hurry to force someone into a manufactured quick fix. God will navigate you through conflict to community.

The House of Leadership: God's Blueprint for Creation

Proverbs 3:19–20

HAVE you hardened your heart toward God and made a string of foolish choices? Has the ensuing conflict left you confused? Do you feel disconnected from Him? If so, He is ready, willing, and able to offer you healing.

The House of Leadership is God's blueprint for success. This was His design when He created the earth: "By wisdom the LORD laid the earth's foundations, by understanding he set the heavens in place; by his knowledge the watery depths were divided, and the clouds let drop the dew" (Proverbs 3:19–20). God's House of Leadership restores our marketplace and ministry lives where He transforms us from pride to humility, from foolishness to wisdom, from confusion to understanding, and from disconnection to knowledge.

This was the apostle Paul's prayer: "For this reason, since the day we heard about you, we have not stopped praying for you. We continually ask God to fill you with the knowledge of his will through all the wisdom and understanding that the Spirit gives" (Colossians 1:9). However, our entrance to the House of Leadership is impossible outside a fully surrendered relationship with God in Christ because: "There is no wisdom, no insight, no plan that can succeed against the LORD" (Proverbs 21:30).

Are you willing to surrender what you have been holding back from God? Simply say to Him, "I can't. You can." *I can't* is repentance. *You can* is faith. God will answer your prayer by giving you a new heart in Christ and equip you to humbly bring wisdom, understanding, and knowledge to others in need.

Pray or Prey?

1 Peter 5:7–10

THERE is something about worry or anxiety that screams our need for God. When conflict in our hearts arise, our response is either to pray or become prey of the enemy. The apostle Peter clearly understood this internal battle.

Peter wrote: "Cast all your anxiety on him because he cares for you" (1 Peter 5:7). Anxiety is a divided inner being. It's like having one foot in and one foot out with God. Usually, we trust in ourselves more than we trust in God. Peter experienced this when he disowned Christ three times after His arrest (Mark 14:66–72). Relaying the stress he experienced, Peter communicated to anyone overcome with anxiety, "Pray."

Peter's rejection of Christ included adamant denial, cursing, and weeping. We often do the same, denying the opportunity to turn to Him when we are tempted to trust in ourselves, becoming vulnerable to Satan's attack. Peter warned: "Be alert and of sober mind. Your enemy the devil prowls around like a roaring lion looking for someone to devour" (1 Peter 5:8). In essence, Peter said, "Don't fall prey to the enemy!"

Satan wants nothing more than to destroy our intimacy with God. Recognizing this, Peter offered a prescription for suffering believers tempted to go it alone: *resist* and *stand firm*. "Resist him, standing firm in the faith, because you know that the family of believers throughout the world is undergoing the same kind of sufferings" (1 Peter 5:9).

When we pray, resist the devil, and stand firm in the faith, we experience God's grace, His undeserved love, His unmerited favor, that heals our hearts and makes us new again: "And the God of all grace, who called you to his eternal glory in Christ, after you have suffered a little while, will himself restore you and make you strong, firm and steadfast" (1 Peter 5:10).

Are you full of worry and anxiety? Pray so you don't become prey to the evil one. The Spirit of Christ is ready, willing, and able to deliver you from your vulnerability, guarding your heart like a military fortress, to restore you to His design for your life. Just like He prayed for Peter to turn back from Satan's prey in order to bring His restoration to others (Luke 22:31–32), so He prayed for you and me to do the same (John 17:20–21). That's why each of us can turn to Him and claim what Peter did: "Lord, to whom shall we go? You have the words of eternal life" (John 6:68).

In Christ to Instruct: Four Barriers to Evangelism and Discipleship

2 Timothy 2:1–2

HOW do you plan to equip and release future generations with the gospel of Christ? Rarely is this question addressed because we remove ourselves from the responsibility for at least four reasons captured in the following statements: "I'm not worthy," "I'll create conflict," "I don't have time," or "I don't know enough."

First, we feel *insignificant*, deeming ourselves unworthy to communicate anything about God. Second, we pray to God with *discontentment* our efforts will create conflict and further discontentment. Third, we choose to control our time, the lives of others, or the intended outcomes, resulting in our lives being *out of control*. Fourth, we are often *insecure*, fearing we do not know enough about God or the Bible to even think about first steps toward equipping and releasing one person from the next generation with the gospel message of Christ.

As a result of these four barriers, we do not choose, think, pray, or want the advancement of the kingdom of God in younger people, thereby breaking apart our relationship with God from our relationships with others. Still, the question lingers, "How will we equip and release future generations with the gospel message of Christ?"

God's answer to this question comes through the apostle Paul and lies in the cross, a symbol of the vertical intersecting with the horizontal. In his last will and testament, Paul communicated God's timeless evangelical message to his disciple Timothy, the pastor of the church at Ephesus: we are called to be in Christ to instruct. "You then, my son, be strong in the grace that is in Christ Jesus. And the

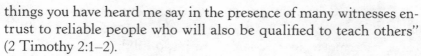

things you have heard me say in the presence of many witnesses entrust to reliable people who will also be qualified to teach others" (2 Timothy 2:1–2).

First, we must vertically surrender our lives to Christ as Savior, Lord, and Teacher. Second, we need to horizontally instruct others with His wisdom. Write down the name of the person from the next generation who God has prompted you to instruct. Pray for them to be open to your investment.

In Christ to Instruct: Learn to Teach

2 Timothy 2:1–13

WHEN we are in Christ to instruct, we *learn to teach*. Learning is the vertical component of the cross; teaching is the horizontal. In order to learn, we must engage in the grace of Christ. Paul wrote: "You then, my son, be strong in the grace that is in Christ Jesus" (2 Timothy 2:1). There is no other place or person where we can receive the grace of God.

When we fully surrender our hearts, desires, and lives to Him, He becomes our Teacher; and His instruction includes a purpose. We learn in order to teach others. Paul continued: "And the things you have heard me say in the presence of many witnesses entrust to reliable people who will also be qualified to teach others" (2 Timothy 2:2). We are to entrust the wisdom of Christ to others who will also be in Christ to instruct. As ministers, we were designed to learn to teach.

This will not come without opposition and challenges, so we must *endure* and *empower*. Paul warned: "Join with me in suffering, like a good soldier of Christ Jesus" (2 Timothy 2:3). *Endure* means "to be tenacious," like a warrior who battles for the advancement of Christ in the lives of others (2 Timothy 2:3–7). We are *empowered* with the resurrection of Christ and His unchained word so that we may empower others (2 Timothy 2:8–13).

First, ask yourself, *"Who is my teacher?"* Is Christ instructing you through a parent, grandparent, an older sibling, a coach, a professor, a friend, a life group leader, or a pastor? Do you even have a teacher? If not, pray to God and seek guidance. Survey your relationships for someone who could help teach about the heart and life of Christ. If

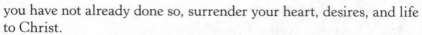

you have not already done so, surrender your heart, desires, and life to Christ.

Second, ask, *"Who is my student?"* Are you intentionally teaching anyone about Christ? If so, pray about how to best help him or her to grow in wisdom. Seek the Bible passages that are most suitable for the needs of your disciple. If you don't have a student, then pray to God and ask for one. Make your muscles move with your prayers by examining your relationships with those who could benefit from your investment. As you study your personal contacts, pray to discover God's prompting.

In Christ to Instruct: Getting the Word Into Our Words

2 Timothy 2:14–21

Hour often does the wisdom of the Bible flow into your words? When we are in Christ to instruct, we get the *Word into our words*. The Word represents the vertical, our words the horizontal. We are to keep reminding others of what we glean from the Word, warning them before God against quarreling words that have no value and actually ruin those who listen (2 Timothy 2:14). Paul instructed Timothy: "Do your best to present yourself to God as one approved, a worker who does not need to be ashamed and who correctly handles the word of truth" (2 Timothy 2:15). This helps us avoid godless chatter in our words, empty talk that, left unchecked, perpetuates a progressive ungodliness (2 Timothy 2:16–18). Instead, we confess Christ who cleanses us to be used for God's purposes (2 Timothy 2:19–21).

The apostles of Jesus who were used for God's purposes communicated that we are equipped to instruct others when God's Word gets into our words. Peter taught that God's Word is true (2 Peter 1:19–21). Paul stressed that all Scripture is inspired by our Creator and useful for teaching, rebuking, correcting, and training in righteousness, so all who are in Christ may be thoroughly equipped for every good work, including the instructing of future generations (2 Timothy 3:16). The writer of Hebrews noted that God's Word is living and active, able to sharply penetrate the heart, judging its thoughts and attitudes (Hebrews 4:12). When God's Word gets into our words, we are equipped to instruct others.

First, get into the Word. Delve into a book in the Bible that you could apply to the needs in your life. If you need wisdom, pursue

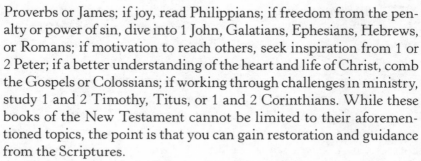

Proverbs or James; if joy, read Philippians; if freedom from the penalty or power of sin, dive into 1 John, Galatians, Ephesians, Hebrews, or Romans; if motivation to reach others, seek inspiration from 1 or 2 Peter; if a better understanding of the heart and life of Christ, comb the Gospels or Colossians; if working through challenges in ministry, study 1 and 2 Timothy, Titus, or 1 and 2 Corinthians. While these books of the New Testament cannot be limited to their aforementioned topics, the point is that you can gain restoration and guidance from the Scriptures.

Second, memorize a verse to assimilate the Word into your words. Speak the text of Scripture humbly and wisely. The more you get into the Word, the more it will get into your words, replacing godless chatter and making you useful for God's purposes.

In Christ to Instruct: Heart to Heart

2 Timothy 2:22

WHEN you communicate with others, do they connect with God's heart?

When we are in Christ to instruct, we connect *heart to heart*. We engage with God's heart to reach the hearts of others. God's heart is the vertical component of the cross; the hearts of others represent the horizontal component.

How do we connect our heart with God's? In order to be in Christ to instruct, we must fully surrender our hearts and our desires to Him. Paul described this pure heart condition, the object of our search, and the resulting satisfaction of full surrender to Christ when he said: "Flee the evil desires of youth and pursue righteousness, faith, love and peace, along with those who call on the Lord out of a pure heart" (2 Timothy 2:22). When we flee our evil desires of proudly searching for satisfaction apart from Christ, we humbly turn with a pure heart to our Savior, Lord, and Teacher in whom we find satisfaction of our desires.

Why does heart to heart work? *Righteousness* is what is right in God's sight, which is *truth* that satisfies our desire for *security*. *Faith* is trusting in God rather than ourselves for *control*, and that brings *power*. *Love* is self-sacrificial serving where we discover our ultimate *significance*. *Peace* is absence of strife in our relationships, satisfying our desire for *contentment*. When we are in Christ, He endows us with His heart.

Surrender your heart and desires to Christ, and His Spirit will connect your heart with His and those you encounter, in order to connect their hearts with Jesus.

In Christ to Instruct:
Connect With the Heart of Others

2 Timothy 2:22–26

HAVE you ever tried to debate someone into the kingdom of heaven? Perhaps, what started out as a healthy exchange of different experiences led to a foolish argument that didn't honor the heart of Christ.

Paul taught we connect with the heart of others by avoiding stupid arguments that produce quarrels (2 Timothy 2:23). We are designed to be kind, able to teach, and not resentful (2 Timothy 2:24). We are called to gently instruct people who oppose Christ in the hope that God will grant them repentance, leading to a knowledge of truth (2 Timothy 2:25).

Instructing with the gentle heart of Christ provides an environment for those who oppose Him to come to their senses and escape from the trap of the devil, who has taken them captive to do his will (2 Timothy 2:26). They, too, can be in Christ to instruct future generations if they fully surrender to Him as Lord, Savior, and Teacher.

In order to equip and release future generations with the gospel of Christ, we are called to be *in Christ to instruct*. First, we must vertically surrender our lives to Christ as Savior and Lord, embracing Him as our Teacher. Second, we need to horizontally instruct others with His wisdom. We reveal the cross when we learn to teach, get the Word into our words, and connect God's heart with the heart of others.

Solomon Pursued Earthly Knowledge for the Sake of Contentment

Ecclesiastes 1:12–18

H AVE you ever encountered God, yet pursued knowledge, possessions, might, money, or pleasure apart from Him to satisfy your desires? No one in history did this like Solomon.

Solomon was the Son of David and Bathsheba; named Jedidiah, which meant "loved by the Lord" (2 Samuel 12:24–25). He became Israel's third king who led its most prosperous forty years (1 Kings 11:42), renowned as the wisest man who ever lived before Christ (1 Kings 4:31).

Solomon encountered God who appeared to him twice (1 Kings 3:5–15; 9:1–9; 11:9). In his first encounter, God offered Solomon everyone's dream: "Ask for whatever you want me to give you" (1 Kings 3:5). Due to the conflict he would experience as king, Solomon asked for a discerning heart (1 Kings 3:9), and God granted that request (1 Kings 3:12). In Solomon's second encounter, God responded to Solomon's prayer of dedication for the temple (2 Chronicles 6:24–25, 36; 7:14). Despite those intimate encounters with God, Solomon pursued life apart from Him in at least five arenas that remain a risk for us today.

First, Solomon pursued earthly knowledge for the sake of contentment, leaving him discontented: "I, the Teacher, was king over Israel in Jerusalem. I applied my mind to study and to explore by wisdom all that is done under the heavens. What a heavy burden God has laid on mankind! I have seen all the things that are done under the sun; all of them are meaningless, a chasing after the wind. What is crooked cannot be straightened; what is lacking cannot be counted. I said to myself, 'Look, I have increased in wisdom more than anyone who has ruled over Jerusalem before me; I have experienced much of wisdom and knowledge.' Then I applied myself to the understanding

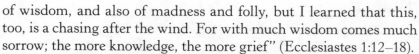

of wisdom, and also of madness and folly, but I learned that this, too, is a chasing after the wind. For with much wisdom comes much sorrow; the more knowledge, the more grief" (Ecclesiastes 1:12–18).

Contentment means "held together." We think if we are smart enough, we can hold it all together on our own, and we often end up on autopilot apart from God, the only One who can offer us true contentment in the peace of an intimate relationship with Him through Christ.

Solomon offered wise advice to many world leaders who traveled to meet him (1 Kings 4:34). He authored Proverbs, Ecclesiastes, Song of Songs, and two Psalms (72, 127). The king spoke 3,000 proverbs and wrote 1,005 songs (1 Kings 4:32). He described plant life (1 Kings 4:33) and taught about animals, birds, reptiles, and fish (1 Kings 4:33). Yet, he still pursued knowledge apart from God. One millennium later, James compared two kinds of wisdom: Godly and worldly. The former is selfless; the latter is selfish (James 3:13–16).

Pursue intimacy with God by reading the Bible daily, perhaps the chapter in Proverbs that corresponds to the date of the month. Allow the wisdom of Scripture to grow your selfless heart and never lord it over others as you rest contented in Him.

Solomon Pursued Possessions for the Sake of Significance

Ecclesiastes 2:4–8a, 11

HAVE you ever pursued the accumulation of possessions for significance? Significance includes the word, *sign*. In essence, significance says, "Hey, look at me." Sometimes, we think possessions will bring us the attention and meaning we seek. No one has attempted this at the level of Solomon.

The King of Israel constructed the temple in seven years (1 Kings 6:38); however, he invested thirteen years to build his palace (1 Kings 7:1). He constructed the wall around Jerusalem (1 Kings 3:1), built a fleet of ships (1 Kings 9:26), and developed many cities (1 Kings 9:15–18). The fact that kings and queens sought out his advice was evidence of his renown. He was a formidable leader. The community of Israel was climbing the ladder of socio-economic power, proving Solomon's influence to even the harshest of skeptics.

Solomon reflected: "I undertook great projects: I built houses for myself and planted vineyards. I made gardens and parks and planted all kinds of fruit trees in them. I made reservoirs to water groves of flourishing trees. I bought male and female slaves and had other slaves who were born in my house. I also owned more herds and flocks than anyone in Jerusalem before me. I amassed silver and gold for myself, and the treasure of kings and provinces" (Ecclesiastes 2:4–8a).

The pursuit of significance apart from God left Solomon empty, feeling insignificant: "Yet when I surveyed all that my hands had done and what I had toiled to achieve, everything was meaningless,

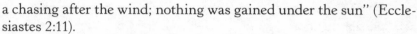

a chasing after the wind; nothing was gained under the sun" (Ecclesiastes 2:11).

True significance is only found in love, so unmerited and undeserved that it is called grace. Jesus Christ is the love of God (John 1:14; 3:16; 2 Corinthians 8:9). He offers us eternal significance when we say, "Hey, look at Him."

Ask yourself a simple question about your possessions: "Do I own the stuff or does the stuff own me?" Remember to trust in the Giver, not the gifts.

Solomon Pursued Military Might for the Sake of Control

Ecclesiastes 8:9b

DO you ever abuse control? When given more responsibility, do you exercise more and more authority over those around you? *Control* means "to roll against." When seeking control, we roll our will against others. Pursuing the development of his own mighty hand, Solomon experienced control issues.

Israel's king ruled over God's people (1 Kings 1:35), whom he overtaxed and drafted into the military, as he steamrolled foreigners into forced labor (1 Kings 9:20–23). He constructed 4,000 stalls for chariot horses and collected 12,000 stallions and mares (1 Kings 4:26; 10:26). This cut against God's desire (Deuteronomy 17:15–16) for a theocracy where He would rule (1 Samuel 8:7). To keep control of his borders, Solomon also built the strategic fortress cities of Hazor, Megiddo, and Gezer (1 Kings 9:15–18).

Solomon's pursuit of control apart from God led to a life out of control. In his last will and testament, he reflected: "There is a time when a man lords it over others to his own hurt" (Ecclesiastes 8:9b). However, when we surrender control to our Creator, we experience Christ the power of God is greater than our desire for control (1 Corinthians 1:24–25).

Are you lording it over others to your own demise? Whereas you probably do not have a military at your disposal, you most likely have enlisted many friends and acquaintances into a social one. This becomes convenient when relational challenges come your way. In your interpersonal conflict, beware of powering-up in relationships. Avoid rallying the troops around your selfish cause. Ask a trusted confidant: "Do I power-up on others?" Take their answers to God in prayer, surrendering all control to Him, as you experience the restorative power of Jesus Christ.

Solomon Pursued Money for the Sake of Security

Ecclesiastes 5:10; 7:12

WHERE do you turn for security? Is it a person, a place, or a thing? *Security* connotes "safety, refuge, or a sanctuary." Oftentimes, we seek security from money.

Solomon was wealthier than any other king on the planet (1 Kings 10:23). "The weight of the gold that Solomon received yearly was 666 talents" (1 Kings 10:14). This is the equivalent of 49,950 pounds, or about twenty-five tons. Solomon's annual income in gold alone exceeded $1.2 billion in today's value.

All the gold, silver, and bronze in the world was not enough to satisfy Solomon's desires: "Whoever loves money never has enough; whoever loves wealth is never satisfied with their income. This too is meaningless" (Ecclesiastes 5:10). His pursuit of security apart from God left him insecure.

Thankfully, Israel's king searched elsewhere, discovering true lasting security in the wisdom of God: "Wisdom is a shelter as money is a shelter, but the advantage of knowledge is this: Wisdom preserves those who have it" (Ecclesiastes 7:12).

Too often, we buy into the empty promise that financial security will someday allow us to enjoy our wealth. Unfortunately, someday never comes because financial security doesn't exist.

Seek Solomon's alternative to financial security: wisdom. In every thought, feeling, choice, and prayer, pursue wisdom: God's heart intersecting with street smarts. Commit to reading a chapter of Proverbs each day, correlating with the date of the month, for the next 365 days. You will read through the entire book each month, replicating your journey twelve times over the next year. The more you get into the Word of God, the more it will get into you, revealing the heart of Christ, the wisdom and truth of God, and the only One who can truly satisfy your desire for security.

Solomon Pursued Pleasure for the Sake of Gratification

Ecclesiastes 2:1

WHAT kind of pleasure do you seek in order to gratify your desires? Too often, we seek happiness apart from God. Solomon sought pleasure from wine, women, and song: "I said to myself, 'Come now, I will test you with pleasure to find out what is good.' But that also proved to be meaningless" (Ecclesiastes 2:1).

Solomon married the daughter of Pharaoh (1 Kings 3:1) and took a total of 700 wives and 300 concubines who led him astray (1 Kings 11:3). This act violated God's plan (Deuteronomy 17:17), but Solomon raised his debauchery to another level when he built temples to their deities (1 Kings 11:7–8, 33). His heart was not fully devoted to the Lord who divided his kingdom (1 Kings 11:4–13). His love for God turned love for worldly pleasure became legendary (Nehemiah 13:26). Solomon had even penned: "Whoever loves pleasure will become poor; whoever loves wine and olive oil will never be rich" (Proverbs 21:17).

Solomon's pursuit of pleasure for the sake of gratification is relevant today in terms of our intimate relationships. Only Christ can truly satisfy our desires. Consequently, we must first pursue intimacy with Him through His Word, His Spirit, and His people. Then we must make our muscles move with our prayers in obedience.

Pass along intimacy with Christ to the next generation. If you parent a teenager, help her or him determine how they want to pursue and be pursued, before there's an emotional connection. Let your teen children know you will measure the success of any relationship by answering these questions: "Does it improve your relationship with God, your parents, your siblings, or your friends? Does it improve your grades or extracurricular activities?" God will use your foresight to guide you and your teen children in the pursuit of His desire for your lives.

What Can We Learn From Solomon?

Ecclesiastes 12:13–14

LIFE apart from God is meaningless. A divided heart led to a divided kingdom. It's the first sin. It's the wide gate. It's love of the world. King Solomon pursued earthly knowledge for the sake of contentment, possessions for the sake of significance, military might for the sake of control, money for the sake of security, and pleasure for the sake of gratification apart from God, the only One who could truly satisfy his desires.

David's first words to Solomon (Proverbs 4:3–9) and his last (1 Kings 2:1–4) were to keep God's commands. Even God Himself repeated this same charge to David's son (1 Kings 9:3–9). It's no wonder that Solomon's Last Will and Testament of Ecclesiastes summarized: "Now all has been heard; here is the conclusion of the matter: Fear God and keep his commandments, for this is the duty of all mankind. For God will bring every deed into judgment, including every hidden thing, whether it is good or evil" (Ecclesiastes 12:13–14).

God is faithful but we are not. That's why we need Christ to pursue life with God (Psalm 127:1), bringing us in communion with Him (Ecclesiastes 3:11) and community with others (Ecclesiastes 4:12). Christ never fails. When we surrender to Him, He will be with us, always.

Solomon's Secrets to Leading Leaders: Love a Pure Heart

Proverbs 22:11

HAVE you struggled with influencing your boss? Are you unable to effectively communicate with your spouse? Does the coach of your team seem immovable? In our sinful nature, we have a tendency to respond to conflict with other leaders in three foolish patterns. First, we act with an impure heart, one with mixed motives, mostly selfish at the expense of the interests of God and others. Second, we frequently use hateful speech, words and tone that tear down rather than build up our counterparts. Third, we react in an untrained manner by not investing in the growth of our God-given skills, let alone our wise conflict management muscles. To compound our problem, the challenging people in our lives often operate with these same three liabilities. Consequently, when our wills conflict, we pursue a pathway toward catastrophic encounters that hinder us from leading the strong personalities in our lives. Solomon shared the solution to this dilemma by offering three secrets to leading leaders.

First, Solomon taught to love a pure heart: "One who loves a pure heart and who speaks with grace will have the king for a friend" (Proverbs 22:11) A pure heart has no mixed motives because it is fully surrendered to God, free from selfish motives, and ready to serve another person's needs. The Bible uses the word "pure" most frequently in reference to precious metal, usually gold. Precious metals must be refined to become pure. This process involves intense heat that brings impurities to the top, so the refiner can remove them. The deepest impurities rise last after an intense time of heat. Just like the crucible is used for silver and the furnace for gold, so God tests our hearts to discover whether they are pure—wholly devoted and surrendered to Him (Proverbs 17:3). The apostle Paul warned us to not be led away from our pure and sincere devotion to Christ (2 Corinthians 11:3).

Our ultimate example of a pure heart is the heart of Christ. The Bible tells us that Christ is pure in heart (1 John 3:3; Hebrews 7:26). He demonstrated a fully surrendered heart with unmixed devotion to the Father. Jesus taught: "Blessed are the pure in heart, for they will see God" (Matthew 5:8). The God of the universe demonstrates His kingdom in the hearts and lives of the pure in heart. They see Christ in themselves. This is illustrated in the molding of silver or gold. The metal refining process continues until the refiner can see his reflection in the metal, and then the metal is fashioned in its useful state.

As the refiner of the heart, God removes our impurities until He sees the reflection of Christ's pure heart in us (Romans 8:29). When God sees Christ in us, we see God. David communicated that God would show Himself pure to the pure in heart, but He would judge those with mixed devotions (2 Samuel 22:27; cf. Psalm 18:26).

In order to have a pure heart, we must surrender our impurities, or mixed devotions. Ask God to search your heart for any mixed devotion and to renew in you a pure heart—one that is fully devoted to Him. You will be satisfied through your unmixed devotion to the Creator who will reveal Christ in you.

Solomon's Secrets to Leading Leaders: Speak With Grace

Proverbs 22:11

IN order to lead leaders, we must also speak with grace. This is held at a premium in world today. When the heat of interpersonal conflict rises, we have a tendency to speak with a harsh tone, one that demands what we want. Wisdom offers a different way.

Solomon counseled: "One who loves a pure heart and who speaks with grace will have the king for a friend" (Proverbs 22:11). A pure heart receives God's grace—His underserved love, His unmerited favor, which frames our speech. Our words become loving, full of favor, and focused on the advancement of God's heart in others. Christ, who fully surrendered all to the Father, is the grace of God (2 Corinthians 8:9). It is Christ in us who will lead leaders to Him.

Surrender your heart and mouth to Christ. Follow Paul's teaching: "Do not let any unwholesome talk come out of your mouths, but only what is helpful for building others up according to their needs, that it may benefit those who listen" (Ephesians 4:29). *Unwholesome talk* is juxtaposed with *building others up*. Consequently, unwholesome talk is not merely coarse language, but words that tear others down, usually in order to lift ourselves up, the opposite of benefiting those who listen. When you speak with grace, The King of kings will use your words to draw others to Himself.

Solomon's Secrets to Leading Leaders: Develop Our Skills

Proverbs 22:29

To lead leaders, we must develop our skills. Solomon invited: "Do you see someone skilled in their work? They will serve before kings; they will not serve before officials of low rank" (Proverbs 22:29). How do we become skilled in leading leaders?

First, we work hard. Solomon observed: "Lazy hands make for poverty, but diligent hands bring wealth" (Proverbs 10:4). Hard work develops our God-given skills and helps us wisely manage conflict.

Second, we work smart. Solomon continued: "He who gathers crops in summer is a prudent son, but he who sleeps during harvest is a disgraceful son" (Proverbs 10:5). We have often heard this verse summarized in the axiom, "Make hay while the sun shines." Working smart delights other leaders: "A king delights in a wise servant, but a shameful servant arouses his fury" (Proverbs 14:35).

Solomon shared: "The horse is made ready for the day of battle, but victory rests with the LORD" (Proverbs 21:31). When we work hard and work smart, all credit belongs to God. By humbly accepting this truth, we are much more effective in leading leaders because they are drawn to the Holy Spirit in us.

Fully surrender the development of your skills to the One who makes a king your friend. Work hard: schedule time in your calendar

to go the extra mile in your relationships. Start your day an hour earlier to focus on growing your skills. Read the Bible, pray, seek a mentor in your chosen area of desired growth. This time will increase the intensity of your focus during the day. Work smart: don't perpetuate bad habits, becoming trapped by the tyranny of the urgent. Define and prioritize the most important values in your life. Find a wise confidant to help you with a hard reset of your calendar to include what you value most. Delegate tasks that drain you to someone who would be energized by them. All the while, give credit to God your Creator, Redeemer, Sustainer, and Restorer.

Solomon's three secrets to leading leaders teach us that when we love a pure heart, speak with grace, and develop our skills, we won't be the ones leading; rather, it will be Christ in us. In order to be effective leaders, we must be good followers. The apostle Paul summed it up this way: "Follow my example, as I follow the example of Christ" (1 Corinthians 11:1).

The Invitation

Matthew 22:1–10

W HAT have you done with your invitation to the biggest celebration on earth? In a discussion with the religious, self-righteous leaders of His day, Jesus addressed this question in The Parable of the Wedding Banquet (Matthew 22:1–14).

The Invitation Rejected (Matthew 22:1–7)

Jesus began the story by setting the scene. He described a king's invitation to a countrywide wedding celebration for his son. The party would last for several days—probably an entire week. The food would be exquisite. The hired chef was expected to perform at the top of his culinary game. He would have to return his fee plus a penalty if he embarrassed the king. Guests would drink undiluted wine from expensive glassware. Even the invitations were delivered with fanfare. Each guest received his invitation well in advance of the celebration with notice of others who had been invited. Either the day prior to or the day of the festivities, a second invitation was delivered by a messenger who brought a personal summons from the king.

Jesus's story brought a countercultural surprise. The people had rejected the king's first and second invitations with flippant excuses and some with fierce hatred. This was indicative of the Pharisees' response to Jesus. The story's enraged king brought forth death and fire—his most serious penalty for treason or revolt against his kingdom. Jesus's imagery probably referred to the eventual destruction of the Jerusalem Temple in 70 AD.

What excuse are you using to reject the invitation to the kingdom of God? Is it a desire to maintain control of your time, talent, or treasure? Is it manifested in an illicit relationship, a click, a drink, a smoke, a toke, a binge, a cut, a pop of a pill, a morsel of gossip, a rollercoaster commitment to a career, or even religion? Whatever the excuse, it flows from a proud heart.

The Invitation Readdressed (Matthew 22:8–10)

The king had deemed the proud rejecters, the privileged few, as undeserving of his invitation (Matthew 22:8). These were Israel's religious, self-righteous leaders and any who had followed them in hardness of heart. Next, the king did something radically uncharacteristic of a monarch in Palestine. He invited everyone to the celebration, both good and bad. He commanded his servants to go to the street corners and invite "Anyone you find" (Matthew 22:9), which they did until the wedding hall was filled to capacity (Matthew 22:10). Jesus had continually preached this availability of the kingdom of God to all sinners (Matthew 9:12–13).

Are you delivering God's open kingdom invitation to anyone you find? If not, you probably have rejected His invitation to the celebration of His kingdom inaugurated by the coming of His Son.

The RSVP

Matthew 22:11–14

IN Jesus's Parable of the Wedding Banquet, during the celebration, the king observed the guests who had jammed the wedding hall. To his dismay, he had found someone without proper wedding clothes. The king treated him in similar fashion to those who had rejected his invitations by ordering his death sentence. At first glance, the sentence of the wedding guest who had come directly off the streets seems harsh. However, we must view Jesus's story through the lens of His day. In Palestine, wedding clothes were customarily provided by the king (Genesis 45:22). The man not wearing wedding clothes had been offered clean garments and yet had proudly rejected them—an external sign of his internal condition.

Our righteousness is like filthy rags to a holy God, the King. The only acceptable RSVP to the King's invitation to the celebration of His Son is humility (Matthew 18:1–4). We must humbly receive the righteous clothing of Christ (Romans 13:14; Galatians 3:26–27).

Jesus concluded His parable with one of His most frequent sayings: "For many are invited, but few are chosen" (Matthew 22:14). *Many* is translated from the Greek word, *polloi*. This was a common word used as an inclusive expression in Israel. It meant *all*. The King invites all to the celebration of His Son, but He chooses only those who humble themselves to the righteous clothing of Christ.

How will you RSVP to the King's invitation? Will you proudly reject it with an excuse pulled from a list of self-absorption, or will you humbly receive the righteous clothing of Christ who gave His life for you? Confess your proud excuses for rejecting the King's invitation to His kingdom. Humbly receive the righteous clothing of Christ and invite anyone you find to the King's celebration. It won't be you, but Christ in you, making the invitation.

Desires Are Not for Our Gratification: Avoid Sexual Immorality

1 Thessalonians 4:1–3

THE apostle Paul likened marriage to the relationship between Christ and the church, teaching that a husband desires respect from his wife, and a wife desires to be loved by her husband (Ephesians 5:31–33). Still, our culture is performing an all-out assault on this covenant, exploiting the desires of both genders. Since a man is attracted by sight, he risks falling prey to the pandemic of porn that is infiltrating western males, both young and old, at an unprecedented rate. Because a woman is attracted by what she hears, she risks an attraction to chat rooms or another male who will listen intently to her feelings.

Paul taught that desires are not for our gratification, nor their elimination, but for our transformation. God's design is that we would experience His desires: holy, sanctified, and fully surrendered to Him (1 Thessalonians 4:1–8). This transformation process begins by fully surrendering our desires to pleasing God with our lives: "As for other matters, brothers and sisters, we instructed you how to live in order to please God, as in fact you are living. Now we ask you and urge you in the Lord Jesus to do this more and more. For you know what instructions we gave you by the authority of the Lord Jesus" (1 Thessalonians 4:1–2).

Paul preached that desires are not for our gratification: "It is God's will that you should be sanctified: that you should avoid sexual immorality" (1 Thessalonians 4:3). *Avoid* meant "to empty out." *Sexual immorality, porneia* in Greek, implied both fornication prior to marriage and adultery during marriage. In essence, it is any sexual gratification outside marriage. The writer of Hebrews reminded his readers to keep the marriage bed pure, free from sexual immorality, meaning that no foreign substance would be brought into the holy place of intimacy (Hebrews 13:4).

For the purpose of illustration, let's examine the process of an electrical transformer. An electrical transformer either steps down or steps up the voltage it receives as determined for its use on the other side. This is a picture of the transforming power of the Holy Spirit who either steps down or steps up the electrical current that we bring to Him. The Greek word *hagiasmos*. Meaning *sanctification* or *holy*, is used four times in 1 Thessalonians 4:3–8. Therefore, Paul is communicating that, in order to be holy, we need to take sexual temptation to the Holy Spirit who will step down the voltage and transform it to empower us to avoid sexual immorality. To believers in Rome, Paul taught that they should not conform to the world, but be transformed to God's holiness (Romans 12:1–2). This has always been in the heart of God for His people. Peter referenced the Old Testament law when he wrote: "I am the LORD your God; consecrate yourselves and be holy, because I am holy" (Leviticus 11:44a; cf. 1 Peter 1:16).

Is there any sexual temptation at the forefront of your life? Are you clicking where you shouldn't? Do you take extra time with a co-worker that's leading to more and more of a physical attraction and an emotional connection? Surrender that temptation to the Holy Spirit who will transform your desires for your spouse, or future spouse if you are single, and empower you to avoid sexual immorality.

Desires Are Not for Their Elimination: Control Your Body

1 Thessalonians 4:4–5

THE electrical current of sexual temptation travels from our world's images straight to our desires, equipped with enough voltage to kill. However, this is nothing new. When Paul wrote to the Thessalonians, the Greek sex culture was perverted, especially in Thessalonica, even at its religious sites. Marriages were arranged between girls thirteen to fourteen years old and men in their mid-twenties. Oftentimes, they had never met. Consequently, it was expected that married men would have sexual relations with prostitutes, female slaves, or mistresses outside the marriage. Demosthenes (384–322 BC) wrote, "Mistresses we keep for our pleasure, concubines for our day-to-day physical well-being, and wives to bear us legitimate children and to serve as trustworthy guardians over our households." The Stoic philosopher Cato (95–46 BC) praised men who gratified their sexual desires with a prostitute rather than another man's wife. As a result, income from prostitution was substantial for the economy, especially for innkeepers and cook shop owners.

Judaism struggled with sexual immorality as well. In first century Judaism, women were stereotyped as instigators whenever sexual sins were committed and were labeled as lacking the spiritual and moral fiber needed to uphold the law. Notice the absence of the woman's lover in the story of the woman caught in adultery (John 8:1–11). Allowances were made for men who experimented with sexual adventures, but this was forbidden for women. Augustus (63 BC–14 AD), Emperor of Rome, instituted the "Julian Laws" in a failed attempt to reform sexual misconduct. It's no wonder Paul taught the church to avoid sexual immorality through the power of the Holy Spirit who would step down sexual desires outside God's design (1 Thessalonians 4:3).

After revealing God's will that believers avoid sexual immorality (1 Thessalonians 4:3), Paul continued his teaching: "That each of you should learn to control their own body in a way that is holy and honorable, not in passionate lust like the pagans, who do not know God" (1 Thessalonians 4:4–5). *Control, ktasthai* in Greek, means "to acquire," or, in our electrical transformer illustration, "to step up," to honor God through the transforming power of the Holy Spirit. What separates the fully surrendered from the partially surrendered is not superior self-control—single phase electricity for the sake of our illustration—but intimacy with God. In other words, we do not pretend that we do not have the desires; rather, we humbly submit them to the Holy Spirit. Paul said that the heathen lust because they do not know, or experience intimacy with, God in their hearts. Jesus preached that sexual immorality flowed from one's heart (Matthew 15:19).

God's design is for a husband to leave, cleave, and weave his life with his wife's (Genesis 2:24). During sexual intimacy, endorphins and enkephalins rush to the excitement and risk center of a man's brain, the preoptic neuron, filling it to the highest possible level. A man's brain glues what he sees during sexual intimacy to what he is experiencing. God's idea is for this to be only his wife (Douglas Weiss, *Sex, Men, and God*, Lake Mary, Florida: Siloam Press, 2002, 15–16).

What would it look like if the Holy Spirit would step up your desires to honor God? How could you learn to control your body with a heart that is intimate with Christ?

Desires Are for Our Transformation: Live a Holy Life in the Holy Spirit

1 Thessalonians 4:6–8

HOW can we honor God with our longing for sexual intimacy? Paul taught that desires are for our transformation: "And that in this matter no one should wrong or take advantage of a brother or sister. The Lord will punish all those who commit such sins, as we told you and warned you before. For God did not call us to be impure, but to live a holy life. Therefore, anyone who rejects this instruction does not reject a human being but God, the very God who gives you his Holy Spirit" (1 Thessalonians 4:6–8). Paul called believers to love others by not harming them through sexual sin. He warned of God's punishment for sexual immorality and called the church to love God and live pure and holy lives by the power of the Holy Spirit. Notice the present tense: "Gives you his Holy Spirit" (1 Thessalonians 4:8). Paul tied this giving to his original thought of living in order to please God (1 Thessalonians 4:1). The Holy Spirit is our spiritual transformer, empowering us to live in a manner that honors God with our bodies.

Are you ready to move from a single-phase life, going it alone, to a three-phase life that experiences a fully surrendered relationship with the Father, Son, and Holy Spirit? Make a commitment today to tap into the transforming power of the Holy Spirit who will step down sexual temptations, helping you to avoid sexual immorality; step up holiness to help you control your body in a manner pleasing to God; and be transformed to loving your spouse, God, and others. God will use three elements to make you new again.

First is the Spirit of God. Pray. Confess any temptation and seek His power to transform every temptation into obedience (2 Corinthians 10:5). Ask Him to redirect your desires to your spouse. See or hear everyone at the heart level. Men, refocus your eyes from any temptation to your wife. Become an active participant with your wife and daughters when it comes to dressing modestly. Ask the question, "Is it too tight, too short, or too revealing?" Couples, pray audibly together to increase your intimacy with each other and Christ.

Second is the Word of God. Quote Scripture to battle temptation, just as Jesus did (Matthew 4:1–11). Couples, study the Bible together to grow in wisdom. The Holy Spirit will deepen your relationship with God and your intimacy with each other.

Third is the People of God. Experience authentic community within a small group of believers who can provide a safe place to confess and restore.

Desires are not for our gratification, nor their elimination, but for our transformation. The result of surrendering to the transforming power of the Holy Spirit will be wives who respect their husbands; husbands who intimately love their wives; and marriages, families, and communities who love God.

The Who, What, and Where
of Wise Confrontation

Proverbs 27:9; 10:32; 16:23; 25:9–10

DURING interpersonal conflict, do you struggle with confrontation? *Confront* literally means "face to face." Only after first taking your conflict to God, ignoring insults, turning the other cheek, and overlooking an offense, can you wisely and lovingly confront another person.

Who should you confront? Examine the relationship you have with the person involved in your conflict. Have you earned the right to be heard? Solomon counseled: "Perfume and incense bring joy to the heart, and the pleasantness of a friend springs from their heartfelt advice" (Proverbs 27:9). If you have invested in the relationship, prior to any confrontation, then it is likely you have built a bridge to your friend's heart, making it relationally appropriate for you to walk across and offer sincere advice.

What should you say in confrontation? Choose your words wisely. Your words must be fitting: "The lips of the righteous know what finds favor, but the mouth of the wicked only what is perverse" (Proverbs 10:32). *Fitting* is translated from the Hebrew word, *ratson*. The NASB translates *ratson* as *acceptable*, which means "bringing favor, or good will." When your words are fitting, you bring favor and good will to your conversations.

When you have wisdom in your heart, your words will be wise and convicting through the power of the Holy Spirit. Solomon taught: "The hearts of the wise make their mouths prudent, and their lips promote instruction" (Proverbs 16:23). Your most powerful source of instruction is the Word of God. The more you get into the Word,

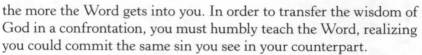

the more the Word gets into you. In order to transfer the wisdom of God in a confrontation, you must humbly teach the Word, realizing you could commit the same sin you see in your counterpart.

Where should you confront? Be sure to confront in private, just between the two of you, in an nonthreatening setting, not in front of others. Jesus taught: "If your brother or sister sins, go and point out their fault, just between the two of you. If they listen to you, you have won them over" (Matthew 18:15). In doing so, you must not betray another party's confidence. Solomon warned: "If you take your neighbor to court, do not betray another's confidence, or the one who hears it may shame you and the charge against you will stand" (Proverbs 25:9–10).

Ask the Holy Spirit for guidance regarding who you confront, wisdom for what you should say, and discernment in where you confront. He will navigate you through conflict to community.

The When, Why, and How
of Wise Confrontation

Proverbs 25:11

WHEN should you wisely confront someone during interpersonal conflict? Timing is everything, so your confronting should not take place too early, too late, or in the heat of the battle. Solomon penned: "A person finds joy in giving an apt reply—and how good is a timely word!" (Proverbs 15:23). The wise king warned of reaching out too early: "If anyone loudly blesses their neighbor early in the morning, it will be taken as a curse" (Proverbs 27:14). He illustrated the value of the right word spoken at the right time: "A word fitly spoken is like apples of gold in settings of silver" (Proverbs 25:11 BSB). In order to speak the right word at the right time, you must have one ear toward God and one ear to those you encounter, avoiding confrontation during the heat of the battle (Proverbs 29:11).

Why should you wisely confront? Ask yourself, "Is it for your benefit or theirs? Is your motive to advance the heart of Christ?" Solomon revealed: "A person may think their own ways are right, but the LORD weighs the heart" (Proverbs 21:2). God examines your motives. Consequently, you must verify through the Holy Spirit that your intentions are noble, for the benefit of others and to advance the heart of Christ. If not, you will confront out of your own pride, under the illusion that you will feel better on the inside. However, that is rarely the case.

Paul reasoned: "If it is possible, as far as it depends on you, live at peace with everyone" (Romans 12:18). God desires that you reconcile, owning any contribution you have made toward the conflict. You will be tempted to go on autopilot with those closest to you and confront harshly, so avoid that coarse sandpaper of the soul by first defining your conflict, determining what two objects are attempting to occupy the same space at the same time.

How should you confront wisely? Communicate humbly and gently in your nonverbal cues. Do not confront by text, email, social media, or letter, unless there is no other option. Tone of voice, body posture, hand gestures, eye contact, and facial expressions should communicate humility and gentleness. Solomon noted: "A happy heart makes the face cheerful, but heartache crushes the spirit" (Proverbs 15:13). He also taught: "A gentle answer turns away wrath, but a harsh word stirs up anger" (Proverbs 15:1).

When you communicate humbly and gently, your speech is gracious. Solomon said: "One who loves a pure heart and who speaks with grace will have the king for a friend" (Proverbs 22:11). He noted: "Fools give full vent to their rage, but the wise bring calm in the end" (Proverbs 29:11). Paul taught: "Brothers and sisters, if someone is caught in a sin, you who live by the Spirit should restore that person gently. But watch yourselves, or you also may be tempted" (Galatians 6:1).

When you confront wisely—only after taking your conflict to God, ignoring insults, turning the other cheek, and overlooking an offense—the Restorer will use you to advance His kingdom in the hearts and lives of those around you, as He deepens your communion with Him and your community with others.

MITCH KRUSE is the founder of House of Leadership, Inc., a nonprofit organization designed to create wisdom and leadership content for marketplace and ministry leaders. Mitch's television program and podcast, *The Restoration Road with Mitch Kruse*, airs online and on sixty networks throughout the world, where he teaches the Bible through stories of restoration. Mitch's first book, *Restoration Road* (Credo House Publishers), chronicles his story paralleled with Jesus's Parable of the Prodigal Son. His second book, *Street Smarts from Proverbs: How to Navigate through Conflict to Community* (Faith Words/Hachette Book Group), teaches Solomon's purpose for Proverbs through twelve key concepts.

Mitch was the youngest licensed Realtor in the nation and the first person to sell a vehicle for a documented $1 million cash while he earned his Bachelor of Science degree in business administration from Indiana University. For seventeen years, Mitch Kruse was owner, CEO, and auctioneer of Kruse International, the world's largest collector-car sales organization. After selling his company to eBay, Mitch earned his Master of Arts and Doctor of Religious Studies degrees with high distinction from Trinity Theological Seminary. Mitch and his wife, Susan, live in Auburn, Indiana and have four daughters. You can visit his website at *mitchkruse.com*.